THE

APPROACHING CRISIS:

BEING

A REVIEW

OF

DR. BUSHNELL'S COURSE OF LECTURES,

ON THE BIBLE,

NATURE, RELIGION, SKEPTICISM,

AND THE

SUPERNATURAL.

BY

ANDREW JACKSON DAVIS,

AUTHOR OF "NATURE'S DIVINE REVELATIONS," "GREAT HARMONIA," "ARABULA," "STELLAR KEY," ETC., ETC.

SECOND EDITION.

BOSTON:
WILLIAM WHITE & COMPANY,
BANNER OF LIGHT OFFICE,
158 WASHINGTON STREET.
NEW YORK AGENTS—AMERICAN NEWS COMPANY.
1870.

McCrea & Miller, Stereotypers.

AUTHOR'S PREFACE.

THE GREAT QUESTION of this age, which is destined to convulse and divide Protestantism, and around which all other religious controversies must necessarily revolve, is exegetically foreshadowed in this Review; which is composed of Six Discourses, delivered by the Author before the Harmonial Brotherhood of Hartford. Religious truths present themselves naturally to a good mind; and by such a mind they will be most accurately comprehended. Men of the greatest talent and learning frequently reason themselves into the profoundest errors, by commencing with the confusing impression that Truth is complex and supernatural. He who would apprehend the simplicity of Truth and worship at her shrine, must be ready at all times to divest his mind of prejudices and of preconceived opinions, whenever Truth reveals their falseness. The author's method will be found to be plain, because such is truly the seal of reason.

The views presented concerning the "Word," it may be remarked, are mainly connected with the external peculiarities thereof, as the occasion does not now demand a deeper criticism. The author is acquainted with a more spiritual *Logos*, within the original symbolical expression (ὁ λόγος τοῦ Θεοῦ, "the word of God," to be found, with identical meanings, in the Zenda Vesta, in the Vedas, also in the Bible), which lies quite untouched in the present work. Indeed, the spiritual "Word" here alluded to, as originally signified by JOHN, is not (ὁ λογος and λόγοι) Divine "Truth" and "Reason" dependent upon the paper and ink habiliments of the Old and New Testaments; but upon the intellectual progress and religious development of the human soul—a growth of parts into a completeness. The *organizing*, *unfolding*, and *energizing* Spirit of God (which is the true translation of John's meaning) will surely be more manifested, or *inworlded*, in a New Dispensation than in any conceivable number of sacred canons. Supernaturalism adheres to the form; the Harmonial Philosophy seeks the spirit.

Among all the author's recent impressions, there stands no one question so *important and conspicuous* as that set forth in the succeeding pages. The most external and superficial aspect is first presented; but deeper investigations are certain to follow. There is much to illuminate our present existence, and far more to joyfully anticipate.

A. J. D.

THE APPROACHING CRISIS.

CHAPTER I.

INTRODUCTORY REMARKS.

Religious reformation the greatest question of the age.—A letter to the Rev. Dr. Horace Bushnell.—Object of this work.—The Crisis approaching.

FAITHFUL to my spiritual impressions, I watch, with constantly deepening interest, all the important and momentous changes of this eventful Era.

All superior intelligences regard the origination and universal application of the Art of Printing, as a power of immense and never-ending value. By it, the world is fast becoming illuminated with the scintillations of wisdom, and with the principles of a spiritual republicanism. By it, the early Alteration in the Church became widely diffused—an alteration, which, owing principally to educational convictions, the Catholic Church stigmatizes as the great "HERESY." But all Protestants know, from the various sources of civil and religious experience derived therefrom, that the alteration alluded to was a decided improvement or "REFORMATION" in all matters pertaining to Christianity. Printing first enlightened the people concerning the irreligion and atrocious ceremonies practiced by the early Church. And the world has at last come to see that religious *reformation* is both possible and beneficial. This conviction has attained a high place in nearly all well-educated and healthy minds.

Changes and consequent improvements in almost every department of human interests, are confidently expected by those who live in the Nineteenth Century. While those who are confessedly mortgaged to the dogmatic organization of Old Opinions, can not bring their minds to contemplate Reformations in any thing as possible without being accompanied by some overwhelming disaster either in the Church or State. The enlightened and *clear-seeing* intellects, however, can read the events of this epoch,—recognizing plainly, in the long, well-defined shadows which approaching changes cast before them, the peculiar crisis or *interregnum* that is certain to precede the establishment of a higher form of ecclesiasticism and a nobler type of republicanism and religious freedom.

Religious reformation is demonstrated to be both practical and beneficial to mankind. Deeply impressed with this conviction, and believing also that the *highest point* of improvement, in social arrangements and religious institutions and faith, *has not* yet been reached by man, I obey my inflowing impressions, and strive to help move forward the ponderous Car of human progression. Accordingly, hearing that HORACE BUSHNELL, D. D., of the City of Hartford, had in contemplation the delivery of a course of lectures, bearing, as I supposed, on the great general question of religious Refor mation, I made it a point, by interior direction, to be present on all the occasions, and listen to his disclosures.

Immediately after the pronunciation of his introductory discourse, I penned and addressed the following letter through the Hartford Times; the import of which will appear on perusal:—

A LETTER TO REV. DR. BUSHNELL.

A SUGGESTION.

HARTFORD, December 15, 1851.

DEAR SIR,—The simple announcement that you had in contemplation the formation and deliverance of a course of lectures "On the Naturalistic Theories of Religion as opposed to Supernatural Revelation," gave me much pleasure. Nor did that pleasure experience any diminution on hearing the first lecture of the proposed course, delivered by you last evening. Indeed, I can scarcely express the gratification excited in my mind by the clearness of your definitions, the broadness of your premises, the fairness of your statements, and by the goodness of your intentions, manifested in the introductory discourse to which I now refer.

Your *position* in the question is, it seems to me, entirely *unlike* any other ever assumed by the clergy of Christendom. And your *appreciation* of the magnitude and importance of the subject—nay, its intrinsic momentousness to the welfare of mankind—is also vastly different and far more just, it seems to me, than I have ever before discovered in any other member of your exalted profession.

That the clergy of this city have manifested wisdom in the selection (by suggestion and compliment) of yourself as the person most calculated to approach and treat this great question with ability and candor, is very evident; and that the enlightened portion of this community will be attracted, gratified, and instructed by the manner and method you design to adopt, there can be no doubt.

You approach the subject, define your position, and declare your intentions and arguments in a manner considerably unlike the method pursued by most clergymen, viz., with a firm reliance upon *your own reason* or judgment, with which you design to address the *corresponding* faculty in the mind of the hearer. This, as you must be aware, is quite *a new method* to adopt in the analysis and examination of a Bible question, so undoubtedly important.

Although you seem not to acknowledge the "Sovereignty of Reason," in matters pertaining to a supernaturalistic revelation and faith; yet you very evidently rely upon *that* faculty (reason) to perform its appropriate functions in order to convince your audience of the soundness and legitimacy of your conclusions.

In addressing you thus publicly, I aim not at discussion or controversy; but simply to make a suggestion to you, and also to the Hartford community, that this course of lectures be delivered by you in a place where all parties interested can have an opportunity, should they desire it, to analyze and examine *before the same audience* the various positions you may assume in the discussion. As the case now stands, the matter at issue is not properly apprehended by half the number of minds that may listen to your discourses. The people do not so clearly realize that very many thousands are more or less involved in the insinuating *infidelity* of this age; indeed, I was myself surprised at the statistical information which you imparted on this head. Hence, to most minds, the question has not yet attained that imposing magnitude which, in your own opinion, and in fact, it undoubtedly possesses. I concur entirely with you, and with the clergy of Hartford, that the *greatest* question of this day is the one you have resolved to answer, viz.: Whether Rationalism or Supernaturalism shall be triumphant? You propose, as I apprehend you, to *reconcile* the two forms of faith, and show that *Miracles*, in the theological definition of the term, are not inconsistent with the operations of unchangeable law and system.

Now I think, Reverend Sir, that you will most willingly accede to the foregoing proposition; inasmuch as you affirmed, toward the termination of your discourse last evening, that in announcing the course of lectures, you had no design to draw people to the North Church, or to imply that you undertook the task from any consciousness of personal qualification. But you very nobly and ingenuously took upon yourself this work of reconciliation from a love of truth, or from an unmixed sense of the magnitude and vital importance of the question to the generality of mankind. I perfectly harmonize in the latter conviction; and, therefore, suggest the FREE analyzation and discussion of the question proposed in your lectures. Will not the citizens of Hartford adopt some method which will secure to all parties an opportunity of free speech? Will they not obtain some large and commodious hall; and would you not, Sir, in such case *repeat* the introductory lecture of last evening; because you therein lay the foundation broad and satisfactory, and in a manner so frank and truthful, that I would recommend its frequent repetition. I do not know that any persons would avail themselves of the liberty of speech proposed, and say any thing by way of criticism on the subjects involved in your discourses. I have at present no design to do so myself; but I simply ask, for the parties interested, that the *same* audience may hear the Pro and Con of the greatest question of the age. I know no other way to obtain a rational verdict.

Very respectfully, A. J. Davis.

The breadth and comprehensiveness of the greatest question of this age, and the bold, independent statement thereof by Dr. Bushnell in his introductory lecture, sent a thrill of pleasure through many truth-seeking and liberty-loving minds. And, necessarily, the result of the foregoing letter was anticipated with no little interest. But no response was received. At the time the letter was penned, I had received no impression to write any discussionary criticism of the Lecturer's propositions. It was only after it became evident that no heed would be given to the above suggestion, that the interior direction came to me to proceed with a plain, unadorned examination of Dr. B——'s principal positions.

Many hundreds have listened with considerable interest, but with more anxiety, to the affirmative treatment of this high theme; whilst only a small portion of that number heard the analyzations of the main arguments on that side, which constitute the contents of this work. Rationalism versus Supernaturalism. This is the great religious question of the age. And considering the position of the church, and the condition of faith among the people respecting it, the subject has been approached and treated by Dr. B——, in a manner as fair and comprehensive as could be reasonably anticipated from that source. Yet he will perceive, it is believed, that a deeper and more candid examination must be instituted before those who have become accustomed to independent thinking, can, with a confiding mind, look to the pulpit for sound argument and practical reform.

The *first* lecture of his course was delivered by him on the 14th; the *second*, on the 21st of December, 1851; the *third*, on the 4th; the *fourth* on the 18th; and the *fifth*, on the 25th of January, 1852. The course is supposed not yet completed. But the lectures, thus far, do not solve the most essential problems, which lie at the basis of what is termed, "Infidelity"; and, hence, it is deemed wisdom briefly to analyze the positions assumed, and state the various difficulties which threaten to prevent the solution undertaken.

The author attended the delivery of these lectures; but he has had no *external* access to the MSS. This *Review* is, therefore, wholly the result of an *interior* effort on the part of the author; and yet it is written in a style adapted to the popular understanding, being free from elaborate and tedious disquisitions.

Since the Norman conquest, there have been evident advancements made in every thing, except, perhaps, in supernaturalistic revelations. The seal of infallibility must be broken away, before a new light and beauty can enliven and embellish the mystical disclosures of any seer, prophet, or evangelist; whose soul may be able to reflect the symbols of many truths. Owing to the dogmatism of infallibility, the Bible is taught now-a-days as it was nearly four centuries ago. And although very many minds have escaped from the old faiths and creeds, and left the priests to their idols; yet the strength of popular or external sentiments is such that the seceders are usually constrained to remain very quiet; and thus they pass in society for very good "lukewarm" Christians, unless, indeed, they have the courage to stem the central current, and establish a new form of worship. If so, they are likely very soon to become respectable, and antagonistic in their turn to those who may prefer a still greater latitude in their theological opinions.

It is confidently hoped that the talented mind, whose recent labors have suggested the succeeding criticisms, will find therein some points—or intended-to-be points—of argument on his part, which may require much reconsideration, in order to subserve the objects for which his lectures were avowedly designed—viz.:—to remove doubt and skepticism from the rising generation, and give a new philosophic light to the *rationalistic* Christian. He may rest perfectly assured that no captious or merely controversial spirit has dictated this review.

On the contrary, the present work is expressly and conscientiously designed to convince him, and the investigating world besides, that Spiritual Rationalistic positions are as invulnerable and satisfying as his doctrines are unsound and insufficient.

CHAPTER II.

FIRST REVIEW.

Truth and custom.—Mental equilibriums.—The modern Martin Luther.—The grounds of supernaturalism.—The defective text.—The sacred canons.—The Greek philosophers.—The foundation of Christianity. Combe's gospel on the Constitution of Man.

STRICTLY speaking, there are, and always have been, in this rudimental and undeveloped world, *two* classes of minds. One class, being improperly situated in society, and mentally trammeled and undeveloped, always love and *reverence* Custom more than Truth. The other class, being endowed with superior powers of mind, combined with social advantages and high conceptions of Justice, always find it easy to *reverence* Truth independent of Custom—nay, independent of the horrors of exilement or the keener *terrors* of the Vatican. The former desire custom to become Truth; the latter, *Truth* to become custom. The votaries of custom are invariably and universally the mightiest in numbers, and most always in power. Hence this party, being in the majority, universally rule the other portion of mankind; and determine, with an iron scepter, what the more truth-loving and advanced party shall do and believe.

The custom-serving mind is certain to oppose all attempts on the part of a truth-loving mind to assert its independence in matters of faith. Every effort—no matter how quiet and wise it may be—to break away from the multifarious restraints, which have held the church and the world in darkness and degradation for long centuries, is, by the vast majority, invariably condemned, precisely as the Pope censured Galileo,—as "absurd in itself, false in philosophy, and formally heretical, *because* declared and defined as contrary to Sacred Scripture!"

The Roman church is not the *only* earthly example of religious apprehensiveness and sectarian intolerance. Protestants love to draw comparisons between the Roman and the English church—showing, by means of *contrast*, the horrid *deformity* and *intolerance* of the one by holding up, before the people, the superior nature, organization, and liberties of the other. Now to this Protestant course I make no objection; but, what I mean to teach is—that the *two classes of minds* alluded to are *not* necessarily churchmen; they are substantially the citizens of the world—a result, when philosophically considered, of the imperfections or rather gradations, consequent upon a universal system of progressive development in minds and morals. There must be *low* and *high*—*intolerance* and *liberty*—*men* and *angels*, stationed along the rectilinear, but spirally ascending, line of *spiritual* and *material* creations.

The car of progress will roll speedily, determinedly onward; and you, my friends, may feel the utmost security in taking seats therein, because conservatism and intolerance are always ready, with their mighty strength, to press the "brake upon the wheels," and prevent the sad, social and religious disasters which might otherwise occur.

This pushing and pulling, this progression and retrogression, this fearlessness and cautiousness, are manifestly all incorporated with, and developed by, the universal providence of the Living God. In mechanism it is a well-known fact, that *all motion* is created and maintained by what has been termed a constant destruction of equilibriums. But unless these equilibriums are properly adjusted, the *motion*—proceeding from their successive and alternate disturbance—is defective and incapable of a useful application. The motion is good and useful *only* when the equilibriums are harmoniously arranged and disturbed. So also, the human race: when agitated by the *improper* arrangement of the progressive and conservative characteristics of mind, it is necessarily very discordant and miserable. But when, like the wise and skillful mechanic, the enlightened members of humanity shall give a truer form and better direction to these mental equilibriums, the whole race will experience more happiness and easier progression. All this is mathematically certain. Now, therefore, as you will perceive, conservatism and even intolerance (in a certain sense) are not to be dogmatically condemned, nor yet *progression* or mental *independence;* but only their wrong development and misapplication. This is the matter to study and to determine.

The application of the foregoing will be seen when I come to tell you, that I am now impressed to review Dr. BUSHNELL; not on the ground or presumption that his conservatism is wrong in itself, but that it is exceedingly at fault in its *present mode* of manifestation. I speak now as mankind's advocate. In conducting this review, let it be remembered, I am not contending with the local positions, private opinions, and confidential statements of an individual; but with an *individual* definition of the various positions, doctrines, and principal *conclusions*, which, unquestionably, are entertained and inculcated in different forms by the most enlightened members of the Christian sects.

That Dr. BUSHNELL is, in several respects, the Martin Luther of to-day,—in the church of which he is a recognized orthodox member,—is evident from the resemblance he theologically presents to that early reformer. Therefore, not *as Dr. Bushnell*, be it remembered, but *as the leader* of a new and more liberal form of conservatism, do I approach the great QUESTION which he defined and amplified in his recent lecture.

In the lecture—to which I above refer—it was very clearly, frankly, and ingenuously acknowledged, that the greatest question of this era is: that which is suggested by the modern "Rationalistic Theories of Religion as opposed to Supernatural Revelation and Faith." A more lucid version would render the question in substance this: "Whether Rationalism should be permitted to supplant Supernaturalism, and preside henceforth over the minds of the people, and give direction in all matters pertaining to religious teaching, discipline, worship, and social organization?" This is the plain statement of the question as I am impressed to apprehend it. It is exceedingly simple; but none the less important. And it is enough to say, by way of special criticism, that Dr. B—— stated this powerful problem at length; with much clearness, beauty, and force of expression; with much originality of appreciation and method; and, above all, it was almost wholly free from that presumptuous and dogmatic style, which most clergymen employ, in describing the tendencies of the various innovations and the claims and positions of the *reformers* of the day. He was frank in his statements; noble in his realization of the present colossal proportions of the Progressive Party; and fraternally disposed toward those who think differently from himself. And yet, it would not be improper to remark, that, although his language and method were free from uncharitableness and every species of church denunciation, still there was betrayed some severity toward the Progressive reformers, in the *tone* and alternating modulations of his voice.

I mention this fact merely to show, that, internally and privately, he experienced sensations of opposition to the different forms of social reform and Progress: from which we may also safely infer, that he desires to establish a species of infallible Conservatism, or theological immutability, contrary in effect to all free thought and mental independence. A man may be very *artistic* and *guarded* in the choice of language by which to express his thoughts, and the expression of the muscles of the face may also be considerably controlled by the will; but how true it is that the *eyes* and *voice* are the never-failing indexes of the soul's paramount sensations!

As I am impressed, Dr. B—— proposes to reconcile, by a course of philosophical argumentation, the various forms of what he terms "Infidelity" with the received claims of "Christianity, as a system of salvation or redemption." He thinks he can, or earnestly prays that he may be able to, show conclusively "that the miracles, the incarnation of God in Christ, redemption, special providence, and prayer," are all perfectly consistent with established system and reconcilable with unchangeable principles. In other words, he thinks he can demonstrate that there is nothing which can prevent a *reasonable* reconciliation between "*natural* and *revealed*" religion; between modern Rationalism and the supernatural system of Revelation and faith.

Now one of two things is certain; either Dr. B—— does not fully realize or comprehend *his own position* in the premises, or else, he is not sufficiently single-minded to the demands of truth, and faithful to the silent convictions of his own soul. Because, in the matter of *reconciliation*, which he has in contemplation, there is surely nothing intrinsically opposed to the fundamental teachings of Rationalistic Christianity.* The Harmonial Philosophy—which, be it remembered, includes both ancient and modern spiritualism—has done this to the perfect satisfaction of its most enlightened students and believers. Miracles, the Incarnation, Redemption from sin, through the exercise of the Christ-principle, Special Providence through angelic ministrations, and Prayer even, are all embraced by the Harmonial Philosophy, as explainable upon unchangeable principles, which have proceeded from Deity into and through the universe. If Dr. B—— designs to assume this *rationalistic* method of explaining supernaturalism;

* The reader may not altogether like this name; but I follow my impressions in conforming to the use made of it.

why then—I ask—does he *excite* the apprehensions of his hearers by describing the *various forms of an insinuating* and potent "Infidelity," which loads the mental atmosphere we unconsciously breathe with pestilential infections and dangerous skepticism? If he apprehends no intrinsic antagonism between "Pantheism," when properly interpreted, "Physicalism, Geology, and the Sciences," and the system of a Supernatural Revelation and its corresponding teachings; then—I inquire—why does he, in stating the great question, create a general prejudice against these features of modern Rationalism? Why create a *false issue* in the premises? Why not say frankly, that, in his opinion, the position of the Harmonial Philosophers and Spiritualists, is substantially correct; but that he would prefer to receive the new doctrines with some modifications, and to clothe them, in order to make them his own, in his own peculiar and classical nomenclature? If he sincerely believes the two forms of faith to be reconcilable, and not incompatible; then I hesitate not to affirm that Dr. B—— has created a *useless* question of distinction, without a difference, and an issue almost wholly false in the minds of his people. But if, on the other hand, Dr. B—— means by the system of Christianity, that definition of supernaturalism which is generally accepted as orthodox in all Protestant countries, or among all enlightened sects; then he has undertaken a work destined to be utterly *valueless* to the thinking world—because he would be striving to prove that *possibilities* and *impossibilities* are merely twin-brothers in the great rationalistic or supernaturalistic system of the All-wise Creator.

To apprehend Dr. B—— as admitting, however remotely, the general doctrines of rationalistic Christianity, would be, as I am impressed psychometrically to regard his mind, very *distasteful* and disturbing to him. He would prefer, doubtless, to be apprehended or interpreted,—(for it seems to me that many of his statements require considerable interpretation,)--to mean this: that he *does not reject* any scriptural definition of Christianity, nor *any portion* of the scheme of "redemption" therein disclosed. Nay: but at the same time, he must be understood to be the special architect of his own theological temple: the rearer and framer of *his own* theology and Christianity. He believes firmly in the purity and divinity of the Bible-materials. But with those materials *no one* can construct or *erect* a spiritual ZION to meet his wants, *except himself!* Hence he *differs* quite conspicuously from all his brethren; not, however, intrinsically and really, but *externally* and apparently. This fact alone makes him a modern Luther; a reformer, not in spirit and in truth, but merely in the FORM or symbols of Christianity. Let us, then, do Dr. B—— the justice to apprehend aright what he designedly signifies by Christianity. He means precisely what any other *Bible-believer* means. And let us, also, do him the justice to comprehend his *meaning* correctly, when he asserts, in substance, "that Infidelity, in its many and varied forms, is pervading and permeating the minds of the people." He means in reality precisely what any other churchman means by that term, viz.: any *thing opposed to the form of conservatism* which he has erected, or which is now in the process of erection, in his own particular mind.

Again I say, that I feel no inward opposition to *the*

principle of conservatism, considered as a law of mental equilibrium; only to its *misapplication*. And I repeat, that I am impressed to regard Dr. B—— as the leader and embodiment of a *new* and more interesting form of *Conservatism* than has ever been constructed from the fossil vestiges of oriental theologies. But this theological superstructure,—which he now contemplates and designs to erect in his own mind, and in which he supposes he will always find Christianity in its *purest* and *highest* form,—is happily not yet completed. It is now in the process of formation. And the hopes of the True Reformer, concerning the future usefulness of the mental labors of this *Martin Luther* to the world, must be suspended on the *mere possibility* (which unfortunately is very slight), that, when he comes to *frame* and *adjust* the superior portions of his theological temple, he may discover that the compartments are too contracted, and the dome too low, to suit the *real* wants of his expanding and aspiring nature!

It is now my impression to examine the introductory lecture of the course alluded to, on the foundation which he therein laid before the people, viz.: *Rationalism as opposed to Supernaturalism*,—contemplating the ultimate reconciliation of the two theories. For to apprehend him to mean, by supernaturalism or Christianity, any thing really *different* from the generally received opinions on that head, is to impeach the soundness of his judgment regarding his own position in the premises,—to do which I have no inclination. I rather desire to believe him to be not fully aware of the deeper workings and convictions of his mind. I come now to the closer criticism.

The lecturer foreshadowed the whole question, and his future answer thereto, in this comprehensive passage—which he selected from the *first* chapter and seventeenth verse of Paul's epistle to the Colossians,—"And he is before all things, and by him all things consist." Of this scriptural assertion he discovered a parallelism, or correspondential indorsement, in the third verse of the first chapter of John; where it is asserted that "All things were made by him, and without him was not any thing made that was made." Now if Dr. B—— really believes that Christianity, "as a system of redemption," was originally laid in the wisdom of the Infinite Mind before any thing was made; and if he believes that, when that Mind elaborated the world, Christianity was incorporated into the very soul of creation; then why does he allow himself to betray, or to experience, any FEAR as to the *safety* of that system which God himself created and sustains? If Dr. B—— believes Christianity to be a PRINCIPLE of Love and salvation, incorporated *in* and unfolded *out* of the system of the world; then he unquestionably occupies Rationalistic grounds, in interpreting his theology; and so there is an end to all cause of difference between us, on the fundamental points at issue. But he evidently *does not* occupy this position; because he manifested great concern for the welfare and success of Christianity, as a scheme of redemption.

Furthermore, if Dr. B—— believes Christianity to be a SPIRIT, and NOT a *form*—a *principle* operating between God and Man; not confined to a *mere combination* of books called "the Bible;" then he is clearly a believer in the fundamental teachings of the Harmonial

Philosophy; and thus, again, ends all cause of controversy. But I am impressed not to identify him with that which *he himself* did not originate and acknowledge; for evidently he is never insensible to the LUTHER feeling—the marking out of an independent course to suit *his own* affections and gifted intellect.

There is no disguising the plain, palpable fact, that Dr. B—— is not yet emancipated from the customary or POPULAR FORM of Christianity; that is to say, he regards the Bible as the precious relic of what occurred twenty and more centuries ago—the Casket of a "system of Redemption," whose supposed jewels must not be examined; except by the EYE of a confiding, unreasoning faith. If he is to be received as the representative or exponent of his own thought; then the above statement of Dr. B——'s present position, is perfectly accurate. A mind thus trammeled, and thus manacled by the *paper* and *ink* habiliments of the Christian religion, can not adapt itself to the workings of the law of Progress. He must, alas! close his *eyes* to the operations of a progressive Christianity; the great law of human destiny! He must step blindfolded along the path of error, describe a circuitous and zigzag course in the fields of humanity and thought; and, whilst the resplendent beams of an orient sun are lighting up the highway to social harmony and human happiness, he must close his eyes, and pretend not to see any "world-saving truth" in the sublime principles of modern reformation!

Dr. B—— is not yet, I repeat, emancipated from the *paper* and *ink* relics of Christianity. The New Testament is the only orthodox remains thereof; the only

SKELETON to remind one of the departed spirit. Alas! what a "foundation of sand" to build a spiritual Zion upon. Every wind of doctrine threatens to demolish the splendid superstructure. The Egyptian pyramids have withstood for long centuries the whirlwinds of the desert; though they approach from "all directions" at the same time. But this is man's work. Surely, if the *Bible* is the pyramid of Christianity which God himself has erected on the moral desert of this world, then can Dr. B—— really believe that the "whirlwind of skepticism and infidelity, coming at once from all points of the compass," can overthrow the God-made superstructure? To this question I earnestly solicit a reply. I know that there are watchmen on the towers of the modern Zion of ancient construction, whose cry is, "It is a Christian duty to hold reason in subjection to faith!" Yet the building is in danger, because, forsooth, TRUTH alone can withstand the surging billows of TIME, of independent investigation, and remain forever unmoved and unchanged.

Let us look at another point. If Dr. B—— sincerely believes the New Testament to be a God-made book, and that the authority thereof should not be questioned by an enlightened reason, he surely was very injudicious, to say the least, to object, in the very outset, to the *defective* translation of a portion of the text which headed his discourse. Nothing can be more productive of absolute faithlessness—especially in the youthful mind and rising generation—than the shadow of a suggestion that a passage of Scripture has been imperfectly or incorrectly translated by the talented English scholars. In one part of his discourse, the lecturer stated, in a *tone* of voice somewhat ironical and sarcastic, that "Rationalists rejoiced and luxuriated in all good men," and that, when "it suited their convenience, they would even quote passages of Scripture." Now I object to such essential unfairness, especially when draped in very respectful and honest-sounding language. Surely, a reasonable man is always pleased and at liberty to adopt the words of any author, in or out of the Bible, should these words express his own promptings and convictions. As for example: Dr. B—— quoted from Paul a passage which plainly declared *his own* intellectual pre-conceived convictions; with the qualification, however, that "had the translation rendered the word 'by,' 'IN,' as it is in the original, the idea would be much stronger;" and, consequently, far more suited to the intellectual conception which the Lecturer had formed of the system of the world, and the relation of God to it. Here, then, is an orthodox example of the *rationalistic method* of quoting Scripture, "when it is convenient," or illustrative of some particular thought or theme. Again, I can not but remark upon the *injudiciousness* and incautiousness of that mind, which—while it professes to believe the Bible to be the pure and unalloyed Word of God—yet so openly ventures to affirm that a passage therein is not correctly or infallibly translated. In this instance, the mistake of the translators is not essential. But what assurance have we that greater mistakes have not been made in other passages?

Let us now think of the text. It was asserted that it imparted a clear "outlined conception" of the system of the world. Also, that it showed conclusively, that the whole "structure and plan of Christianity" were contemplated before the world was made; and that it is, consequently, an institution laid within the constitution of things. To this I am moved again to reply, that, if Dr. B—— means, by Christianity, a PRINCIPLE OF LOVE—that redemption from sin is practicable through a personal and universal *exercise* of that principle—a principle unfolded in the progressive developments of nature and humanity; then, he is *with* us, and we *with* him, and thus satisfactorily ends the controversy. In this case, his whole question, together with all his apprehensions about "Infidelity" and "Christianity," are based upon his own intellectual misconceptions; the issue is false, and hence unnecessary. But that *he does not* take this ground has already been shown from his method. By Christianity he *means* precisely what every other Bible believer means by the term. Hence, in order to be perfectly sound and reasonable in his conclusions, Dr. B—— must admit that the Deity actually planned—in the holy labyrinths of his wisdom, "before the world was made"—the Garden of Eden; the fall of man; the misery of his offspring; the deluge; the confusion of tongues; the vicarious atonement; and the unutterable miseries of hell. Does this category of evils seem like the handiwork of an all-wise and perfectly good Creator? But—no matter! It must be so—that is, if the text under consideration is, in very truth, *the Word of God.* For "He is before all things, and *in* Him ALL THINGS (not a portion of things, remember, but *all* things) consist." If Dr. B—— were a rationalistic Christian, the text would clash with no truth which his affections might feel, or judgment comprehend. But as he is not, his position is exceedingly painful, inconsistent, and untenable. Indeed, the conflict which will inevitably be generated in his mind, by the entertainment of such hostile sentiments, and the attempt to reconcile them, will be sufficient, it seems to me, to force him either into rationalistic doctrines or else into a deeper and more incurable conviction of the asserted truth of the Persian tale of total depravity. That he may never find himself confirmed in the latter faith—in the slough of Despair—in company with the giant bearing that name—is my fervent prayer and hope.

The text in question plainly asserts that, "He is before *all things*, and by (or IN) him all things consist." Now, I ask: How does Dr. B—— know that this text foreshadows a truthful conception of the outline or frame-work of Creation? Does he adopt the rationalistic or *eclectic* method of quoting Scripture, "when it is convenient," to body forth the sentiments of his own mind? Or, does he take Paul's Epistle to the Colossians as divine authority? If the former, then he is a Christian rationalist—a strict follower and advocate of the Harmonial Philosophy. If the latter, then he is standing upon a foundation as impermanent as the changeful sand. Unless he is very careful and sound in the assumption and establishment of his premises, the youthful minds of his congregation, and the rising generation of investigators, will surely find it out. If he takes St. PAUL for his authority, and believes that the text is true *on that ground*, then I must remind him of a fragment of church history, with which, as a scholar, he must assuredly be well acquainted.

When the pure Hebrew tongue ceased to be vernacular, and the Jews had returned from Babylon, there was immediately formed a sacerdotal organization, and a committee of Rabbis was appointed to collect and preserve all the known Hebrew manuscripts. This was done; and the parchments placed in the Sacrarium. It was not, however, until many years after the return of the Jews from the Babylonish captivity and exilement, that most of the *books* of the *Old* Testament were heterogeneously bound together. This was, properly speaking, the "Babylonian Canon;" because it was originally made by the Chaldeanic Rabbis. But many years subsequent to this collection, there arose some considerable dissatisfaction and discussion among the younger Rabbis concerning the heterogeneousness of the first canon. Hence, by permission of the sacerdotal authorities, they *rejected* some books, arranged others in a *different* order, interpolated a few passages, and made another Testament. This is properly termed the "Jerusalem Canon;" because it was made by the Jews of Palestine. During all this time,—owing to *local* oppressions and *temporary* emergencies,—books, by the Jews, containing multifarious speculations and national prophecies, multiplied very rapidly. Parties and preferences became numerous, and began to create *dissatisfaction* in regard to the *last* Canon which was formed; and so, apparently to keep up with the demands of the times, another *Old Testament* was formed—the "Alexandrian Canon"—in Egypt. All these compilations, be it remembered, were different. At this time the book of DANIEL was generally regarded as the creation of an eccentric old

Jew, who was talented, and a seceder from the regular priesthood. Hence, that interesting part of the *present* orthodox Old Testament, was not then universally received as containing reliable inspiration.

Now I feel moved to inquire: Does Dr. B—— design to take the ground, that the Bible is the actual and immutable *foundation* of religion? Or, that the New Testament is the only foundation and evidence of Christianity? Does he believe that, when we reject the *paper* and *ink* clothing of Christianity, we thereby lose the soul or principle?

Christianity, as it is in fact—and as regarded by all intelligent rationalistic philosophers—never exerted *so much saving or reformatory power upon the human mind as it did in the first century*, when there *was no such a thing in existence as a New Testament.* Christianity is one thing; the New Testament is quite another. In fact, the *New Testament* is a name which does not signify a book; but a DISPENSATION. St. Paul did not write his speculations, concerning faith and redemption, to be read and adopted by all generations after him. His thoughts and epistles were developed by, and written for, special and particular occasions. His epistles—to the Romans, to the Thessalonians, to the Colossians, &c. —were especially adapted to the existing wants of those respective churches, but they are not adapted to the wants and requirements of the people in this Nineteenth Century. Indeed, the writings of Paul were twice *rejected* as authority; and at last it was fully determined by the bench of Bishops, under the Emperor Constantine, that Paul should be placed in the gallery of the old theological masters, as an inspired penman.

Here, then, is the important point to settle before proceeding further, viz.: Does Dr. B—— quote from St. Paul a text, axiomatically, as a motto, because it expresses the impressions of his own mind? If so, what necessity is there for creating a *seeming* difference between our rationalism and his supernaturalism? For in such a case he manifestly assumes the "sovereignty of reason" as superior to Bible revelation. This is the crime—the only crime—of the so-called infidels. Or, does he take the New Testament to be the "Word of God," and the text in Colossians as divine and immutable authority? If so; how will he explain *the human formation of the Bible*, and the *unsatisfactory* translation of the text? My impression is, simply, to solicit the Lecturer's attention to the solution of these important considerations in the premises, in order that he may the more perfectly cure the skepticism and rationalism existing and developing in this world.

When Dr. B—— rolled up the curtain, which permitted us to view the Greek theater, how artistically did he cause to be enacted the strange drama—almost the tragedy—of "Speculation and Superstition." He showed "the ingenuity" with which the abounding myths and Egyptian superstitions of still earlier times were caused to disappear by the Greek philosophers and sophists. Or, in other language, how the speculatists, having "some regard for the religious feelings of the people," concluded to resolve the furies and myths into symbols and presiding deities. Then the Doctor showed his audience what the furies, thus symbolized and classified, did "above ground" and also under the earth. And the Greek sophists—said the Lecturer—

finally succeeded in making God and Creation one and the *same* thing; reduced every thing of a religious nature to a common level; and ingeniously demonstrated all things to be moving in harmony with the "unchangeable laws of an endless cycle."

Now arises a question. Why did Dr. B—— allude to this piece of Greek history? Why did he dwell on the terms "speculatists, philosophers, and sophists," and the reduction of all religious things to "the unchangeable laws of an endless cycle?" Surely his *text* teaches precisely the same doctrine. "In him all things consist," says the text; which is merely a synoptical or synthetical method of asserting, that "Nature is bathed in the Spirit of God—is penetrated and sustained by him; that all things exist and operate according to unchangeable law." The talented Doctor. subsequently considered this doctrine of modern rationalism; acknowledged "that HUME was *right* in affirming that nothing could possibly occur contrary to established law and system;" and substantially confessed, also, a belief, in the Harmonial doctrine, that there can not be any real *conflict* between Nature and Supernaturalism, when the two are properly comprehended. Now why did he—with such a text, with such convictions, and with such noble concessions—roll up the Greek curtain, to show to the young minds of his congregation the "ingenuity of the Greek Philosophers" in *sifting*, *rejecting*, and *symbolizing* the RELIGION of that era; which, he said, they called "Superstition?" Was it to give them an idea of history? Was it to display his ability to trace out and comprehend the whole origin and scope of Rationalism? Far from it.

His only design was this: To draw a prejudicial parallelism between the Philosophers of Greece and *those* who are to-day denominated philosophers; to make the people see that the exposition of superstition, by modern "speculatists," is achieved by "ingenuity," and not by Truth; to create an impression that that which is termed Harmonial Philosophy, is merely the revival of old ideas and long exploded speculations; to prejudice the people, in a word, against almost every thing of this century, which bears the general features of a rational reformation; and yet, the Doctor, it seems to me, is too highly endowed with a love of truth and benevolence to permit him to draw the parallelism too bold and rugged, or to enforce too earnestly its acceptation. The enlightened mind, however, can not but regret any such attempt on the Lecturer's part; because it shows conclusively, that his mind has not yet attained that moral growth which is capable of conducting a perfectly free and impartial investigation. Nevertheless, he is far superior to the popular species of clerical opposition to new truth; and declares himself "no enemy to science;" nor yet jealous of the truths uttered by Pantheists, or Humeites, or Physicalists, or by Phrenologists even, whose "gospel," said the Lecturer, "is Combe on the Constitution of Man." These concessions give promise of something like a religious reformation.

That I have apprehended and interpreted Dr. B—— aright in his parallelism, may be seen from the question he asked in that department of his discourse—viz.: "Is Christianity, as a system of faith and redemption, to meet with the same fate?" That is: is it to be *re-*

solved by modern speculatists—as the Greek philosophers *sifted* and *resolved* the then prevailing superstitions—into symbols and things, moving in harmony with the unchangeable laws of an endless cycle?

The Doctor thinks the "Infidelity" of to-day, is hydra-headed; coming from all directions—setting in one strong current against, and threatening to overthrow, the foundations of a supernaturalistic Christianity. Now, whether a supernaturalistic system of Christianity will be hurled from its foundations, in the opinion of Dr. B——, will be decided and determined by what he defines that foundation to be. If he defines the foundation or basis of Christianity to be the Bible; then he may rest assured that *supernaturalism*, as the world defines it, will fall ere long to the earth. But, on the other hand, if he resolves, like the Greek philosophers, the superstitions of Christianity into *symbols;* and, like the so-termed Harmonial Philosophers, accepts the *foundation* of Christianity as resting wholly upon PRINCIPLE, then he can also rest perfectly assured, that the ten thousand and one currents may set in against it, but its *power* upon the human heart will surely be all the more augmented. For assuredly, in this comprehensive sense, Christianity was eternally laid in the Wisdom of the Infinite Mind, "in whom all things consist."

The gospel of "Combe on the Constitution of Man" will contain—if the Lecturer comes to this rationalistic position—no injurious or anti-Christian doctrines; though it proves crime to originate in organization, "confuses," according to his assertion, "duty with penalties and benefits," and leads the reader to social reorganization, as a means of redemption from sin and misery. Surely, Dr. B—— will not desire or attempt to refute these doctrines. A little calm reflection will certainly convince him that mental *organization* and social *situation* has much to do in *molding* and destinating the individual. If the Lecturer comes to see truths just *as* and *where* they are, he will inevitably think better of "Socialism" so called; better of "Revelations about the Spheres," through magnetism; better of "necromantic conjurations" and spirit-seeing; better of "Unitarianism," though it does tardily accept the miracles, believes in a remote Christianity, and *rejects* the person of Christ as a "Redeemer," in the orthodox signification. But whether he does, or *does not*, come to see truths just as and where they are, is a question which his present course of lectures will eventually determine. I, for one, await the result with no little interest; and I can only breathe for than indwelling prayer, that he may work out a system of reform.

In conclusion, I again affirm that this criticism is not a matter between two individuals. It is human *freedom* and *independence* against a *new* modification of an *old* form of *conservatism;* the *misapplication* of which, to the present wants of mankind and the Age, is the ground of the present controversy.

Dr. B—— referred to the ingenious manner with which the Greek philosophers detected and dissipated the prevailing superstitions. I would ask, if he remembers the historical statement, that SOCRATES was condemned to swallow the *juice of hemlock*, for teaching the *Athenians* the existence of a Supreme Being? —a doctrine in which I apprehend the Doctor to be a firm believer. The inspiration, then, of God—of the doctrine of the UNITY of God—was extended to the soul of a Greek philosopher! Even so, as "all scripture is by inspiration," may not the philosophers of to-day—having the wisdom and experience of the past before them, and receiving the increasing influx of fresher truths from superior spheres into their souls—bring out a fairer faith, and a PRINCIPLE of greater saving power, than the *forms* and *faiths* of the present age, which are the bequeathments of superannuated centuries? It seems, according to his expressed declarations, that Dr. B—— is not *jealous* of science, nor yet at *enmity* with the general materialistic tendencies of this age. He seems to contemplate a *reconciliation* between Nature and Revelation. This is *possible only* on the ground which I have already defined; which would, of course, be *identical* with the one we at present stand upon; viz., upon Rationalistic Christianity; not upon "Supernaturalistic Revelation," as generally defined as truly orthodox by the Christian world. But what Dr. B—— is destined to accomplish, in the capacity of a modern LUTHER—as a theological reformer—is yet to be developed to our perceptions and understandings. We may say to him, however, and with the most fraternal inclinations, too, that Christianity, as received by the citizens of Hartford, will never prove itself to be a satisfactory system of redemption. For if he will philosophically and dispassionately analyze the origin and nature of man's vices and passions, he will surely discover, in the ultimate analysis, that the *worst* manifestations of character are fortified in the strong intrenchments of religious and social institutions. And the remaining and ordinary evils of mankind, he can legitimately trace to the improper or *ignorant* procreation of our species. I respectfully request Dr. B——'s attention to a calm consideration of the above propositions.

If the high-minded man—who penned that precious "gospel on the constitution of man"—was here, he would speak to us, in his own familiar language, and say:—The clergyman assails the vices and inordinate passions of mankind by the denunciations of the Bible; but as long as society shall be animated by different principles, and maintain in vigor institutions whose spirit is diametrically opposite to its doctrines, so long will it be *difficult* for him to effect the realization of his frequently urged precepts in practice. Yet it appears to me, that, by teaching mankind the *philosophy* of their own nature and of the world in which they live —by demonstrating to them the *coincidence* between the dictates of this philosophy and true Christian morality, and the inconsistency of their own institutions with both—they may be induced to supplant their bad institutions by good ones; thus to *intrench* and strongly fortify the *moral* attributes of man; and then the *triumph* of virtue and Religion will be more complete and certain. Those who advocate the *exclusive* importance of a supernaturalistic religion for the improvement and redemption of mankind, appear to me to err in overlooking *too much* the necessity for complying with the *natural conditions on which all true* improvement depends. I anticipate that, when schools and colleges shall expound the various branches of this philosophy as portions of the natural revelations of the Creator—

when the *pulpit* shall deal with the same principles, show their practical application to man's duties and enjoyments—and when the *activities* of life shall be so arranged, as to become a field for the *pleasurable* practice at once of our philosophy and our religion; then will man attain the position of a rational being, and Christianity achieve her highest triumph!

CHAPTER III.

SECOND REVIEW.

Conflict between the affections and understanding.—The new conservatism exhibited.—The system of Nature *versus* the system of God.—Points of agreement.—The wonders and extent of nature.—A faith above reason.—Human magnetism.—The Mormons.—Shelley.—The Vestiges of Creation.—Confusion in nature.—The question of free agency.—The cramping influence of a false theology.

KNOWLEDGE is progressive; but faith is conservative. I mean that *faith* which the mind has been forced or educated to accept in its early years; a faith which has attained a high place in the affections, where Reason is seldom allowed to enter. There that conservative opinion stands, venerable with age, an idol of the mind; supporting itself by two staffs which it holds in its hands—one composed of the *sanction* of Time; the other, of the *authority* of great names. Now it frequently happens, that when we hear a clear voice emanating from the professional preacher, having all the common features and semblance of pure reason, and causing us to *imagine*, for the time being, that Reason, "that heaven-lighted lamp in man," is really the source of what we hear; yet, after all, we discover that we merely hear the affectionate and conservative voice of that venerable Idol; whose substance is derived from past dogmas and whose life is absorbed from the weaker elements of the mind.

But then there is a far truer *faith;* a pure and progressive *faith;* one which should be forever enshrined in the soul's affections—a *faith*, I mean, which is generated by appropriate and adequate EVIDENCE; a free-born child of the understanding! The fair child of reason is never afraid to expose itself to the inspection of the world; never shrinks from the thought of displacement, should another and a better offspring, from the same parent, seek to occupy its seat in the affections, or to exert its benignant influence upon the intellect. Now, the difference between a faith which *controls* the understanding, and a faith which cheerfully obeys the *voice* of an enlightened Reason—as a dutiful child the mind of its parent—is very conspicuous and unmistakable. The conservative child—to preserve the analogy, whose parents are authority and antiquity—always *employs* the faculties of reason as special advocates and counselors. Let any new discovery appear, and the conservative employs Reason forthwith to use its native wisdom and dignity, in the capacity of an attorney, to argue against the approaching innovation. Let philosophy teach the plain doctrine that the physical and moral government of God is founded upon certain great general laws—teach that obedience to these laws brings its own happiness and rewards, and disobedience its own adequate punishments—and you will see conservatism, with all the erudition and talent it can possibly command, fully aroused to a sense of approaching "*danger*" and the immediate necessity of greater vigilance. Let Geology arise from the sepulcher of earth and stone, and read in a confident voice the gospel which Nature has been myriads of centuries in writing upon the broad tablets of the inner world; and, lo! the child of conservatism is alarmed for the safety of her strong towers, and seeks the startling words—"deception"—"infidelity"—"innovation"—as expressive of its fear of the new manifestation.

Not so with the child of the Reason. Having inherited by hereditary transmission of qualities, the ruling characteristics of its progenitor, the faith of the understanding is always ready to hear, to investigate, and to obey. It feels a religious confidence in the decisions of its progenitor. And although it changes in order to suit the increasing demands of progressive principles, yet it is as fixed and unyielding in its spirit as Truth is immutable and honesty inexorable. It is, therefore, an easy thing to decide in what minds the reason-principle is held in *subjection* to faith, or where faith exists as an effect of knowledge, based upon the reason-principle. We must always judge by the external manifestation.

In my review of Dr. B——'s introductory discourse, on *rationalism as opposed to supernaturalism*, I was impressed to affirm, that I did not regard his conservatism as *wrong* in itself—considered as a principle or characteristic of mind; but that it is exceedingly at fault in its *present* mode of manifestation. This tendency to wrongly use a prudential faculty, by a mind enriched with good native powers and a scholastic education, was very *faintly* foreshadowed in Dr. B——'s first lecture. But in his *second* discourse, delivered by him last Sabbath evening, he developed in bold relief the fact, that he has *not yet attained* that harmonious moral growth which enables the mind to conduct an honest and impartial investigation.

Of the latter discourse I may in this place briefly say, that it was not as well conceived and elaborated as the former; neither did it contain the perspicuity and beauty of expression, the *broadness* of thought, nor the purity of feeling which characterized the opening lecture. Nor was he so ingenuous in his allusions to the positions which the rationalists occupy. On the former occasion, his language was free from unfairness and derision; and only betrayed some severity toward the Progressive party in the modulations of his voice; but, in the second discourse, his method and words were more suited to the *internal* feelings which prompted the anxious and disturbed manner of his delivery. None of this would emanate from a mind which fully realizes that Truth is immortal and God unchangeable; that all things must have a high and happy termination; because the Lord God omnipotent reigneth. Why the Doctor does not fortify himself in this conviction, and set about the discharge of his highest duties with a positive, frank, and calm demeanor, is a question which he can best answer, and reconcile to the inexorable principles of truth and invincible honesty.

Dr. B—— originally avowed the principal object of his lectures to be centered in this thought—viz.: to effect a *reconciliation* between Naturalism and Supernaturalism, to the end that the young minds of the community might be preserved or reclaimed from the vortex of a manifold infidelity. He began very nobly the task before him, and laid the foundation broad and somewhat logically; but it seems thus far that he builds the house with no strict reference to the shape and principles of the primary arrangement.

He does not do himself justice as a theological architect. This can not but be regretted. For there are many honest-minded citizens awaiting and watching the erection of the new Zion; which this LUTHER has promised to erect on the rock of ages—an impregnable and indestructible fortress, in which to place the purest and highest form of Christianity, where it can forever remain unmoved and unchanged by the march of intelligence and human independence. Upon an octagon foundation, he builds a three-cornered house. Upon a foundation large enough to embrace the whole human family, he erects a temple scarcely capable of meeting the internal wants of his own mind. Such inconsistency, alas, is the common, inevitable result of the pernicious habit of maintaining the reason-principle in a state of subordination to educational Faith.

I come now to consider Dr. B——'s second discourse; with strict reference to its inconsistencies and details.

He opened with his text, selected from that classic book attributed to JOB, eleventh chapter, ninth verse, wherein it is asserted that the perfections of the Almighty lie beyond man's limited comprehension. "The measure thereof *is* longer than the earth, and broader than the sea." In this connection, Dr. B—— glanced at the transcendent efforts of the human mind. How it searches and explores the earth; calculates its extents and magnitudes; and mounts on high, to examine the distant myriad orbs whose light has been ages traveling toward and reaching our planet. Mind, he said, has exerted its powers to comprehend the drops in the great fire-ocean, which constitutes the physical universe. But failing to achieve its object, the mind comes back to earth, exhausted and overwhelmed with the contemplation. Still it is not satisfied, and so recovers strength for a fresh exertion. It mounts again, on the wings of fancy, and climbs the rugged sides of the material creation, in order to get at or "*imagine something*" to meet the soul's demands for the mysterious and the supernatural. Hence it sets its speculative faculties energetically into play, and "imagines spheres, &c., entirely above the comprehension of reason."

From this Dr. B—— inferred that Nature could not be "the system of God;" and that man absolutely demands, in the deeper wants and consciousness of his nature, a FAITH independent of, and above, reason or unilluminated judgment. From this proposition the Lecturer derived what he termed his essential "definition of Nature in contradistinction to the Supernatural system." He confessed, that, unless his definition was understood and accepted by the audience, all his *subsequent* reasonings would be obscure and almost valueless. Therefore, as this "definition" is the *main point* or *very foundation* of all he designs to say, in the great work of *reconciling* rationalism with supernaturalism, it is but just to him that we proceed to analyze and examine this corner-stone of the supernatural temple. He said, in substance, that the spirit of God must be "longer than the earth, and broader than the sea;" that extents and magnitudes "expressed" the deific spirit, but did not "include" him; that we, in our speculations, might expand matter or the material creation illimitably, but God was more expanded and more illimitable. In a word, that the "system of Nature by itself *is not* the system of God. Dr. B—— then defined Nature to be a "system within itself." In its inherent laws and material combinations, almost wholly independent of "the supernatural creation, which is particularly the system of God!" Dr. B—— thinks that Nature is a "system of cause and effect; but, that the Supernatural is not subsisting upon, and controlled by, these mechanical forces or reciprocal principles." He thinks, that when miracles are performed, the RESULT is accomplished, *not* by violating or suspending any of the inherent laws of Nature," but by the action of the supernatural kingdom or government of God UPON Nature —producing effects and phenomena therein, which could never otherwise be developed by the unceasing operations of nature's inherent principles. Dr. B——'s definition, therefore, amounts substantially to this: that Nature is a system of matter, mechanism, and forces, operating *outside* of, and a long way *beneath*, the real kingdom and government of God; that the Supernatural system, which is far *greater* and *beyond* the extents and magnitudes of the system of nature, and is the system of God, "operates upon the world"—and produces therein *effects* and *miracles*, varying very prominently from the *usual* progressive developments of unchangeable laws—without disturbing or suspending, in the least degree, the general processes of natural or causative creation.

Dr. B—— was very desirous that the people should *accept* this definition, to the end that his *future* lectures might have the desired effect. Now this is all exceedingly superficial and unsound. I make no doubt but that his reasonings and deductions would be very good and legitimate, in case we *adopt* his premises as fixed and unquestionable truths. But this can not be allowed him. For his premises, are contradicted by every thing in existence; as I will presently proceed to demonstrate. His reasonings and conclusions, I repeat, would doubtless be sufficiently sound and logical, if we should *admit* the foundation as resting in immutable truth. So, indeed, would the reasoning of a man be correct, who should first lay it down as a fixed fact that HARTFORD was submerged in twenty feet of water; and, then, proceed to lecture to the people of New York, stating that none of the houses could be entered or inhabited except on the second and third floors; and that the citizens were obliged to do their trading and visiting by means of boats and various kinds of vessels. But suppose a skeptic should doubt, *not* the premises which the lecturer had assumed with so much confidence, but the general conclusions about going only in boats from place to place. Accordingly he would ask—"Are not some houses built sufficiently firm and tight to keep the water out the lower stories? Are the people in fact all driven from their kitchens and stores to the upper floors?" "Most certainly," replies the lecturer, "for this very good and satisfactory reason: the water is twenty feet high, above the surface of the earth. If the water is so high throughout Hartford, your judgment will enable you to perceive, that it would necessarily flow into the houses through the lower windows, &c.; and that all the effects named must result as a natural consequence, from such an inundation." "True," replies the skeptic, "the inhabitants of Hartford must be disturbed and suffering just as you describe. For if there be twenty feet in height of water in the streets, your reasoning is all entirely sound and conclusive. But I would prefer being better satisfied *first* as to the foundation upon which you predicate the account,—that is, to ascertain if there be an inundation. Now, this skeptic comes directly to Hartford, and discovers, to his great surprise and satisfaction, no water in the streets, —that no such deluge had taken place, and the inhabitants were undisturbed. He therefore says to himself: "the lecturer reasoned very legitimately from his undemonstrated premises; but now, the whole relation falls to earth, because the foundation is shown to be a groundless or untenable assumption."

So with Dr. B——'s definition. His reasonings would be perfectly logical and conclusive—indeed, I may say quite unanswerable—if he first makes it appear satisfactory and certain, that his interpretations of Nature and Supernaturalism are based and grounded in the essence of truth. But a true reformer in thought —a true investigator, one whose *faith* is an effect of a preponderance of adequate evidence, and not of theological and superficial education—must have the *strongest* possible historical, chronological, and intuitive demonstration that Nature is not "the system of God," before the conclusions, or superstructure, which are made to repose upon that proposition, are, in his opinion, entitled to careful consideration and worthy of credence.

His definition of supernaturalism in *contradistinction* to Nature, is not essentially different from the common orthodox opinions on that head. It is sub stantially identical with the written views of all the principal Christian scholars. Hence Dr. B—— is not so truly a reformer *in spirit*, but an iconoclast—a reformer of the FORM. This fact must be a matter of sincere regret to all lovers of free thought, of unre stricted inquiry, and mental progression.

The Lecturer briefly alluded to the "confusion among rationalists" as to what Nature is, or should be defined to mean. He thought this fact "weakened" the force of all their arguments against supernaturalism. But this is evidently a misapprehension. Rationalistic arguments may be sound in *Chemistry*, in *Geology*, in *Astronomy*, &c.; while their individual definitions of the general system of Nature may be as heterogeneous and conflicting as the different learned commentaries upon the Sacred Scriptures. It is my impression, that the Lecturer has not given his "definition" of Nature and of Supernature sufficient reflection. There is an absence of consistency and congruity in his views—a result, it appears to me, of his repugnance to seeing and acknowledging *new truths* in the multiform and stupendous developments of the present era. Does he remember the opening text quoted from St. Paul—"And he is before all things, and IN him all things consist?" Now, if "Nature is not the system of God," or included *within* that system; how—I inquire—can the above text be a perfect and infallible utterance of truth? If "all things consist" in God—how can Nature be *outside* or *beneath* the including spirit? If the supernaturalist means to say, that Nature is the Material Universe, and that the supernaturalistic realm should be understood to mean the Spiritual Universe, —in which the Spirit of God is manifested more *visibly* than in the physical creation; then, he is certainly developing an unreal, and hence wholly unnecessary, difference between Rationalists and Irrationalists. For the above is comprehensively *our* "definition" of the system of Nature.

Upon this basis, the term "supernature" may be reasonably employed to signify any thing which is high and *spiritually exalted*, yet *homogeneous* with the visible and material;—the difference in this interpretation consisting *not* in the kind and quality, but in the DEGREE and condition exclusively. Thus—for example—the human body is called the "physical man," and the human mind the "spiritual man;" yet the *two*, being united by the common ligaments and ties of sympathy and harmony, constitute ONE harmonious system. Even so—on the soul-exalting principle that ALL truth is a Unit and intrinsically harmonious—may we not rationally conclude, that the *material creation*, expanding far and wide throughout the illimitable infinitude, is the "physical universe;" and that the superior and ultimate departments of the *same* identical system—embracing all the *future* habitations and realms of the soul—constitute the "spiritual universe," wherein, more particularly and manifestly, we shall enjoy "the Lord of Hosts"—all the more for then fully realizing the now inconceivably glorious fact, that *in him all things consist?*

This is the *definition* of NATURE which is suggested

by the Harmonial Philosophy. Now, why does Dr. B—— refuse to recognize a definition, which may be considered as the only real rationalistic view of nature known to the world? For all the scientific and philosophic views ever elsewhere presented—except in three or four instances of eminent productions—are mainly fragmentary, speculative, or hypothetical. If Dr. B—— would accept the Rationalistic method of reconciling "naturalism with supernaturalism," he would most assuredly escape the horrid overwhelming vortex of theological inconsistencies to which he is now evidently but unconsciously hastening. Indeed, he would then survive the keener and far-reaching analysis of the rising generations of the earth, and would hold a sacred place in the reasonable affections of his advancing countrymen, as the leader of a principle of Conservatism, which favored the development of science and the application of a pure religious philosophy to the work of human redemption and universal improvement.

But what a low and unsatisfactory estimate did Dr. B—— make of Nature! It would seem that he had *gone back* to Job in order to get a "definition" of the magnitudes and extents of the system of the world—yea, gone back three thousand years, to a period when the people had no ships whereby to learn the *breadth* and wonders of the sea; no systems of measurement to calculate latitudes and longitudes, and the *length* of the earth; no telescopes, wherewith to ascertain the extents and immensities of creation—a period, in short, when the *territories of Oregon* would fill the then prevailing conceptions of Nature, and Lake Erie the general idea of a Sea!

The wondrous immensities and peaceful harmonies of the Universe, the unutterable unity and silent operations of all created things, we are too apt to forget or neglect to properly examine. "What mere assertion will make any man believe," remarks the celebrated HERSCHEL, in his Discourse on Natural Philosophy, "that in one second of time, in one beat of the pendulum of a clock, a ray of light travels over one hundred and ninety-two thousand miles, and would, therefore, perform the tour of the world in about the same time that it requires to wink with our eyelids, and in much less than a swift runner occupies in taking a single stride? What mortal can be made to believe, without demonstration, that the sun is almost a million times larger than the earth? and that, although so remote from us that a cannon-ball, shot directly toward it and maintaining its full speed, would be twenty years in reaching it, it yet affects the earth, by its attraction, in an appreciable instant of time? Who would not ask for demonstration, when told that a gnat's wing, in its ordinary flight, beats many hundred times in a second? or, that there exist animated and regularly organized beings, many thousands of whose bodies, laid close together, would not extend an inch? But what are these to the astonishing truths which modern optical inquiries have disclosed, which teach us, that every point of a medium through which a ray of light passes is affected with a succession of periodical movements, regularly recurring, at equal intervals, no less than five hundred millions of millions of times in a single second! —that it is by such movements, communicated to the nerves of the eyes, that we see; nay, more, that it is the difference, in the frequency of their recurrence, which affects us with the sense of the diversity of color; that, for instance, in requiring the sense of redness, our eyes are affected four hundred and eighty-two millions of millions of times; of yellowness, five hundred and forty two millions of millions of times; and of violet, seven hundred and seven millions of millions of times per second. Do not such things sound more like the ravings of madmen than the sober conclusions of men in their waking senses? They are, nevertheless, conclusions to which any one may most certainly arrive, who will only be at the trouble of examining the chain of reasoning by which they have been obtained."

The earth was originally believed to be the center and circumference of all creation; and the vast *arena* of all the supernatural and capricious miracles of Omnipotence. According to Job's own testimony, the Lord was even engaged in afflicting him, who, while he perpetually—with prayers and complaints—acknowledged himself to be under the special guidance of the Almighty Power, and confessed dependence thereon for existence, diseases, troubles, &c.; yet he prayed for a commutation of the punishments arbitrarily inflicted upon him, as if there then existed between Job and the Ruler of this immeasurable and stupendous Universe, a private amity and confidential correspondence! Now if such an instance of supernatural familiarity and presumptive arrogance was stated to Dr. B—— as having occurred ten days since with a *Hartford citizen*, or with some enthusiast, he would either indignantly repel the account as supremely absurd and blasphemous, and dogmatically set it down to voluntary deception, or else to the longings of the soul after something *supernatural*, transcendental, and above the powers of the reason-principle.

After giving the erroneous impression that NATURE is but an isolated "system of cause and effect"—of godless and inert forms and combinations of matter, the Lecturer then proceeded to show that nothing could satisfy man's internal wants but "a *system of supernaturalism;*" that Man *must* and *will* have something mysterious and miraculous—a faith superior to reason, argument, or judgment. It is necessary to remember, my friends, that we are now examining Dr. B——'s propositions and evidences of the existence of a system of supernaturalism; which, by acting *upon* or *in* the present world, develops the many and varied EFFECTS which Nature, by herself considered, could never accomplish by the unceasing operation of her undeviating and abiding forces. These evidences should be duly examined; and I now proceed to utter my impressions concerning them.

First: that man's prevailing desire for a mystical faith—for a faith in something mysterious and super natural—is a strong presumptive evidence, that such "a system really exists beyond nature."

To this I am impressed to say, that so far is this desire from being an evidence in favor of, it is more perfectly a powerful evidence *against* a system of supernaturalism, as disconnected from Nature. A *desire* for the marvelous is the legitimate child of Ignorance. Every enlightened mind shrinks from incomprehensible mysteries. He loves, and desires, and demands light and knowledge. Miracles do not excite his respect and veneration: they amaze and confound his understanding. He desires new and better developments; but repels every thing that bears the stamp of the supernatural, unless it promises to yield forth a consistent Truth. If he has a *faith*, it is a child of his judgment; the result of preponderating evidences. Hope, that *darling* of his affections, draws its highest nourishments chiefly from the fertile sources of reason. He has a reason for his hope. It is only the uneducated mind that yearns for the romantic, the absolutely supernatural, and the incomprehensible.

Second: Dr. B—— thinks, and openly asserted, that the mysteries of human magnetism constitute one evidence that people long for the supernatural; he thinks, also, that another inferential proof is derivable from the strange career of the Mormons. Now this is all wrong. For the *mysteries* of human magnetism are simply the normal operations of the natural sympathies of the human body and mind. These operations are *mysterious* and *supernatural*, only, to those who *can not* or *dare not* make them a matter of fair and thorough investigation. Dr. B——'s allusion to this subject betrayed very conspicuously the fact, that he had not sufficiently familiarized his mind with the great general *natural* principles upon which all magnetic phenomena invariably depend and undeviatingly occur. As to the Mormons, it is but common justice to say, that, as a peculiar religious people, there is among them no stronger "desire" than a firm determination to improve, if possible, the social existence and governmental arrangements of mankind upon strictly religious principles. Becoming satisfied that Christianity, as now inculcated, could not accomplish this very desirable improvement, they resolved unanimously to embrace something, or *any thing* else, which appeared to furnish an adequate remedy for the prevailing evils, inequalities, and discords of the world. And as to their religious system, national government, municipal laws, &c., I do not see how Dr. B—— can consistently and conscientiously object; because JOSEPH SMITH endeavored to *imitate*, so far as it was possible and locally convenient, the political peculiarities and character of Moses, and the more prominent habits and military methods of the religious chieftain, Joshua.* It was affirmed that Shelley, the great and gifted bard, "having worked himself into Atheism," still could not live happily without the supernatural faith. Hence he "peopled the forests, flowers, and trees with mythologic beings and beautiful elfs." It is very true, the immortal Shelley had too great and cultivated a soul to permit him to believe in the *cruel* and *capricious* God generally worshiped by the Bible Christians. The love of liberty and humanity, combined with a sacred appreciation of the advantages of Reason, as man's highest blessing, compelled Shelley to *dread* the time and land "where kings first leagued against the rights of man, and priests first TRADED with the name of God." And he had the good fortune to become skeptical in the God of priests; because he well knew that "human *pride* is skillful to invent the most *serious* names to hide its ignorance." Nevertheless, the poet did desire, as every

* For further analogies, see the Great Harmonia, Vol. III., Entitled the "Seer"

enlightened mind must, some better and more harmonious *faith* than he could find in the theological world about him—something more congenial with his cultivated affections and consonant with his best reason—and, had he known the Harmonial Philosophy of Nature and Spirituality, it is very probable, nay it is almost certain, that he would have joyfully accepted it; because—yea, *because*—it is so entirely divested of every thing which is uselessly mysterious and supernatural, and because, also, it addresses the cultivated heart *through* the expanded understanding.

Thus far, then, the alleged evidences of man's "desires for a faith in the supernatural" are unsound and fallacious.

But I think it must have surprised his intelligent hearers, when the Lecturer appealed to the serial creation of vegetables and animals as an "*evidence* of the action of the supernatural system upon the world." And in this connection Dr. B—— seemed to *reject* the whole doctrine of *progressive development* in the great operations and creations of Nature, by alluding to the discovery of the fossil remains of a perfectly *vertebrated fish* in one of the lower stratifications of rock. Here the Lecturer also alluded to the want of improvement in the system of *nursing* the young; and asserted that the plan was more perfect, if any thing, in the salmon, which protects its young from the liquid element, during the first week of its existence, by a soft gelatinous envelopment, than in the so-called higher animals, including the helpless offspring of man. All this was evidently adduced to *confuse* the order of progression in the development of animals. Indeed, the confusion would be exceedingly difficult to overcome and controvert, were it not for the important fact that *no such* confusion exists.

Dr. B—— set aside the "Vestiges of Creation," and all similar productions on Geology, by informing his audience that he was perfectly aware of the existence of such a work, and *feebler* attempts at rationalistic speculation. Will the earnest, vigorous minds of his congregation receive *this* as a conclusive argument against the progressive theory? Will they henceforth receive the supernaturalistic theory as proved to a demonstration? The Doctor disposed of the progressive theory in a most summary and gladiatorial manner, and then recommended his hearers to read Hugh Miller's recent work, entitled the "Footprints of the Creator." This work is not at all accepted by those who know any thing of practical geology. For it is merely a *plea* of the clergyman in behalf of his theological faith; an instance of hereditary or eruditional FAITH employing reason to act as an advocate and special partisan.

I have affirmed that *no confusion exists* in the order of creation. True, by the merest accident, a tree may fall from the hill-top to the valley, and be found centuries afterward, standing in an inverted position, buried in many feet of stratified earth. But does that circumstance *prove* that trees do not grow from the root upward? So also, suppose a FISH, the creation of a more recent period, should be found in the rock-formation of a remoter period: does that simple circumstance *confuse* the universal testimonies of Nature to the contrary? Among all enlightened people, where all jurisprudential proceedings are conducted upon the established fact that every case has *two* sides, and that verdicts are to be rendered in accordance with the preponderating evidence, I can not but believe that Dr. B——'s method of demonstrating supernaturalism must be peremptorily repudiated. He brings up the fossil remains of a single fish, to prove that all the uniform testimonies of Nature, in favor of progression, are doubtful or valueless. And then, having given himself the "benefit of the doubt," he turns the case over to supernaturalism; and proceeds to give the impression that the fish could not have been placed in its stony prison, except by the supernatural system of God operating upon the system of Nature! But I have tried to discover the location of that fish-skeleton, and I *do not find such a fact in Nature*, although it is mentioned *in the works* of three or four authors who have endeavored to throw doubt and discord over the philosophy of progressive development. The supernaturalist should be exceedingly careful in the selection of his evidences; because, not being a practical geologist himself, he might very easily be imposed upon by so-called *facts*, which may have no other foundation than the prejudice and conservatism of theologians.

But what shall we say about the NURSING? Why, simply this: that it is not true that the *plan* does not *advance* with the progression of the species. Every advancement in the organization of animals—especially the mammalial types—is attended with a corresponding improvement in the care of the young. The more intelligent the animal, the less is the system of nursing a matter of mechanism and instinct. The Salmon is provided with a natural cradle for its young, because it has not the intelligence to *make* one. The Kangaroo is provided with a pouch in which to carry its young, because it has not the intelligence to manufacture blankets and garments to protect the young body from the atmosphere. Now, will Dr. B—— affirm the human offspring to be less cared for than these lower organisms, because merely the human mother is not provided with those imperfect and cumbrous appendages? Surely, the *plan of nursing* the young is more and *more perfected* as creation advances from the lowest saurian to the human type. To affirm contrary to this, is to impeach the plainest declarations of the universal system.

Thus again, Dr. B——'s evidences of supernaturalism in nature, are shown to be groundless.

But what shall we say about the "acorn" which develops the stalwart oak? The Lecturer seemed to regard the growth of trees as accomplished by supernatural action! He said you might plunge a knife into the *acorn*, and examine it in various ways, still it is nothing but a plain nodule. That is to say, it is a *thing* in nature. But place that *nodule* in the earth, and soon it comes forth, adding length after length of wood; and, while the seasons come and depart, this *tree* stands up in *defiance* of the laws of gravitation and chemistry. I think Dr. B—— was very *obscure* in what he said of this oak. This *obscurity* may be regarded, like a bad hand-writing, as *evidence* of scholarship, but it certainly is no indication of clear thinking or that the individual is naturally and properly a teacher.

If I have exhumed the meaning of the lecturer on this point, it signifies this—viz.: that the Acorn derived its *potency* to build the ponderous oak, from the supernatural system of God. That the oak was the type of other and higher miracles; the prophecy of more spiritual demonstrations of supernaturalism. Now if this reasoning be correct, there can not possibly be any *uniform law* or rationalistic explanation in nature to account for the production of trees. But what are the facts? Why, the growth of trees is a chemical phenomenon. Chemistry has revealed the existence of an *invariable Power* in nature which promotes union between elements and compounds, even though their apparent natures be strongly opposed. This power is termed "chemical attraction;" but I can see no reason why it should not be called the unchangeable will of God operating in nature, like the flowing of blood in the human body, an eternal attribute of the one INDISSOLUBLE SYSTEM. The acorn, or nodule, would not produce an oak, if, instead of placing it in the earth, you should drop it in the water or among stones. There is nothing *supernatural* in the manifestation. Because the growth of trees depends upon certain favorable external conditions; whilst, if that result was ever accomplished by the direct action of God on the world, we should see some variation from the established laws.

Dr. B—— almost ridiculed the idea, that Nature by itself could develop organism endowed with *motion, life, sensation*, &c.; but does he not know that flour, dampened with a little water, will, in a few days or even hours, be transformed into *moving, living, feeling*, organisms? Does he not know that certain kinds of decomposed vegetation in stagnant water, will, if partially exposed to the sun, develop *worms*, *lizards*, and *frogs* incipiently—all, endowed with motion, life, and sensation? If the Lecturer admits this, but attributes the process of organization to *supernatural action* upon nature, then he virtually acknowledges that *Omnipotence* is itself subjected to man's power; because man can arrange the materials to produce these animals, or prevent the phenomena altogether by cleanliness and civilization. And man can develop rye from oats; or *oak-trees* from a combination of chestnut, pine, and walnut. If oats are cast in the ground at the proper season, and kept mowed down during the summer and autumnal months, and allowed to remain undisturbed till the succeeding spring, the oats will completely *disappear*, and a moderate growth of *ryy* will appear at the close of the following summer. Thus, it is by no means safe for Dr. B—— to set bounds to the achievements of chemistry. As a science, it is yet in its infancy. But whether by its aid, man will in the future, *be able* or not to combine Elements and Compounds so as to develop a *wolf*, a *fox*, or a *lion*, if he desires it, is a question which time and science will answer much better than any disciple of oriental dogmas.

In conclusion, I will direct your attention to a *subject* upon which Dr. B—— bestowed the most labor and manifested the greatest enthusiasm—*i. e.*, the *free agency* of the human. In discussing this matter, in its connections to supernaturalism, the Lecturer referred frequently to an *imaginary* portion of his discourse, which he termed "The Argument." I say "imaginary," because it was impossible to understand what he meant by "the argument," unless we adopt the hypothesis that he supposed he had one somewhere in the premises. What else he particularly referred to I can not discover.

The primary and scriptural *definition* of "Nature," be it remembered, was a system of *cause* and *effect*—a means, bringing about ends according to the action of the supernatural system upon, or within, its constitution. As NATURE, however, it was to be regarded as a *system* by itself; possessing inherent laws and fixed principles. At this point Dr. B—— started the subject of *free agency*. He said, in substance, that if he could bring those inherent laws and principles into subjection, it would prove that *he was independent of nature* in the same proportion; and would prove, also, that he was to the same degree *supernatural* and *responsible* to a supernatural government for the right use of his freedom and capabilities.

He said that NATURE never told falsehoods; never constructed *pistols* and *powder*; never loaded these weapons and shot men; but *he could* obtain powder, put it in a pistol and shoot his neighbor, and be hung for it. Whereas, he said, if the Rationalistic doctrine of cause and effect be true, the *powder* was as much to blame for the murder as he—inasmuch as, according to this naturalistic doctrine, he was merely *acting* as an effect; or from the strongest cause or impulse of his organization. Dr. B—— concluded that *man* was perfectly *free* in the volition of his consciousness—and supernatural in his supremacy to nature; and therefore accountable to, and dependent upon, the supernatural kingdom of God for his actions and ultimate redemption from sin.

Now let us see into this. Dr. B—— asserts that he can procure powder, load a pistol, and shoot his neighbor—proving thereby that he is morally *free*, and superior to nature; because he *can* do what nature can not. Nature, by the way, even when considered in her lowest departments, does manufacture powder, or explosive compositions, and nature *does* shoot and kill human beings by her coal mines and volcanic eruptions. And it is true, that the stones, trees, and inferior animals of NATURE do not build ships, &c.; but when the system of creation has progressed to the human species, developing thereby new wants and powers, then NATURE, through the organization of man, does build houses and ships, and unfolds results through the higher instrumentalities of the human in tellect.

By what Dr. B—— says of personal freedom, he displays almost unpardonable ignorance of the con struction and nature of the human mind, and seems to entertain the most confused and contracted view of the relationship and harmonious dependencies of things. When the Lecturer viewed himself as connected with the universe of God by a *chain of causes and effects*, and supposed himself to be let *down* "*into a well*" where he could touch nothing but "the link just above," what a sense of *loneliness* and *abhorrence* did he manifest! But I know nothing in Rationalism so-called to which this graphic comparison is at all applicable; although when I think of *popular theology*, with its mechanism of intercession and redemption, I realize something analogous to Dr. B——'s description of his own sensations.

Rationalism, *or Harmonial spiritualism*, sees MAN as a *microscope*—as a *miniature* universe; being perpetually visited by innumerable friends from the four quarters of the firmament. Man is not compelled to touch merely the next link above; but being constitutionally the HEAD of Creation, he can enjoy the countless relationships which exist, most intimately, between him and external nature; between him and the spiritual universe! He thinks he is supernatural and *perfectly free*, because he can raise a book and overcome the law of gravitation. This he thinks NATURE can not do, because it is bound by the inexorable principles of cause and effect. Dr. B—— should remember that a *tornado* can also *overcome* the law of gravitation, accompanied with terrible manifestations of its power; not only by raising the book, but by raising fifty men —*filled with free agency*—at the same time! But Dr. B—— informed his congregation, repeatedly, that HE WAS A MAN—a *free* man—a MAN that *could shoot* his neighbor—could do, in a word, any thing he pleased. Now, believing him to be a man of unimpeachable veracity, I would solicit a few practical illustrations of his perfect freedom. Will he answer these questions?

Could he, by the exercise of his personal freedom, procure *powder* and pistols if these things were not yet invented?

Can he control, by his will, the conditions of mind known as belief and disbelief? or, the states known as *love* and *hate?*

Can he voluntarily *hate* his best neighbor? Or, can he for ten minutes *love affectionately* a person *revolting* to his whole soul?

Can he, by the exercise of his personal freedom, *disbelieve* in the existence of a Supreme Being? Or, *believe* it at will?

If the Lecturer can not do these things at the instigation of *his will*, then he is in *bondage* to the system of terrestrial *cause* and *effect*. How does he know that there are *objects*, *lights*, *shades* and *colors* in nature? I answer, that he knows these things, through the medium of bodily vision; without which organs, in spite of all *his* personal freedom, he would have in his possession no certain knowledge of them. So, too, is he absolutely dependent upon his *bodily hearing* to learn ideas of sound; upon his limbs for locomotion; upon the cheerful *action* of his tongue to communicate his ideas to the people. If his *tongue* were paralyzed —his *arms* amputated—his *eyes* deprived of their appropriate functions—and his brain loaded with blood; how impotent would be his will should he then *desire* to *shoot* his neighbour, preach to his congregation, or impart his thoughts by wielding the pen! If Dr. B—— can not do *every thing* which he may desire, simply by *willing* to do so,—a *man* who *felt* and declared himself so *superior* to *all* "cause and effect,"— then I do not see how he can escape the *Rationalistic theory*, that all things are *bound together* in the Universal Spirit of God—"in whom," according to his original text, "all things consist."

How depressing, and how unlike an impartial investigator, was the attempt to ridicule the great Bible doctrine that God is "without variableness neither shadow of turning." The Doctor, seemed to have forgotten that this opinion was entertained by the Bible authors, and hence ridiculed it as a Rationalistic Theory. Instead of saying that the Lord "made the heavens and the earth, and all that in them is, in six days," and devoted the seventh to rest (as the Bible expresses it), he ridiculed it *as a naturalistic* notion, that God as a mechanic, had "*made* and *perfected* his MACHINE a long period since, and was now engaged in turning the crank!" Why Dr. B—— ridicules Bible doctrines under the title of Rationalistic Theories, is a difficult question to solve, unless we charitably conclude that he has not familiarized his mind with the opinions of his antagonists. He thought the idea *degrading* and *abhorrent*, that the Lord should have perfected the vast machine of heaven and earth, and pronounced it "good," a long time ago, and had nothing to expect *outside* of its action!

Surely Dr. B—— does not understand the Rationalistic theory; which teaches that God is constantly *improving* and advancing NATURE. If the object is to dethrone rationalism, why does not the Lecturer state its doctrines, and then proceed in a dignified manner to expose their fallacy? To assert that modern philosophers believe that the Deity *perfected* his machine centuries ago, and then assign to the Creator the duty of turning the crank, is all a false and ignoble representation. This is the doctrine inculcated in Genesis, but is vastly unlike the rationalistic theory.

The Harmonial Philosophy teaches that *Progress* is a Law of Deity; that *matter* is *the receptacle* of the Spirit of God; that every thing is perpetually advancing from *bad* to *better*—from *motion* to *mind*, from earth to heaven; that "the machine" can *never* be perfected—that the Deity can not be "turning a crank;" because he is the *great Positive Mind*, enlivening and controlling the *material* and *spiritual* universe, with an unerring and unchangeable government.

Dr. B—— thought that, should he wish to address the Deity, through love and gratitude, according to rationalism, he should be regarded by the Creator as giving expression merely to the emotions natural to his organization—a consequence of the machine, like an island thrown up by volcanic action from the sea. In this view he thought *a man* might as well be something *else*; and KOSSUTH, so far as responsibility is concerned, might as well be smoke curling from the chimney-top! Now I am impressed to object to such unfairness and inconsistency—it should not emanate from a reasonable mind—especially not from one who is somewhat disposed to be a Martin Luther in theology.

Dr. B—— ridicules this system of *cause* and *effect*—of praying and being righteous on the ground of personal organization—and yet, he is an advocate for *schools*, *colleges*, *churches*, and systems of education. He thinks well of *temperance* societies, &c. But wherefore? Because these *institutions* influence the human mind to goodness. Because *good morals* depend upon *good* influences and upon *good* systems of education. Because, in a word, the human mind, like the softened clay, can be *fashioned* and molded into ANY SHAPE, by the action of external *causes* upon it. Thus, while he would, as a Christian scholar, theologically repudiate the doctrine of *cause and effect* as applicable to man, he at the same time virtually acts upon it in his daily existence and professions. In closing, I will merely remark, that this doctrine of human freedom is THE PIVOT, upon which Dr. B——'s whole philosophy of the Incarnation and Redemption depends. This made him sarcastic in his criticisms, and impatient in his utterance. But he has not yet answered all the *objections* which can be urged against his doctrine; nor manifested any ability to make his propositions invulnerable. The latter, being an impossibility, he can not be expected to do. His definition of NATURE and SUPERNATURE, is not to be admitted; because he has not given us the *least evidence* why such a definition should be accepted as resting in truth. And his statement of the extent of nature, is too narrow to answer the conceptions of rationalists, who believe matter to be the external Revelation of God—immeasurable, infinite, eternal. In a word, his theological opinions are cramping and trammeling his own mind, as they have, in *other* forms and modifications, enslaved hundreds of thousands; and which have prevented the introduction of those more reformatory theories, that lie at the very foundation of Christianity and promote the highest civilization.

CHAPTER IV.

THIRD REVIEW.

Retrogression.—The supernatural realm.—A war of words.—Symptoms of reason.—Simplicity of rationalism.—Things and Powers.—The origin of evil.—Insurmountable objections.—The mysterious knockings undignified.—Mental expansion necessary.—A spiritual United States.—Pulpit exaggerations.—The question of evil biblically considered.—A conversation between God and Adam.—The true origin of evil.—Knowledge based upon experience.—Moralism and Christianity.—The social causes of evil.—Rationalism and supernaturalism illustrated.

LAST Sabbath evening, Dr. Bushnell delivered his third discourse upon the Supernaturalistic system of religion. It seems that he has forgotten or neglected to achieve the promised "reconciliation" between the naturalistic and the unnaturalistic forms of faith; and abandoning considerably the philosophical ground, has proceeded in the old familiar work of constructing a theological fabric or system in which to enshrine *his* scholastic notions of religion and revamped theology. Conservatism, therefore, of the unprogressive and unrighteous kind, will probably be, or appear to be, promoted to a higher throne in the kingdom of dogmatism, and receive another coronation as the Emperor of Antiquity and the changeless friend of Oriental Doctrines.

The Lecturer, as you doubtless remember, found a

suggestive title to his discourse in the sixth chapter of Isaiah, fifth verse, in these words—"The Lord of Hosts"—a form of expression very frequently employed by all those who were converted from paganism, or polytheism, to a belief in monotheism and in the Hebrew God.

In his previous lecture, it will be recollected, Dr. B—— acknowledged that his "future arguments" could not be fully appreciated, unless his "definition" of Nature and Supernature was understood and accepted by his hearers. He therefore expressed the definition, and proceeded to build his house of theologic thought accordingly.

For two reasons, I am impressed to regard this method as quite unrighteous and positively antagonistic to the cause of progressive Truth. First, because he introduces, and adopts his pre-arranged definition without in the least consulting or explaining the Rationalistic positions and definitions on the same head. Secondly, because he proceeds to argue, and to build upon, his own theological assumptions and foundation without demonstrating the said ground-plan to be the *only* reasonable and consistent one possible for the human mind to conceive and adopt.

It is very true, that Dr. B—— did present what he supposed to be satisfactory and demonstrative evidences of the voluntary action of the supernatural system of God upon this world of effects and causation. But I have shown, I think, that no such evidences really exist. Hence he has nothing left but an *imaginary* or hypothetical formation—premises, in other words, which are derived principally from scholastic sources of theological speculation, and from certain scriptural suggestions. This method, for the reasons already stated, will never cure the world of skepticism. The natural constitutional instinct or intuition of the soul needs to be addressed; and the Reason-principle must see, and the moral sensibilities must feel, the foundations of Truth.

Of the third discourse, which I am now examining, it may be truly said that it manifested considerable scholastic skill and power of intellectual conception. It contained several interesting and well-elaborated passages; indicated the existence of a subdued veneration in the producing mind; but it was no less free from the unskillful ridicule and unnecessary sarcasm which characterized the preceding lectures. There are times and places, undoubtedly, when a moderate expression of satirical thoughts may work a better temporary result than the soberness of common conversation or description. But in a philosophical dissertation, it seems to me that ridicule and sarcasm should not be permitted to appear, especially when and where pure and honest arguments are pre-eminently required, and earnestly sought by truthful minds. The latter alone constitute the moral and intellectual *pabulum* of truth-loving and reasonable persons.

Let us return to the text. The expression—"Lord of Hosts"—was understood to mean something more than the God or Spirit of Nature. It referred, it was asserted, to the supernatural system. It referred to a spiritual realm; where "exist kingdoms, and thrones, and powers, and principalities;" where there are every possible degree of spiritual life, and every conceivable shade of angelic and phase of seraphic existence. This *realm* was described at considerable length, by the Lecturer, in contradistinction to the fixed and immutable System of Nature visible about us; as the vast world, in short, where alone we are certain to find the throne and supernatural or moral government of God.

Now I am moved to inquire: How does Dr. B—— know that there is any such a realm as he described, in the universe? Has he seen through the dark and shadowy valley of death? Has a ray of immortal light, from the supernatural sphere, descended and awakened his interior understanding? Or, has some enlightened dweller of the spiritual realm approached him in the midnight hour? Did it open his blinded heart? Did it lead him out beyond the changing earth, and point upward to the eternal Mind, that "taketh knowledge of the falling sparrow" and lights the illimitable universe with a kindling glory? If so; why does he not confess, that, like a new-born man into whose nostrils has just been breathed the breath of a higher life, he utters his convictions of the supernatural? If not; then how does he know, how can he be certain, that any such a spiritual dominion exists as he described in his last discourse? Or, has he studied the universal laws of analogy, and the principles of correspondence? Does he base his conclusions upon the psychological laws and constitution of man—upon the spiritual manifestations of this century? In a word, has he any *new and reliable light* by which to see the truths and principalities, and thrones and powers, of the celestial realm?

The negative reply is too distinct. He has received no fresh inspiration, but takes the old and superannuated *Hebrew* expression as authoritatively suggestive of the supernatural system; and then amplifies the idea by using the speculative language of Paul concerning thrones, dominions, powers, and principalities; which, if the apostle ever beheld, he must necessarily have seen by the exercise of the same identical mental power of *clear vision*, which is denominated clairvoyance by modern investigators. Dr. B—— is manifestly seeing through the eyes and thoughts of ancient minds. He does not put sufficient trust in the "ten talents" which he, in common with all the earth's inhabitants, has inherited from the heavenly Father. He too plainly inters his capabilities within the sacerdotal tombs of antiquity. Scholastic education, which is another term for *learned ignorance*, has presided over the funeral, and now prevents a healthy resurrection.

Before inspecting the very few points contained in the discourse referred to, I will briefly direct your attention to the fact, that the ancient Hebrew conception of the "Lord of Hosts" is low and cramping to the benevolence and republican sentiments of the generous mind—especially, when practically believed. The Jewish God is *cruel*, *capricious*, *tyrannical*. His kingdom is more despotic, and more contracted in principle, than the present government of the Russian empire. The earth's inhabitants, who *first* conceived of such a supernatural being, could not have obtained or entertained higher views of a Chief Ruler and directing power, because they were living in the midst of Kings and Empires. Isaiah could only expand upon the idea of an earthly king, and upon a terrestrial empire; though he freed his conception as far as possible of all the iniquities and unrighteousness which pertained to earthly rulers and political governments about him. And so did all the Hebrews who were converted from the pagan sects. The birds do not more naturally build their nests, or the mole dig into the ground, than does the human mind, in its unprogressed and unspiritual states, conceive of a King of kings and a Lord of lords, as residing in the mystical or unseen sphere. The Indian has a Sachem; the patriarch an omniarch; the Hebrew king a Lord of Hosts; the childlike mind a Heavenly Father. Now, according to my impressions and the testimony of history, the Old Testament idea of a Deity is the outgrowth of the despotic stage of human mental development. It is the best idea which could in those times have been entertained; and I am, with you, my friends, exceedingly disappointed that, in a philosophico-theological discourse of to-day, this superannuated monotheistic conception should be appealed to as a living Truth.

If there be in reality a "spiritual realm"—not existing upon the reciprocal principles of cause and effect, in which resides the "Lord of Hosts" with a system of government entirely different from the system of nature—then it is time, it seems to me, that the earth's inhabitants should receive some substantial and unequivocal demonstration to that effect. That there *is* a Spiritual Universe co-eternal and co-extensive with the material universe, which the finite mind can measure or comprehend—the two systems being inwrought and interblended perfectly, and universally harmonious, too, in their essential natures and governments—is a truth, which has been fully and satisfactorily demonstrated to the earth-people in various ways since the world began. This is the sacred conviction of the most enlightened rationalists. It is evidenced in the psychological laws of mind; in the laws of universal analogy; in the spiritual disclosures of the present century; and, more particularly, in all the higher sciences and discoveries of modern times. Every thing evidently is conspiring to a single point—to *demonstrate*, as it were, one infinite truth—viz.: the stupendous oneness and harmonies of the entire universe! The best minds of the age begin to see and acknowledge that there can not possibly exist two independent and antagonistic systems of truth in one universe. But that harmony must reign co-equal and co-essential with the great all-animating principle, which is Deity.

My impression distinctly is, that Dr. B—— would be less unfavorably inclined toward harmonial Rationalism, if his judgment was better acquainted with its fundamental positions and elevating teachings. His last lecture contained a few points of difference; but there was more antagonism, or positive conflict, in the *terms* employed than in the ideas. Indeed, the most of it was a species of literary bombardment—a *war of words*—requiring, merely, an honest and dispassionate comparison of ideas to soothe and restore every antagonistic feeling to peace. For example: the idea of human *progression* throughout the spiritual universe was clearly enough set forth in the words—"thrones, dominions, powers, and principalities"—which correspond, measurably, to the different shades and degrees of *circles*, *societies*, &c., which the Harmonial Philosophy contemplates in the spirally ascending spheres of the spiritual universe. Again: the Lecturer's assertion, that all *spirits*, and *angels*, and *seraphs* were *once* subjected to the discipline, trials, temptations, and vicissitudes of the material world, is perfectly in accordance with the rationalistic theory on that head. Hence, I repeat, that the pending war is, in several respects, altogether confined to language, which a little calm investigation on the Lecturer's part would soon change to the furtherance of truth and religious reformation.

Dr. B—— declared his third lecture to be merely "interposed" to bridge the channel between his previous definitions of nature and supernature—to amplify and describe, in other words, the vast dominion of the spiritual realm, and consider it in relation to external nature and to man. It was very plain that he was laboring to open a place to be hereafter filled by the supernatural system of redemption. He labored to harmonize his scholastic education and religious convictions with the known laws and constitution of nature. But he could not and can not succeed; for it is only the truth that can be made to appear harmonious and consistent.

It is now my impression to examine Dr. B——'s classification of what he termed—"Things and Powers."

It was asserted that "things" are created absolutely *perfect* at once; that they are incapable of further improvement or alteration; and are bound together by the fixed laws of cause and effect. "Powers," on the contrary, are created with self-subsisting and self-directing force—susceptible to eternal change and advancement; and confined to the action of *no laws* in particular, but responsible alone to the supernatural government and moral system of God. "Things are under law; powers are above law." "Things belong to nature; powers, to the spiritual realm." "*Things* are in bondage to the system of nature; *powers*, are self-determining and free agents." The foregoing are substantially the positions assumed by Dr. B——. But how obscure is all this! How unlike the universal testimonies of creation!

Where is the line of demarkation—I ask—between the empire of things and the Hosts of powers? Where do the "perfect" and law-serving "things" cease to exist? And where commences the universe of imperfect and disloyal "powers?" Surely, plants and trees can be and are daily improved; minerals can be greatly perfected; and brutes considerably educated. There is no evidence that a plant is more perfect than a man. The one may be a higher development than the other; but *each* creation may be perfect *of its kind*—alike, capable of being changed, deformed, or improved by the energetic play of external circumstances upon them. We want, therefore, the plain truth. We demand a clear definition of "things and powers"—not a theological and *romantic* classification; but a psychological, philosophical, and *rational* one, which shall be so truthful and so simple, that he who runs may read.

Dr. B—— alluded to his grand and soul-satisfying conception of the spiritual kingdom, in comparison with the *simple* and low doctrine of rationalism; which teaches that all things and powers are subsisting upon, and controlled by, the unchangeable laws of cause and effect. Indeed? "Simple!" Does he admire the plain, unadorned teachings of Jesus? Surely the *simplicity* of the Christian precepts and doctrines constitutes their principal charm and beauty. Truth, it appears to me, is always simple. Undeveloped minds invariably entertain mysterious and incomprehensible notions of almost every thing. But the comprehensive mind sees the unity and simplicity of Truth. Manifestly, it is quite unrighteous to generate prejudice, in the minds of the people, toward a matter of which they have no very definite knowledge; by *comparisons*, which amount in principle to mere ridicule, as based upon educational pride and repugnance to seeing new light in the developments of the current age. It is *because* Rationalism is so self-evident and reasonable that the human mind can easily comprehend and love its disclosures. As *honesty* clothes the good man, *modesty* the virtuous, and *meekness* the man of wisdom; so is *truth* robed in *simplicity;* and, like the shining sun, its rays dissolve the mysterious clouds which obscure the heavens from our vision, and by its power the unity of the whole is distinctly revealed.

Evidently Dr. B——'s definition of things and powers was derived from the Bible and from his own mental abstractions. Had he contemplated the vast panorama of external nature, and then turned his eye in upon himself, and upon the psychological constitution of man, he would have obtained *more truth* and a better definition. As the matter now stands, I have nothing to comment upon in this department of his discourse. The classification of "things and powers" was wholly fictitious, and superinduced, in order to fix a foundation upon which to rest the doctrine of absolute "free agency" and the scriptural or supernatural system of redemption. As he did not appeal to nature and to human experience to support his definition, I, therefore, have nothing to examine or to analyze; because, I repeat, the whole matter was conceived and procreated in the fertile womb of superstition.

Again: Dr. B—— revived the question of free agency. He asserted that all created "powers" are endowed with the ability to act from choice, consent, or will; and then proceeded to consider the various spiritual relations which are supposed to subsist between man and the Lord of Hosts. He thought man's *will-power* was perfectly unrestrained; and nothing was permitted to prevent the "powers" from exercising their freedom, and receiving the consequences thereof, both here and hereafter. He thought a different view—the Rationalistic doctrine of universal dependencies and sympathetic relationships—would convert society, government, all laws, penalties, benefits, and the marriage relation, into unmeaning institutions. He said that these institutions were constructed on the universally admitted *fact* of man's moral freedom. And yet, Dr. B—— conceived the divine government to be acting just above the will. The Divine Will, with its inexorable principles of justice, "overlaid" the mental faculties of choice; and thus the Lecturer introduced or created a demand for the medicine of "redemption" as a remedy for the soul's voluntary sins and iniquity.

In this elaborating conception, it must be acknowledged Dr. B—— manifested some originality of thought. Indeed, he exceeded the wisdom and assumptions of the Bible on this subject; and may, therefore, henceforth be denominated an "infidel"—at least *to the views* of the timid, good, and rigid orthodox members of the Connecticut Association. As the question of man's freedom was the principal point of his last discourse, I will proceed presently to briefly consider it.

I come now to another point—viz.: *the Lecturer's idea of the origin of evil.* It should, however, be constantly remembered that Dr. B—— did not begin his inquiries in a state of mental freedom. This fact obscured his intellectual vision; and caused him to give a false coloring to nearly all the thoughts he presented. He is trammeled, according to my impression, like an artist whose mind can not operate independently of the "Old Masters." He does not start on his voyage of discovery like the intrepid Columbus, seeking truth only, in some heretofore undiscovered continent. Far from it. He sets out, like an engaged attorney, to argue the partial and particular case of his client. *He must not see truth on the opposite side.* He does not set forth with the noble resolution to *follow* truth wherever it may lead. But he has two things to accomplish—first, to *find a place* for a supernatural system, which he determines *shall have* a place somewhere: secondly, he must and will discover an intellectual method whereby to *reconcile* the plan of Christian redemption with personal wants, with the logical deductions, and sinful condition of the race of man. That is to say, he will argue *his side* of the question exclusively as *the side of truth.* He must, therefore—in order to be judiciously Conservative, and sufficiently orthodox to pass current among the people—paint and tint his pictures in accordance with the great general plan pursued by the old theological writers and masters. This, alas, is not particularly and exclusively *his* besetting sin. The majority of men are thus sinful.

The Lecturer's philosophical idea of the *origin* of sin was truly a supernatural, or rather an *unnatural*, conception. He seemed to think that there was no particular danger in creating "things;" but that the creation of "powers" was attended with the awful "possibility of evil;" that sin was a *necessary* concomitant of this branch of God's creation! Indeed, he thought that Omnipotence itself was "environed by the possibility of evil" before the world began; and that the divine Mind *could not* have created free moral agents or "independent powers" without bringing into existence, or without being under the necessity of tolerating, the blight known as sin. Sin, it was asserted, is a necessary, or rather a "possible," consequence of such creations as men, spirits, angels, and seraphs. Thus, sin or evil is *supernaturally* derived and originated! Hence, it requires a supernaturally instituted plan to *overcome* the consequences of sin; and also to *neutralize*, as far as the system of "free moral" creations will permit, the terrible "possibility of evil" which environed the Divine Being even before the creation of the world. Here, then, in the most scriptural and ingenious manner, Dr. B—— opened a place in the affairs of men for the introduction, and for the indispensability, of the Christian plan of redemption. He derived all his fundamental suggestions from the Bible; but it is most evident, that in the subsequent conception and elaboration of this redemptional scheme, the Lecturer again *out-generaled* the wisdom of the Sacred Scriptures. The Bible does not *so clearly* assert, that God was ever environed by the possibility of evil in creating man. Nor that sin is supernatural —except, so far as *Adam's* transgression was a violation of an eternal command or law, to which was mysteriously attached eternal penalties. And even this doctrine of evil is principally the work of clergymen, as I shall demonstrate in the sequel. The Bible furnishes mythologic suggestions; and, then, the professional preacher—the "D. D."—that is, the man who *doctors* divinity—takes up "the wondrous tale," and skillfully manufactures or compounds a *system* of sin, a *system* of redemption, and the absolute necessity for a *systematic* and regularly organized priesthood, in order to guide mankind from hell to the state of heaven. How much better would an organization of all kinds of industry be for the world!

But let us think of the idea. If God was under the *necessity* of making free powers, or human beings, at a tremendous *risk* of involving his moral universe in interminable trouble—if he could not have created man without being "environed with the possibility of evil" —then, I inquire, where is the alleged *Omnipotence* of Jehovah?

Or, if he could have made man, and could have prohibited even the "possibility" of sin, had he *desired* it—then, I inquire, where is the unutterable *Goodness* of Jehovah?

Or, if he would have made man invulnerable to evil, had there been any possibility of so doing, consistently and compatibly with the moral state of free agency—

then, I ask, where is the wisdom or the eternal and universal *Omniscience* of Jehovah?

You may say that I have no right to question the Creator's wisdom or designs on these points; but should accept whatever he has done as the very perfection of wisdom and equity. Nay, not so. Because I am, in common with all my earthly brethren, made with the faculties for seeking and finding, I have reasons for believing that, by asking for truth, I shall find it in due time. Besides, I am truly impressed that the Bible is a compilation of the thoughts, traditions, and opinions of imperfect and fallible men. The doctrine of sin, and the system of redemption, as conceived and elaborated by Dr. B——, was developed, not with the real Lord of Hosts, not with the real Divine Principle which enlivens and controls this immeasurable and harmonious universe; but I can see, by history and otherwise, that it originated with human beings. Hence, I have a right, a heaven-born right, to question the origin and consistency of the scheme; and to expose its horrid and soul-harassing incongruities, too; because the *development* of republicanism and of mental happiness among men, depends very much upon the absence of these dogmatic compilations or fossil relics of an old Hebrew and Chaldean theology. They retard the car of progress, and trammel the higher faculties of thought. I will, therefore, presently proceed to explain the *true* origin and nature of evil.

But let us now think of demonism. Dr. B——, it seems, has ventured to improve, to a considerable extent, upon the old Zoroasterian doctrine of a *personal devil;* which doctrine is frequently alluded to, or quoted, by the evangelists and other New Testament writers. He thinks the true *idea of a devil* is the generalization or combination of evil. All sins combined, organized, and then personified by the term "Devil." This sensible reformation of theology is praiseworthy. It is the Rationalistic method. But Dr. B—— does not seem quite so far advanced as the Persian *author* of the doctrine of a personal devil. Zoroaster said that the devil—called Arhiman—would, in the fullness of the dispensations of time, be completely transformed and converted, together with all his multitudinous subordinates, into *perfect friends* of the God of Goodness, Ormuzd. I think that, if the Lecturer embraces one portion of this doctrine, he certainly should the other.

In the Scriptures we are told that if we "*knock*, it shall be opened." All learned divines, so-called, concur in the opinion, I believe, that this language has an *interior*, spiritual, or correspondential signification of unusual scope and latitude. It means, evidently, that whenever and wherever the honest and truth-loving mind finds a door, which promises to open upon a new territory or region of truth, it will certainly be "opened" unto him, if he will but "knock" thereon, with the simple-mindedness of a child, and with the meekness and lucidity of wisdom. But Dr. B—— declared or affirmed that he would never *consent* to "knock," when he became a disembodied spirit; because, forsooth, it was not sufficiently dignified and noble! When Jesus compelled the devils to flee into the herd of swine, it seems that the swine,—belonging probably to some laboring man,—ran off the precipice, and were entirely destroyed. Now here was a real and absolute "destruction of property," owing, not exclusively to the devils, but to *the power which caused* the devils to accomplish the named supernatural result. But Dr. B—— thought that the devils had "come out" of the swine again, and were nowadays "knocking upon tables, chairs, writing upon turnips," &c.; a matter exceedingly repulsive to his feelings and scholastic notions. He did not, however, undertake to deny that spirits do or can communicate in various ways with the earth's inhabitants. Now, it seems to me, and I express it with due deference to him, that Dr. B—— would be a wiser and happier man, if he possessed more of that simple spirit so pre-eminently characteristic of *Jesus;* who told his followers—"seek, and ye shall find; KNOCK, and it shall be opened unto you."

It is quite essential, my friends, that we keep definitely in our mental view, the precise and avowed object which this champion of supernaturalism has energetically set out to accomplish. It may be summed up in the well-known language of nearly all Christian scholars, commencing—somewhat conspicuously, with the celebrated *Pollok*, who, although he did not live to execute the extraordinary classical projection, yet conceived "A Review of Literature in all Ages, designed to show that literature must *stand* or *fall* in proportion as it *harmonizes* with Scripture Revelation." Dr. B——'s present effort is substantially the same in effect, only differently stated and developed. It is still the scholastic and church idea of "harmonizing Nature with Revelation"—that is, possibilities with prodigious impossibilities; essential truths with the most overwhelming and mind-deforming inconsistencies.

Let us also bear in mind, that the present discussion is not pending between two individuals; whose education and opinions chance to be openly manifested and antagonistic. It is Humanity and mental Independence against a new form of dogmatic Conservatism. The latter has recently obtained an utterance through the mind and mouth of Dr. B——; and the former, in the capacity of an independent spectator and thinker, has appeared in the various criticisms of the reviewer. I pray you, therefore, to elevate your thoughts above the local imperfections of the mere *individuals* engaged, to the end that you may scan, with a more clear and comprehensive vision, the merits and demerits—*the proprium ingenium*—of the *great principles* involved and unfolded in the discussion.

As you probably remember, the theological *Luther* of to-day, in developing his philosophical idea of unphilosophical things—I mean, in giving his reasons for the supernatural origin of sin and discord—said, that, although he was not designing, or at liberty, to discuss whether the race began with one man or with many types, yet he would take Adam as an illustration. Accordingly, the *first man* was marshaled out on the theological ground; and then and there was viewed in the capacity of a pure, immaculate, but undisciplined and uneducated mind. "The experiment of life was now to commence." Adam was a "free power;" not subject to the reciprocal principles of cause and effect; neither to "mere mechanical force," as "things" manifestly are, in the domain of nature. He could *not have known sin*, said Dr. B——; for he was as yet quite inexperienced. Consequently, although the *law of Right* was sounding in his soul with all its original symphonies; yet he sinned—transgressed the law of God—and there he stood, looking at himself in the "mirror of the law"—descanting on his own moral deformity—"and would not even look away,"—so conscious was he of blamable wrong. Thus, the tremendous "possibility of evil which surrounded the Deity in creating the powers," was originated and *actualized*, so to express it, on the footstool. This was Dr. B——'s philosophical explanation of the origin of evil.

Disconnected and devoid of pure moral intuition and philosophy, as this explantion is, yet there appears enough to show the scientific and faithful historian, that the Lecturer listens more to the voice of oriental traditions than to the heaven-attuned music of immortal Truth. Oh, that his vision could be expanded, from the individual, to a comprehensive idea of the *solidarity* of humanity! He is painfully distracted by the annoyances of isolated thought. The grand soul and sources of the human heart are measurably overlooked by the habit of gazing too particularly and constantly at minor points of character. He may ascend the highest eminence to view the surrounding landscape; but the ineffable beauty and towering grandeur of *the whole is lost*, to the eye that sees only spears of grass and points of pins. Dr. B—— is a man of peculiar genius; suffering from certain internal fluctuations of feeling—a conflict, between the vigorous play of his moral sensibilities and his intellectual perception of truth and reason—causing him to draw a strange line of demarkation between Nature and Supernature; and to *depreciate* humanity in the honest effort to urge a misinterpreted Christianity upon the rationalistic philosopher. Assisted by his genius, he occasionally mounts the heights of Thought, and employs a grotesque eloquence in speaking of man's strength and willingness to "pass through burning worlds" to maintain the Law of Right; nevertheless, just when a higher view of humanity is about to break forth from the quivering tongue, the *eye* reverts back to some *local* annoyance or imperfection arising from weak *individual* man, and, lo! the sentence is turned to a theological saying that "the heart of man is desperately wicked, and there is no good in him." Instead of this circumscribed estimate, how liberated would the mind become, should it believe, from a comprehensive survey of, and affiliation with, the whole, that—

> "If rightly trained and bred,
> Humanity is humble,—finds no spot
> Her heaven-guided feet refuse to tread."

On this occasion, I am impressed to examine the church or Conservative philosophy of the origin of evil—with a view to show the *impossibility* of philosophically *convicting* the race of *voluntary sin* on the Bible basis.

A question of great magnitude and importance can not be analyzed and fully elucidated in a brief discourse. It is not only the great general subject itself which requires careful dissection and illustration; but also the *particular* phases of the manifold thoughts that flow up from the principal consideration as its constitutional constituents. One thing, however, is manifestly favorable to a successful explanation, in one lecture, of the question before us. I allude to the fact, which is a source of no little gratification to me, that I am about to address an assemblage of *thinking*, *truth-loving* men and women—a class of citizens that have ventured away from the old paths in thoughts and creeds. While the majority of mankind are wending their way along the shore—fearing to lose sight of the old moorings and landmarks—you put out to sea, taking the compass of Thought to determine your latitudes and longitudes, and the North Star as the never-varying Truth shining over your pathway; and, like the persevering Columbus, the voyage of discovery, which you have thus enterprisingly undertaken, will, while it subjects you to the various vicissitudes and whirlwinds of public opinion, ultimately result in the organization of a Spiritual United States—differing as much from the present system as the *effulgent soul* differs from the material body.

The origin of evil, or sin, is a question that has suggested itself to the mind of almost every person. Everybody is made sensible, from the hour of birth to the moment of physical death, of something out of *order* and out of *harmony* in this world. No one is entirely happy. Disturbances either physical or moral, are experienced by all breathing beings, to a greater or less extent. *Physical disorders*, pains and sickness; *social discords*, wars and inequalities; *mental disturbances*, anxiety, disappointment, unhappiness, and despair. These are the prominent symptoms of some chronic disease in the world. The question is, How did *this disease*, or these endless symptoms and incongruities, originate? *When* and *where* did they *begin* to be? This interrogatory comes home to every one. The *selfish* mind wishes to know *how* to escape these discords, from motives of mere *personal* comfort and consideration; the *philanthropist* prays to *know how they originate*, in order to apply the appropriate remedies; thus to emancipate mankind from the bondage of corruption, and from the dominion of unhappiness and despair. As I have already said, a question of such magnitude and innumerable complications, can not be thoroughly and minutely elucidated in one lecture, nor yet in ten carefully prepared discourses; but the generalizations and philosophy on this head can be given in a concise form; with many things left for your more private and particular examination.

The church assumptions on the primary development of evil, are probably familiar to you all. Learned divines—erroneously so called—have concentrated their time, capital, and talent upon this question. They have laid the foundation deep in the *ignorance* of the people; they have erected a mighty *sacrium* thereon; and all the theological relics of olden times are very carefully labeled, the prices marked up, and carefully laid away upon the sacred shelves,—ready for purchasers. Evil has received all the honors of deification. It has been gazed at by clergymen through the magnifying lens of the vicarious atonement; and, in order to harmonize effects with causes—to make the stupendous and so-called merciful scheme of *Redemption* correspond measurably with the thing which suggested and required it—they have, with much honest motive and inevitable cupidity, promoted *sin* or *evil* to a high primeval position in the realm of the Godhood and the supernatural. The writers of the New Testament are not wholly exempt from this charge of the unnatural and unrighteous *exaggeration* of sin. They have made it a matter of more importance than the subject properly requires or deserves. And the priesthood have followed up the method; they have finally succeeded in wrapping

> "Nonsense 'round
> With pomp and darkness till it seems profound;
> While reason, like a grave-faced mummy stands,
> With its arms swathed in hieroglyphic bands."

And now, with the subject or question of evil so entombed in theological imaginations and church dogmas, how can we divest our minds of the infectious absurdities sufficiently to once more dispassionately inquire into, and correctly ascertain, the origin and nature of discord or sin? Let us strive to do so, and begin by glancing at the Bible doctrine on this head. Let us commence at the foundation, with the Mosaic account, and see whether clergymen have, or have not, sufficient ground for their views and hyperbolical representations of the "original sin," and its eternal consequences.

You have all, doubtless, read the relations in Genesis very frequently. I am now moved to examine those accounts briefly, for motives soon to be developed. The following quotation is derived from the second chapter of Genesis, fifth, sixth, seventh, and eighth verses, as you may see by careful reference:—

"Every plant of the field was in the earth, and every

herb of the field grew; for the Lord God had not caused it to rain upon the earth, and there was not a man to till the ground. But there went up a mist from the earth, and watered the face of the ground. And the Lord God *formed man* of the dust of the ground, and breathed into his nostrils the breath of life; and man became a living soul. And the Lord God planted a garden eastward in Eden; and there *he put the man* whom he had formed."

Now this account is truly *simple*—in more significations than one. It is not only unartificial and unexaggerated, but it is likewise exceedingly *deficient* in describing the exceeding great, momentous, and multiform relations, which are theologically asserted to have been established between God and man at the moment of his creation. It is deficient, I mean, only when the church is regarded as *correct* in its doctrinal suppositions. Christian scholars universally agree that *sin* is either a *voluntary departure* of a free moral agent from a recognized principle of rectitude; or else, a manifest *neglect to discharge* known duties and divine commandments. Sin, therefore, when viewed in this light, is certainly a tremendous reality—a supernatural transaction—the creature against the Creator! If sin is this terrific thing—is the peace-destroying and heaven-subverting power which the church represents it to be—then, most assuredly, He who "made man," or the sinning-substance, being All-wise, must necessarily *have known* the unutterable awfulness and the prospective endless consequences thereof.

But let us ask—Did the Lord God make Adam acquainted with the church theory of sin? Nay. For "the Lord God planted a garden," * * * "and took the man and PUT him into the garden of Eden to *dress* it and to *keep* it." From this it appears, that Adam *did not commence life* a free moral agent. His feelings and attractions were not at all consulted. The Lord God did not even ask him whether he *would* willingly and voluntarily go into the beautiful Eden; but the Lord "*put him in it*," as a master would his serf. Nor was Adam questioned as to his willingness to choose horticulture as an occupation, or to be a gardener; which liberty of *choice* is alone compatible or reconcilable with the church theory of man's moral freedom; but, on the contrary, "the Lord God took *the man* whom he had formed, and put *him into the* garden of Eden to dress it and to keep it."

We are gradually approaching the origin of evil, as developed in Genesis.

Freedom is not consistent with slavery. A free mind is its own commander. Coercion or constraint, of any description, can not be consonant with the unlimited scope and principles of freedom. According to this self-evident conception or definition of liberty, it appears that man was not made in the beginning a free moral agent. The question of "free agency" I am not now discussing. I am examining the Mosaic account of the original sin, and comparing the relation thereof with the church theory; which holds that sin is a willful transgression of divine law—a voluntary apostacy of man from the *known* rules of rectitude or duty. Now, I ask, what are the Bible statements on this head? Why, simply, that the Lord God put Adam into the garden, and constrained him to labor. Did the Maker consult the moral freedom of the creature? Here is the answer. "The Lord God *commanded* the man, saying, Of every tree of the garden thou mayest freely eat. But of the tree of the knowledge of good and evil, thou *shalt not* eat of it; for in the day thou eatest thereof thou shalt surely die." Here is a plain *implication* that the Lord God *had* planted good and evil in the world, before the creation of man. This idea was quite prevalent in the early stages of the world. Persian and Chaldean myths are nearly all based upon this superstitious belief. But we let that pass, and inquire: Did the Lord treat Adam as a free moral agent? Was the free-born mind consulted as to choice? Far from it. For "the Lord God *commanded the man*," &c.; which implies the *servitude* of the creature to the power that formed it; the power of the potter over the moistened clay.

If sin is the tremendous reality it is alleged to be, and if the All-wise Lord had a prevision and pre-realization of sin's terrific consequences upon man and the world; why did he not describe to Adam—in characters of fire, and in a voice so accordant, full, and penetrating, that nothing could ever silence the sound thereof in the soul that once had heard it—the intense and never-ending consequences, the discords, the abortions, and eternal agonies, which would inevitably flow from the *first* transgression? Instead of this, the account says, the Lord simply told Adam, that if he ate of "the tree of the knowledge of good and evil," the consequence would be death. Now this *is all* very obscure and ambiguous. The *nature of the tree* and the *kind of death* are neither described nor treated with any marked importance. The *tree* and the *death* are left to the fertile imagination of commentators and ambitious clergymen. The world is to-day replete with sectarian animosities and jargon, mainly owing to the ambiguous and unsatisfactory relation of this so-called supernatural and infallible account. One sect is decided that the "death is spiritual;" another, that the apple, or the first sin, introduced "the phenomenon of death into the world." Others are very positive, that "death, temporal and spiritual"—external and eternal—resulted from Adam's voluntary transgression of the divine command. We can, therefore, trace the origin of much sectarianism and mental discord to the ignorance of the world in regard to this biblical relation. For differences of opinion people will sacrifice the friendship of friends, and yield themselves to the dominion of local hatreds and cruel persecutions—all, because the world does not yet know that the Mosaic record of creation is nothing but a compilation of Persian and Chaldean cosmological myths and theologic speculations.

Do you ever think, my friends, how replete the Scriptures are with absurdities and contradictions? Your clergyman has probably concealed them from the popular gaze, with the imposing livery of Dr. Somebody's commentary, and by the constant pronunciation of a classical eulogium upon the best and brightest truths that decorate the sacred pages. But you should look with your own eyes; and use the talents which God has given you. The New Testament exhorts us to become "perfect even as our Father in heaven is perfect." This is a glorious and ennobling motive for spiritual advancement. I love and accept it as a high exhortation. But do you remember what the Lord God is alleged to have said after Adam had sinned? Do you recollect the *consequence* of eating the apple? "And the Lord God said, Behold, the MAN IS BECOME AS ONE OF US, to know good and evil; and now, lest he put forth his hand, and take also of the tree of life, and eat, and live forever; therefore [that is, because man had become like the heavenly Sovereigns], the Lord God sent him forth from the garden of Eden, to till the ground from which he was taken." It seems also that man's moral freedom to take hold of the tree of eternal life, was peremptorily denied. Now comes the moment for serious, fervent inquiry. Did the Lord of Heaven —the Eternal Spirit—the Almighty Mind—the God of Truth—act toward the first man, and magnanimously consult his mental attractions, as he should have, on the church supposition that man is a free, self-determining, and self-acting power! Nay. Man was made without his consent—forced up from the quiet solitudes of matter, without having his voluntary powers consulted as to the wondrous and hazardous undertaking. And when he became a living soul, how unceremoniously and peremptorily was he "put into the garden," to work it and keep it clean! It might possibly have been decided by Adam, had he been properly *conferred with prior to his earthly existence*, that he would not be created at all—especially, had he been duly informed by the Lord, as a free moral power should have been, of the tremendous "possibility of evil" which inevitably presided over "the creation of powers" from the beginning. Inexpressible thought! The religious world does not—I fear, it can not—realize the wondrous inconsistencies involved in its cardinal teach ings.

The Lord God, who is believed to be the "beginning and the end" of all things—"in whom all things consist"—who, being perfectly *omniscient*, must see all things *as* and *where* they are, just *as* and *where* they are eventually destined to be, should, in order to *escape* the eternal condemnation of being *unloving* and inexpressibly *unmerciful*, have illuminated Adam's mind, *before his creation*, and acquainted him of the eternal evils which would certainly flow from his simple eating of the forbidden fruit. According to the popular supposition, the creation of Adam was *the beginning* of an eternity of the most dismal *evils* and of wondrous *wretchedness*, which no man can imagine or pencil illustrate. Surely, the *omniscient* Creator must have known the *end* from the beginning. There is no escaping this conclusion. To assert that the Lord made man to be *his own eternal master, and left* the *future* consequences altogether to his decisions and acts, is manifestly the utterance of *imbecility*. It would do to *impute* such recklessness and absence of wisdom and goodness to some mythologic Being. But to associate such a thought with the Eternal Mind of this beautiful and magnificent universe, is, to my mind, *more blasphemous* than the oft-repeated oaths of the thoughtless man. The Lord, according to Moses, gave *Adam* no *adequate* and *influential reason* why the apple should not have been eaten. He says, "in the day thou eatest thereof thou shalt surely die." Now, how could that inexperienced and unilluminated mind *under-*

stand what were the horrors and convulsions of death —temporal or spiritual?—physical or eternal?

The serpent "was more subtile than any beast of the field." According to the myth, the serpent contradicted every thing which the *Lord* had communicated to Adam. "Ye shall not surely die," said the loquacious serpent. Now it appears from the account, that *the woman* had never had *any* conversation with the Lord on the subject of sin, nor received any commandment from him, except, perhaps, at second-hand, through her husband; and hence, she, seeing that the tree was *good* [not EVIL, remember, but *good*] for food, and that it *was pleasant* to the eyes, and a tree to be desired [not for mere *physical gratification* and *selfish luxury*, but] to make ONE WISE, took of the *fruit thereof*, and did eat, and gave also unto her husband," &c., * * * * "and the eyes of both were opened." It is honestly supposed by many that the "serpent" was the "devil," tempting Eve to violate a *known* commandment or *law* of rectitude. But let me ask, Who created that wicked and subtile being? Where did *he get his power* to deceive? Did the "supernatural sin," in its enormous strength and subtile windings throughout the domain of unfolding beings, develop that *creeping*, *deceiving*, *venomous* monster? Far from it. The Mosaic myth is sufficiently explicit on this head; and I am not a little surprised that Christian scholars, and honorable men in the church, do not confess to the literal truth.

Adam and Eve were the last or final creations. Every thing else *in* the *heavens* above and *in* the *earth* beneath—"every creeping thing"—was completed before the introduction of man. "And God saw *every thing* that he had made, and, behold, it was VERY GOOD" and satisfactory. Now, what does the account say concerning the beguiling serpent? In the beginning of the third chapter of Genesis, it is distinctly affirmed, that "the *serpent* was more subtile than any beast of the field which [not the supernatural sin, but which] the Lord God had made!" The serpent was subtile; but the Lord had made him so! And why the poor, unfortunate beast—not being created in the category of so-called free moral "powers"—was subsequently "cursed" with such an almighty determination, and condemned to a life of wretchedness in the *mud* and *dust* of creation; is a question which some biblical *commentator*, more versed in *Greek* and *Hebrew* than in *science* or philosophical intelligence, can best answer to the perfect satisfaction of those who have not yet learned the art of independent thinking.

But to the important question. Did the *first* human pair violate a *known* law of duty and rectitude? According to the superficial and unexaggerated letter of the Mosaic account, I affirm that they did not. They were not mentally illuminated. The education, which a proper *amount of experience* can alone stamp upon the human intellect, they had not yet acquired. They had no certain *data* from which to infer *and* thing definitely as to what sin is, or would eventually result in; for no person had yet *died* either a physical or moral death. Consequently, when the *Lord* gave them their so-called "*moral freedom*," associated with a *powerful* temptation to influence them to *misuse* it, and also the penalty of inevitable "*death*" as a sequence of the latter result;

he gave them a matter which they could not have understood, in all its theological lengths and breadths; and the supposed effects of the original sin are now towering far above the world as a frowning and everlasting rebuke to that Power, which, without consulting man's freedom in the first instance, did not exercise sufficiently the attributes of *goodness* and *wisdom* in creating the human world. According to this oriental myth, I say, the *first pair* did not do that which would constitute a theological definition of the supernatural sin. They did not transgress any *known* law of God. The woman had not received any inspiration as to her duty. The first conversation which, according to the account, Eve indulged in after her creation was with the "subtile serpent" which the Lord God himself had made. What shall we say, then, to the world's theology? Whence came it? I reply. We must charge it mainly to the *learned ignorance* and to *the honest cupidity*—if I may so use the expressive paradoxes—of the popes, and priests, and sacerdotal orders of men, who have elaborated the present system of theology. They suppose they find a wondrous system of Redemption in the world. This is designed, they think, to do away with something equally as wondrous. Accordingly, the "original sin" must be *magnified* and exaggerated to conform, with a certain amount of philosophical proportion, to the stupendous scheme which is designed to achieve the great universal regeneration. Thus, clergymen have filled the world with soul-cramping theories and systems of ethics, and the people have become so thoroughly "salivated" with it, as the allopathic physician salivates his patients with calomel, that nothing but years of obedience to the laws of Nature and reason can effectually accomplish the perfect eradication.

The theological method of convicting the world of supernatural sin, to be consistent, the system should assert that Adam's advent upon the earth was a matter of previous personal consent; that the *Lord* actually opened his understanding as to the exact principles of Right, causing him internally to *know* them; and then depicted the eternal and horrible consequences certain to follow the first transgression. According to the true conceptions of justice to man in the premises, with which my mind is now impressed, I will briefly describe the *conference* which the Lord God should have had with *Adam* prior to his introduction on the earth.—I mean, *on the supposition* that the church doctrines of moral freedom and voluntary sin are unequivocally true. It is not inconsistent that the Lord should converse, on the hypothesis that Moses is a faithful historian; for his "voice was heard" by the citizens of Eden, while "walking in the garden in the cool of the day," &c.—implying that the Lord, as a man, is capable of walking and conversing with mortals face to face. I am now to describe, I repeat, the conversation which the Lord should have held with Adam, in order to leave the Divine character unimpeached, and man at liberty *to do, or not to do*, the will of God.

Among all the innumerable "Hosts of powers" in the supernatural realm, it may be supposed that the Lord God had, after completing the creation of the heavens and the earth, selected a spirit, named Adam, to go upon the earth and commence the generation of mortals.

Calling this spirit to his side, the Lord may be imagined to have addressed him, according to the inculcations of popular theology, in the following language:—"Adam, in the dim and shadowy immensity, I have just completed a world with fields, seas, hills, valleys, and mountains. It is lighted by a sun, by countless stars, and a moon. The fields are clothed with herbs; the beasts roam among the hills; the fish sport in the liquid element; the air is pierced and transpierced by birds of song; the viper crawls in the dust; and a beauteous luxuriance emanates from every thing which I have made; and I have pronounced the whole creation to be 'very good.' But, Adam, there is not A MAN to till the ground. It requires attention, and the earth needs to be subdued. Now, I have a proposition to express. I desire that you should *consent* to go to the earth, and take your position as Lord of the creation. But you are a free son of God. You are a free moral, self-determining power; not subject to mechanical force, nor to the earthly system of cause and effect. You are at liberty *to go, or not*, as you may desire. You may remain in this heavenly country to all eternity, or you may go to earth. If you 'consent' to accept my proposition, and become the *Lord* and *sole* proprietor of the earth, and of all its possessions, you should do so understandingly. I see the 'end from the beginning'—and, that you may be fully enlightened as to the nature and consequence of the enterprise, I will relate what will inevitably occur in the rolling away of centuries.

"If you go to earth, remember, you go on your own personal responsibility; for, being a free moral power, I have *no right* to restrict your individual movements.

In the best place thereon, I will plant a beautiful garden. I desire you to dress and clean it; but you are at *liberty* not to do it if you so desire the contrary.

"In that garden I will plant a tree, which will bear a beautiful fruit. This *fruit* I shall put there as a strong temptation to your disposition. I shall also *form* for you a female companion, and bless you both. Then I shall leave the rest to you and your wife.

"Now, *hearken*, while I relate what will surely result from your undertaking. You will eat the fruit, which, as I now inform you, will result in the *total depravity* of the myriads of generations which shall succeed you. The human Race 'will surely die,' both *physically* and *spiritually*, in my estimation. But, in order to *maintain justice and show mercy*, I shall send to earth my *only begotten* Son. He will suffer every thing. He will take upon himself the sins of the world; and his righteousness will be imputed to the sinner. But, Adam, notwithstanding all this, you will inevitably destroy the beautiful order of the physical creation, and be the *primary* cause of the eternal and unutterable wretchedness of countless multitudes."

Adam, overwhelmed with the perils and mountainous evils which would attend or succeed the adventure, begins to grow feeble in his heart, and almost resolves not to be "formed" on earth. And yet, *not* realizing the truthfulness of the relation which the Lord had just pronounced, it may now be supposed that *Adam* replied thus:—

"My eternal Lord, I acknowledge the perfect freedom of my soul to *accept* or *reject* your proposition; although it is hard for me to realize, in view of all this rolling ocean of eternal Love whereon Wisdom shines with such ineffable majesty, how it can be possible for Omnipotence to be so oppressed and circumscribed in its strength and operation as to permit a single free power, like myself, to disconcert the earth, and fill the future realms of darkness with unutterable wretchedness and woe."

"Concerning this, I will enlighten your understanding," says the Lord.

"It is *within* my power, Adam, to *prevent all* the evils and atrocious crimes, which will result from your transport to earth; but I am, in the deep, sober comprehensiveness of my *Wisdom*, constrained to obey certain *laws of consistency* among the 'Hosts' of self-causing powers. Although I most fully comprehend the prodigious calamities consequent upon your going to the earth, and eating the *fruit* which I shall deny to you; nevertheless, to be consistent with *your moral* freedom, I must proceed to people the earth without *seeming* to know the end from the beginning, or interfering with *your consents* and choice. I say this, that you may adopt my proposition in the light of your own freedom and reason."

Adam replies: "The latter I can now understand. But the former, my Lord, the eternal consequences of eating of that simple *fruit*—this is still beyond my comprehension. It is presumption to think that a spirit's *minute* and *feeble* faculties, wrapped around with the dim and shadowy clouds of finite things, can comprehend at once the mighty scheme, and all the results thereof. Lest, therefore, I may be led astray by false reason, or captivated by ten thousand deceitful things, and fail to live the just life, I pray you my *finite vision* to unscale, and, through the interminable avenue of coming centuries, let me behold the Terrors which have cast their hideous shapes upon thy all-seeing mind."

We may now imagine that the Lord God touched Adam's mind, and gave it the power to view the scenes of his future course.

Adam gazed. He beheld the earth in its primeval beauty, all as it had been told him. The luxurious garden all ready for the final preparation to accommodate his presence. He saw the irresistible tree of good and evil. Its *fruit* sparkled in the shining sun; and when his companion gave him it, he did eat. Now, there spread a deepening gloom over the world. He had *fallen*, in the love and estimation of his heavenly sovereign. Eternal Justice was offended; and all things began to bear thorns and thistles, or to wither and to decay.

Still he gazed. And in the distant time, he beheld the *wars*, *cruelties*, and *abominations* of man. He saw the deluge; the confusion of tongues; the scattering of the nations; the line of seers and prophets; the Incarnation of the Only Son; his life of trial and wretchedness; and his death upon the huge cross. The vision was sickening to his soul, and fatal to his resolution. But further on he saw, reflected in the literature of the world, the horrid realities of the bottomless gulf. And soon, he beheld the abyss itself in all its *flaming* terror. The mountainous wall of burning adamant struck a sickness to Adam's soul, and he found no words to express the consequences of his *first* transgression. His heart turned within upon itself; and he could only adopt the weak language of POLLOK in relating what he beheld :—

"Upon that burning Wall,
In horrible emblazonry, were limned
All shapes, all forms, all modes of wretchedness,
And agony, and grief, and desperate woe."
* * * "Wide was the place,
And deep as wide, and *ruinous* as deep.
Beneath he saw a lake of burning fire,
With tempest tossed perpetually, and still
The waves of fiery darkness 'gainst the rocks
Of dark damnation broke, and music made
Of melancholy sort; and overhead,
And all around, wind warred with wind, storm howled
To storm, and lightning forked lightning crossed,
And thunder answered thunder, muttering sound
Of sullen wrath; and far as sight could pierce,
Or down descend in caves of hopeless depth,
Through all that dungeon of unfading fire,
He saw most miserable beings walk,
Burning continually, yet unconsumed;
Forever wasting, yet enduring still;
Dying perpetually, yet never dead!"

You involuntarily shrink, my friends, from this horrid picture; but you should remember, that *it was originally painted* by a talented clergyman. What an expenditure of mind and thought! What an abuse of imagination! But let us, for the present purpose, *imagine* the foregoing to have been Adam's vision previous to his approach to our earth. Surely, if he had "*consented*" to take the earth for his habitation, after having viewed, thus prospectively, the disastrous and overwhelming consequences thereof; then, indeed, would there exist some rationalistic ground for *the theological scheme* which has obtained a footing in this lower world. But does Moses furnish any such premises for the original sin? Was Adam, according to that account, *consulted* and treated in the commencement, *as a free moral power should have been*, in view of all the perils of his enterprise? Nay. The Lord God *forced* man into this existence; *breathed* into his nostrils the breath of life; *put* him into the garden to dress it; and then *commanded him not to eat the fruit* for the fear of incurring a mystical penalty, of which his *inexperienced* and *unilluminated* mind could not form the least reasonable conception! Therefore I affirm, that, granting the Mosaic account to be perfectly true to the letter, there *is no foundation* for the vast theological superstructure of "original sin" and "Redemption" as claimed by the entire clergy of Christendom.

The *first part* of my discourse on this subject is now nearly completed. I have shown you that we must seek for the "origin of evil" outside of any scriptural statement, and separate from all modern theological speculations, if we would arrive at the plain, unvarnished truth. The Bible account of creation is a very interesting myth—mainly a *plagiarism*, from the early traditions and cosmological doctrines of the ancient Persians and Chaldeans. But to regard the first chapters of Genesis as a divine revelation of truth, is to press to your hearts a pagan relic, which should no more command your serious respect than the ancient doctrines of Fetichism. This assertion is susceptible of the fullest confirmation; not only by the *high au-*

thority of an enlightened reason, but also by the philosophical spirit of history.

The eternal Deity, my friends, amply demonstrates to us the character of his Religion! His *creed* is written all over the firmament. It is expressed in the *order*, *beauty*, and loveliness of Nature. It flows up from the depths of the pure soul. All indications testify fully, that the *true religion* is *Justice*, and *joy*, and *peace*, and *beauty*. If we would study this creed, let us go forth and meditate in the open fields—let us *look up*, and contemplate the *works* and *ways* of Nature's God. We are never so *free* and *happy* as when we bring our spirits into direct sympathy with the forms and flowers of nature.

It is evident that the *decorations* of the earth and the heavens were not unfolded in vain. They must subserve some useful and elevating purpose. They must be the manifestations of some universal Spirit or Principle of Beauty and Truth. Chance is not such a skillful builder! No! the Divine Mind is the fountain source—who, in his universally published creed, is certainly no gloomy Orthodox, or Quaker. For instead of causing Creation uniformly to wear a *drab dress*, or a dismal expression foreboding evil, he has bedecked the hills and dales with ineffable loveliness, and placed a shining crystal on the breast of the granite mountain!

Nor are the Birds *monotonous* either in their dress or song. The sturdy oaks, too, put forth their boughs in *diverse* ways, and spread out the foliage of gladness and youth. Surely, there is a principle of Beauty in Nature! And its perpetual breathings prove that a Perfect Deity is both its Author and Friend. It appears, I repeat, that the Deity is the GRAND SOURCE of all beauty and loveliness. But why is it so? Certainly, he can not be what is generally termed, *an Orthodox* in his Religion. He can not be eternally conscious of the existence of a pandemonium just beyond the boundaries of his glorious dominion! He can not see the eternal "*destruction*" of the wicked, and yet send forth a principle of *love*, *truth*, and *beauty* into this world—causing the birds to sing the songs of gladness, and the fields, to teem with blushing loveliness! No; the thought is impossible! For if there were a hell in the neighborhood of heaven, as asserted by mis-impressed and wrongly-educated clergymen; and if that *abyss* contained but *one*—just one—lost soul; we *know*, granting the Lord to be unable to save, that the angels in heaven—our departed brothers and sisters—would *weep tears enough to extinguish the fires of hell;* and, upon the swelling bosom of *an ocean thus formed*, that once lost soul would ride triumphantly into the courts of heaven!

Supernaturalism, as scripturally derived and philosophically explained by clergymen, utterly fails to account for the origin of evil, on the supposition that every human being is a free moral and self-determining power. Adam did not absolutely *know*, by any personal experience or spiritual prevision, the entire laws of eternal justice and rectitude; and hence, when he began to put into practice the normal liberties and voluntary powers of his nature, he did so experimentally; just as we first taste of food to ascertain its flavor, or smell the growing plant in order to learn the nature of its fragrance. If doing that which we *know* to be wrong, *is sin*, then, as knowledge is based upon absolute experience and foresight, Adam does not come under the condemnation. Adam was told not to eat the fruit under penalty of inevitable death. The account asserts the information, or positive commandment, to have been openly communicated by the Lord God unto the man whom he had formed. The external *authority*, therefore, was of the very highest order. But did the man, with his mind wholly undeveloped and inexperienced, *know* that the Lord had told him the perfect truth? You may reply, that the Lord caused Adam internally to feel the truth and the importance of the commandment. But this is going beyond the primary assertions of the foundation of supernaturalism—the Bible; and so, in a discussion of this particular and exceedingly momentous character, no such reply is in any way admissible.

In a very obscure and mystical method, Adam was informed that the *effect* of eating the forbidden fruit, was *certain death*, and that is all! Nothing is said about the asserted consequences of that sin, to be experienced by all subsequent generations, and throughout the interminable centuries of eternity. The latter information might have strengthened Adam's mind, and energized his soul to the everlasting obedience of what he might have supposed to be the laws of supernal justice and right. But according to the account, the *first man* had no such inducements to be righteous: neither any mental enlightenment as to the true principles of rectitude, the laws of existence, or the ways of happiness. The penalty of certain *death*, as a logical sequence of eating a beautiful and inviting fruit, was "all Greek" to both Adam and Eve. It is like seriously informing *a new-born babe*, that the fire will burn; or the desert Arab, that thunder issues from the concussion of surcharged clouds.

Rationalism, as opposed to supernaturalistic revelations and faith, is, therefore, obliged to supplant all mythological theories of evil and redemption, and shed its light over the rugged, ascending pathway of mankind's progression. The sins and evils in the world must first be *rationally* explained, as to their origin, before the world can *rationally* set about the work of extermination and human deliverance. For eighteen long, dark, wearisome, eventful centuries, the Bible, or the church *medicine*, has been administered to the sin-sick soul. But the "disease" still prevails; and the "Doctors"—of divinity, I mean—continue to feel the public pulse, and to prescribe the old nostrums. While science and philosophy—those darling offspring of the human mind—have, by the invention of printing, by the science of navigation, by the discovery of steam, &c., civilized and advanced this portion of the earth; Christianity, as now understood and interpreted, on the contrary, has been, in the hands of its champions, the great Conservative power in the world,—retarding the march of freedom, and vilifying every member of humanity who has successfully out-rode the storms of the church, and who now ventures to apply new remedies to existing disorders among men. Without further premising, I will proceed to utter my impressions concerning the true *origin* and nature of evil.

In order to give an intelligent and decisive solution to this question, your minds should first recognize a few philosophical preliminaries, respecting the subordinate system of Nature, especially as unfolded in the earth. A permanent foundation for all true and enlightened reasoning may be easily discovered somewhere in the vast world or systems about us; but, unless we are certain as to the basis or premises, we are not likely long to retain and cherish the superstructure as a temple of truth and reason.

The earth, in its primeval condition, was a mere combination of liquid elements—a blazing comet, rolling upon its axis and flying eccentrically about the Sun from which it originally was eliminated. For many ages our earth was in this state. If any one of you could then have gazed this way, from the beautiful planet Saturn, which was then peopled, you would have seen a conglobated combination of fire-mist, sending off, in all directions, glowing emanations of light as from a blazing substance. You need no longer fear that this world will in the future be consumed by the dissolving flame. For it *has passed that point*, and the principle of progress never permits an actual retrogression in any thing existing. This description of the origin of our earth you may consider wholly destitute of adequate proof. But I assure you to the contrary, and affirm, that all astronomical discoveries—the physical constitution of the sun, the immense territories of luminous *nebulæ* in space, the eccentric comets, &c., combined with all the geological discoveries of this era—demonstrate conclusively, or as far as an external method of research can bring forth reliable deductions from well-ascertained data, that the earth was originally a vast globe of flaming elements!

In accordance with the laws of progress and development, the heated, flowing substances gradually began to lose their *ignigenous* properties, and the process of cooling and stratification imperceptibly commenced. It would be very interesting to notice in detail all the extensive and wondrous changes which resulted from the process of primary stratification of the earth's surface, but this would not subserve our present purposes. We must pass rapidly over very many ages, and contemplate the earth subsequent to the hardening of its circumference.

There was nothing orderly or symmetrical. One portion of the planet was covered with water; another, pierced the upper air with towering mountains. Every thing was angular—full of grotesque forms of matter—irregular and unequal as the thoughts of the inebriate. This was the primary condition of the earth—a stage, when properly denominated, of *wildness* and universal eccentricity.

But soon the beautiful process of crystallization commenced. The earth, however, contained no rounded and symmetrically shaped *particles* of matter; and so, as a natural consequence, the minerals and crystals which were formed—by the chemical action of existing gases in connection with the pervading heat and the sun's influence—were all replete with angles and sharp projections. The first forms were necessarily irregular and almost indescribably fantastical. In proportion, however, to the modifications in the atmosphere, the refinements in the mineral kingdom, and the improvements in the general physical conditions in nature; in the same proportion did the productions of

Nature assume a more orderly and harmonious appearance. When atoms of matter became intrinsically improved, the result was forthwith manifested in the development of *higher* forms in the fields of creation. The highest crystallization or mineralization of particles merged into the lowest form of vegetable life. If you compare the physical construction of a mineral body with any species of plants or vegetation, the coatings and fibers of the latter will appear distinctly, though incipiently, in the former. How like the leaves and fibers of plants do the crystallizations of frost appear on the window-glass! But you never see mineral bodies so distinctly exhibiting animal organizations. Because, in the order of progress, the mineral kingdom immediately precedes the vegetable kingdom; and the latter, the animal creation; which, in a vast variety of particulars, indicates its parentage and ancestral relationship.

In the plant and animal are exhibited many points of likeness. The rounded limb; the external surface and the narrow; the circulation of fluids and gases through the body; the drawing of nourishment from the earth, and the absorption of the surrounding atmosphere—these are the most conspicuous features of similarity. But a closer anatomical inspection would reveal certain analogous physiological processes and habits, so to express it, which clearly demonstrate the nearness of the relationship between the two kingdoms.

Now you perceive how gradually the principles of progress and development elaborate higher and better productions, from the primary particles which were exceedingly gross and grotesque. But at a point where the animal kingdom ceases to go on, there the *human kingdom* commences its eternal march of being. What a moment—what an epoch—was this, when the mortal put on immortality! The animal became the human; and the new creation asserted its supremacy! You may not now—at this late day of creation—see *the exact point* at which the animal glided into the human type; because the *transition* species have become nearly extinct; but even yet, when you contrast the *lowest* types of humanity with the *highest* animal organizations in nature, you will be greatly astonished at the *brotherly* likeness presented. The same anatomy and physiology are exhibited; also analogous attractions and habits. I will not now present any particular elucidations on this head; but proceed directly to assure you that there is a *unity*, and a progressive harmony, in the System of Nature.

By the foregoing sketch, you can not but recognize the progressive development of all things from the *lowest* grossness in the primary condition of the earth to the *highest* refinement in the human creation. But you ask—what has all this to do with the origin of evil? Be patient with me, and I will fully manifest the application. Gross and angular particles of matter make mineral organizations. When the atoms become more symmetrical, they pass into the formation of plants. The vegetable kingdom achieves an alteration and improvement in the shape and condition of the particles, and then the latter ascend the scale of being, and unfold the animal. From *this point* of atomic refinement, the human kingdom commences; and this connects the material and the spiritual—the mortal with immortality! Now the human Race has gone, or is now passing through a similar system of progression. All development goes by cycles; the *links* in the endless, spirally ascending scale of progress. All things throughout the immeasurable domain of terrestrial and celestial existence—with their forces, laws, movements, and developments—are reciprocally related to, and inseparably connected with, each other; and so there is formed or constituted a magnificent, *unitary* system of existence and causation, of which the Divine Being is the great positive Life-principle and regulating Power.

In the subordinate departments of nature, the order of the system stands thus: Earth, Minerals, Vegetables, Animals, Man. The same identical system of *cycles* has been, or is being, manifested by the progressions of mankind. The order stands historically and absolutely, thus: Savagism, Barbarism, Patriarchalism, Civilism, Republicanism. The same system is exhibited in the normal life of every individual, thus: Infancy, Youth, Adolescence, Manhood, Maturity. The analogy is none the less perfect in the development and association of moving principles, thus: Motion, Life, Sensation, Organization, Intelligence.

I am impressed to present these analogies in order to impart a clear conception of the system of the world; in contradistinction to the supernatural theory of specific creation of perfect things, and subsequent *discord* by the workings of sin. When the individual is yet in the Infant stage of growth, how *angular* and *grotesque* are the external manifestations of character! Inconsiderate, impatient, impetuous, reckless. Thoughtlessly, the inexperienced mind tastes or grasps the first thing presented. It would drink milk or vitriol, so far as its knowledge goes, with an equal degree of readiness. The milk would nourish; but the vitriol would impair or destroy life. Behold, in this simple illustration, the whole mystery and philosophy of evil's origin. The child plays with the *viper* as unconsciously of danger as with a beautiful ribbon. The undisciplined hand reaches forth to grasp the *flame* of the taper as willingly as "the burnt child" studiously avoids the contact. If the mouth should receive only the milk, the organic laws of the physical economy would then be obeyed; but the vitriol, although drank with the same degree of willingness, would possibly subvert, temporarily, the organic harmonies, or terminate the bodily existence. If you should *command* the child not to drink the vitriol under the penalty of certain *death*, and still leave the inexperienced mind to act from its voluntary impulses; the child not *knowing* any thing definitely about the nature of vitriol or the phenomenon of death, would be very likely to drink the forbidden beverage, should it be the most attractive to all external appearances. As the progress of the Race is typified in the individual; so is the origin of evil, or disease and discord, with mankind, manifested in the acts and impulses of the uneducated child. If the child impairs its constitution by various transgressions of the physical and organic laws of its being, then the generations succeeding it will surely receive the results of the disturbance, through the laws of hereditary descent or transmission.

You ask—"How did evil originate?" What do you

mean by "evil?" Do you mean the diseases, the wars, the cruelties, the discords in the world? If so, then I reply, in accordance with my impressions, that they are the *consequences* of a regular system of progressive development in Nature—just as *angular crystals, sharp and craggy rocks, irregular vegetation, cumbrous plants with thorns, huge animals, and imperfect developments of the human species*, are the steps of a *transcending* law of progress, in its majestic march from the deepest recesses of grossness and materiality to the highest eminences of refinement and spirituality. I will presently elucidate this point more particularly. The human race, in its passage from savagism to civilization, has been subjected to the laws of *experience* as the only source of absolute *knowledge*. The civilized nations, as they are termed, manifest still the consequences of their journey; they show, in their laws and institutions, certain predispositions of character which remind us of the early stages of man. Savagism is the *great great grandfather* of Civilization. The offspring bears distinct traces of its parentage! The laws of national hereditary transmission of qualities are immutable. The evils, or rather the numerous *misdirections*, of savagism, are now nearly extinct among civilized nations; but the features of Patriarchalism are still discoverable in the religious and political organizations of the most advanced inhabitants of the earth. One Era sits in judgment against the preceding, as the youth judges his father. The *angularities*, or *misdirections*, of savagism are condemned by those persons who outgrow them in the order of progress. The American Nation—if it can be termed a nation—to-day sits in judgment against all the nations of the earth—rebuking them for their evils, their discords, wars, and tyrannical institutions. But America is also condemned by still more liberty-loving spirits for her slavery and local disorders. We do not know what wrong or misdirection is, until we outgrow it in our minds and morals. The doctrine of evil, therefore, is a local and arbitrary matter, which the succeeding generation will alter to suit the standard of another construction.

Surely, you see the truth of this statement. How do you *know* that milk is *better* than vitriol for babes?" "By experience," you reply. Do you *know* by *personal* experience? "No." How, then, do you know? "By the experience and well-authorized attestations of others." Yes, this is almost knowledge; because it is based on the experience of the race to which you belong, and in which you unconsciously confide. So, you learn that *slavery is wrong* by a *knowledge of liberty* and of its blissful concomitants. Again, I affirm that *evil* is altogether an arbitrary term, which men apply to those inequalities and misdirections which they have themselves, morally as well as intellectually, outgrown, but which others far less developed may still continue to perpetuate. There is a vast difference between *perceiving* a wrong by the intellect, and *resisting* that wrong by an exercise of the moral sensibilities. One person may be *morally and intellectually above* the act of theft. In such a case, the mind has nothing to resist; for *the act* is held by the individual as beneath the dignity of his inward nature. Another person may equally *know that theft is wrong*, according to the laws of the land; but, when the opportunity presents, he finds his moral feelings not very strongly opposed to the act—in fact, he does not consider the deed beneath his dignity at all.

Clergymen, knowing almost nothing of man's spiritual character, in connection with the laws of progress and development, are very sanguine as to the correctness of the Bible-idea of sin: and the people are compelled to labor under gospel vituperations and clerical denunciations of every description, without knowing how, or daring to obtain a better idea of the sins complained of by their shepherds. It is now my impression to relate, briefly, the real origin of what is termed evil—commencing, as the clergymen do, with the beginning of the human species. What has been said, thus far, is concerning the philosophy of sin or discord as developed in the system of Nature.

The doctrine, that the race began from a single pair of originally pure and heavenly beings, is vastly far from the real truth. You, who have intellectual discernment and comprehension adequate, should not allow your minds to misread Nature, which is the book of deific origin. Creation shows, very explicitly, that the commencement of any thing is gross and imperfect. Nothing begins existence with prominent spiritual characteristics, and terminates in the depths of grossness and materiality. I speak now of the great universal system of Nature. The first trees, the first animals, the first men, were quite imperfectly formed and as unrefined. The same is true of every thing invented by man. The first agricultural implements, the first steamboats, the first locomotive, &c., were exceedingly defective and cumbersome. Progression proves that "that is not first which is spiritual, but *natural*, and afterward the spiritual." Accordingly, I discover the first types of the human family to have been dwarfed or unadvanced in mental development; but gigantic and powerful in their physical structure and organic constitutions. They were giants in every respect, except in mind. They were to the present race of men what the megatherium, the missourium, and the mammoth were to the present existing types of animals. Progression in mind brings *physical* refinement; thus, the animal-man becomes extinct in proportion as the spiritual-man obtains the ascendency. All this I have shown you in considering the *unity* of the system of Nature.

Asia, as all mythologic traditions and history truly indicate, cradled the first born of the human species. By the first born, I do not mean any special creations by a deific hand; but the first type of the mammiferous animals which approached sufficiently near the human type, to be properly denominated the "first born" of the race to which we belong. There were *two* distinct molds or forms of the mammiferæ organization that ascended at the same time rapidly toward the human organism. One tribe existed in Eastern, the other in Western Asia. They did not discover each other until a long period after they had established independent nations or tribes. One race was more effeminate than the other. And when, like the race of modern Gipsies, the former tribe traveled over the fertile country of Asia, and discovered the stronger race, an immediate *union* was formed; and thus the two types, combined, commenced the production of the different nations that subsequently peopled the earth. Still they were savage in habit and ferocious in disposition. They were far more animal than human; the spiritual was as yet undeveloped, and the material greatly preponderated. They lived peacefully and harmoniously so long as the various wants of their physical constitutions were plentifully supplied. When these material conditions were not fully complied with, they would like the beasts of the forests, or, perhaps, more as the inhabitants of the Cannibal Islands, manifest the unrefined and savage custom of quarreling and warring with each other and with nature for what they considered to be their rights. But I must hasten away over several centuries; during which period the youthful types of man employed the natural, or rather *rudimental* language—such as motions, gesticulations, configurations of the countenance, &c.; which, by not involving much complicity, they contrived to use, without any distinct modification or trouble, until they discovered their ability to make a vast variety of vocal sounds. This discovery was at first hailed with delight. Accordingly, they very rapidly abandoned their primitive habit and form of expression; and forthwith began to communicate their thoughts by vocal effort. And now, behold, what a great fire a little matter kindleth!

When the early inhabitants used only gesticulations, assisted by a crude form of hieroglyphical language, as means of individual communication, the simplicity and fixedness of the agents employed, prevented *all misunderstanding* as to the real import of each other's thoughts. Vegetables, animals, birds, mud-images, objects worked out of soft stone,—such were their books, their history, their creeds and schools. But with vocal expression came also misunderstanding! Their minds were not yet sufficiently developed to establish grammatical order and intelligent sounds; and it was soon discovered that different persons would make different oral sounds to signify the same thing. Not properly understanding each other's natures, each held the other responsible for intentionally, and with premeditation, varying the sound of the voice when referring to any specific thing. Many of the youthful nation soon became impatient—honestly supposing that the vocal expressions were breeding falsehoods and deception. They rapidly became displeased with each other; and socially miserable and antagonistic. They became envious, cruel, and deceptive; because their intellectual endowments were not enough developed to account for, and properly prevent the abounding misunderstandings. However, there was a chieftain in their midst who declared that they were possessed by a strange and wicked being, who floated in the invisible shades of night in the air, breathing a malignant element into their minds. This piece of mystical speculation the chieftain taught them by using their cast-off hieroglyphical images. Thus commenced a discord which caused the youthful family to separate and wander abroad over the earth. One tribe blamed and denounced the other as *the cause* of the discord; and thus was formed the *first* theory in this world of the origin of evil. The separated tribes soon multiplied and established small nations, each developing a *different* language in order to escape the hypothetical evil of the first vocal sounds employed; and so originated the different nations and the early discords among the human species. All this is demonstrable by the history of races and language.

The facts herein disclosed and set forth, concerning the origin of the *first discords* among the foundation-progenitors of mankind, can be, I am impressed to say, substantiated by reference to various sources of outward or external information. All ethnological researches into the derivation and distribution of the different races and families of men; all archæological investigations into the mysteries and science of antiquities; all philological discoveries concerning the origin, science, and affinities of the different languages; all geological disclosures, and the science of comparative anatomy, each and all stand as so many unexpected and unsought sources of demonstration, that the foregoing statements respecting evil are grounded in historical Truth. Indeed the science of the origin of language, of the different races of men, of the diverse religions and mythologies in the world, essentially require, in common reason, something like the above *substratum of historical præcognita* or ascertained *data* from which to commence a train of logical inferences and deductions.

Furthermore, how intrinsically *probable* is this revealment of the origin of discord when compared to any theory now received. The Old Testament asserts the *different* languages and races of men to have originated, subsequent to a universal deluge, by a supernatural "confusion of tongues" and scattering of the tribes engaged in building the Babel-tower. Geology, be it distinctly remembered, unfolds evidences against the *possibility* of a universal inundation; and besides, the atmosphere could not have sustained watery vapor in sufficient quantity to cover the whole earth on the event of condensation. On the score, therefore, of mere natural reasonable *probability*, the account, which I have been impressed to relate, must stand pre-eminently recommended to your understanding and credence. Because, moreover, it appears in the line of all archæological and geological discoveries with which this age is so exceedingly enriched—a powerful presumptive evidence of its truth, which should not be overlooked by impartial minds.

In offering these historic suggestions, as so many conspiring evidences of the verity of this philological revealment, I design not to trouble the reader of this work with the many argumentations which appear adducible. There are, however, a few passages, bearing directly and favorably on this question, which I quote from an admirably written and *rationally* disposed work,* entitled "God in Christ," opening with a very valuable dissertation concerning the natural *origin* and spiritual significancy of human language. In speaking of the origin of vocal sounds, the author says: "It is undoubtedly true, as many have asserted, that human language

---

* A friend first called my attention to this work, because its author, Dr. BUSHNELL, has expressed, in the initial chapter, corresponding ideas respecting the *disputes* and *differences* which arise from the arbitrary nature and indeterminate use of vocal expression. From the representations, given, I can not see how he can refuse to acknowledge the *tractability* and *probability* of the foregoing statement in regard to the origin and establishment of the different languages.

is a gift of God to the race, though not, I think, in the sense often contended for. It is by no means asserted, in the Scriptures to which they refer, that God himself pronounced the sounds, or vocal names, by which the objects of the world were represented, nor that He framed these names into a grammar."

Again, in alluding to the instinct of language in the first man being developed by having his mind directed to objects around him, the writer says: "He was, himself, in this view, the occasional cause of the naming process; and, considering the nature of the first man to have been originally framed for language, he was the creative cause; still the man himself, in his own freedom, is the immediate, operative cause; the language produced is as truly a human, as a divine product. It is not only *for* the race, but it is also *of* the race—a human development, as truly as knowledge, or virtue, or the forms of the social state."

The writer is truly aware of the troubles among philological investigators concerning the parentage of vocal expression; and thinks "the fact, that there are living languages, between which no real affinity can be discovered, still exists in its integrity"—forcing us to "either admit the existence of races originally distinct, or else we must refer these languages to the Scripture solution of a miracle." This conclusion the writer, like a truly philosophic rationalist and thinker, manifests no particular proclivity to accept; but considers no mystery in the idea that the "different languages are so many free developments of the race." On this head, he remarks: "Nor is there any so great impossibility or mystery in this matter of originating a language, as many seem to suppose. I hope it will not offend the romantic or marveling propensity of my readers, if I affirm that a new language has been created and has perished in Connecticut, within the present century." Still further on he says: "Nor is there any reason to doubt that incipient and rudimental efforts of nature, in this direction, are often made, though in cases and modes that escape attention. Indeed, to believe that any two human beings, shut up wholly to each other, to live together until they are of a mature age, would not *construct a language*, is equivalent, in my estimation, to a denial of their proper humanity." All this, as the reader perceives, favors the rationalistic solution of the question.

As to the tendency of vocal expression, *to produce discord and unintentional derangements* among men, the writer remarks: "men are so different, even good and true men, in their personal temperament, their modes of feeling, reasoning, and judging, that moral bitterness, in its generic sense, will not be a state or exercise of the same precise quality in their minds. Some persons will take as bitterness in general, what others will only look upon as faithfulness, or just indignation. And, then, in the particular case to which the word is to be applied, different views and judgments will be formed of the man, his provocations, circumstances, duties, and the real import of his words and actions." "Words," continues the author, "are legitimately used as the signs of thoughts to be expressed. They do not literally convey, or pass over a thought out of one mind into another, as we commonly speak of doing. They are only hints, or images, held up before the mind of another, to put *him* on generating or reproducing the same thought; which he can do only as he has the same personal contents, or the generative power out of which to bring the thought required. Hence, there will be different measures of understanding or *misunderstanding* according to the capacity or incapacity, the ingenuousness or moral obliquity of the receiving party—even if the communicating party *offers only truth*, in the best and freshest forms of expression the language provides." From the foregoing paragraphs it is reasonable to infer, that Dr. B—— has *rationally* meditated upon the causes of "the interminable disputes of the theologians;" and has seen, no doubt, several insurmountable difficulties, which he has labored not to see, standing in the way, preventing the reconciliation of an infallible revelation with the arbitrary and indeterminate nature of the language in which that revelation is clothed and forced upon the vast contrariety of intellects that compose the human world.

Analogous troubles are often generated, by similar trivial causes, among children who just begin to use vocal expression whereby to communicate their thoughts. You will see them playing together, delighted with each other's society, until something is suggested to be attempted in their gambols, which they have not the words or the power to clearly express and define. In their haste and impetuosity, they *misunderstand* each other's intentions, and the disturbance quickly embroils and embitters the whole party. Each feels the other to be clearly at fault; and so, the little angels change their peace into a domestic war. Thus were commenced the first troubles among mankind.

The church theory of evil, on the contrary, attributes or involves a defect in the divine goodness, or in the divine power. One creed represents God allowing evil to appear in the creature-man in order to openly display his own prowess and sovereignty. Another creed represents God as designing to make man morally good, but *had not the power to do so* consistently with the creature's moral freedom. Consequently, evil walks into the creation in spite of the Creator; being, according to the supposition, a counterpart or necessary result of the good he would create.

My present impressions can not be more intelligibly or practically worded than they have already been by an independent thinker and vigorous writer of this century,* and as set forth in the following extract: "Thus moralism is the parent of fetichism, or superstitious worship, the parent of all sensual and degrading ideas of God, the parent of all cruel and unclean and abominable worship. Leading me as it does to regard my inward self as corrupt, to distrust my heart's affections as the deadliest enmity to God, it logically prompts the crucifixion of those affections as especially well pleasing to Him, and bids me therefore offer my child to the flames, clothe my body in sackcloth and ashes, lacerate my skin, renounce the comforts and refinements of life, turn hermit or monk, forswear marriage, wear lugubrious and hideous dresses that insult God's daylight, and make myself, in short, under the guise of a voluntary and mendacious humility, perfectly ulcerous

---

* See "Moralism and Christianity; or, Man's Experience and Destiny." By HENRY JAMES. pp. 160, 161, et seq.

with spiritual pride, a mass of *living* purulence and putridity.

It is, I repeat, simply inevitable that moralism, or the doctrine of man's subjection to society, should produce these effects, should enormously inflame the pride of one class of its subjects, and as enormously depress that of another class. For if I, being a morally good man, that is, conscientiously abstaining from all injustice or injury to my neighbor, come to regard that character as constituting a distinction for me in the sight of God, as giving me a distinction there above some poor devil of an opposite character, it is easy to see I must become as inwardly full of conceit and inhumanity as a nut is full of meat. How can it be otherwise! If the All-seeing behold in me any superiority to the most leprous wretch that defiles your streets, then clearly I have the highest sanction for esteeming myself above that wretch, and treating him not with fellow-feeling, but with condescension and scorn.

I know the unctuous cant, the shabby sophistry, which prevails upon this subject. I know it will be replied that I "ought not" forsooth! to do thus, that it "would be wrong" forsooth! for me to exalt myself above this poor wretch on the ground of my superior morality. But wherefore wrong? If that morality really distinguish me before God, if it constitute a superior claim to the divine favor, then it were flat inconsistency in me, it were flat treason to God, not to acknowledge it in my practice. Can God's judgment be unrighteous? Wherefore then should I hesitate in any case to conform my conduct to it?

"Ah!" replies some one, "but *you* do not see as God sees. If you saw all the temptations that have beset that poor wretch, if you could see in the first place, the superior intensity of his passions to yours, his comparative intellectual disadvantages, his depraved circumstances from infancy up, and so forth, you would possibly regard your difference as small, and abate somewhat the tone of your triumph." This is all true. This is exactly what I myself say. But then if the circumstances here alleged should affect my judgment of my poor friend, much more should they affect *His* judgment to whom they are so much better known! If I cease on these grounds to exalt myself over my fellow, how much more must God cease to exalt me! But if this be so, what becomes of your moral distinctions in His sight? If He have no higher esteem for me, a morally good man, than he has for you, a morally evil man, then it is clear that the moral life is not the life He confers, the life of which He is chiefly solicitious.

You perceive that you are here in a dilemma. Either God esteems me a virtuous man above you a vicious man, or He does not. If He does, then inasmuch as all His judgments are right, and designed for our instruction, I should instantly learn to esteem myself above you, that is, to withhold from you sympathy or fellowship, in which case I become inhuman by virtue of a direct divine influence. If, on the other hand, He does not esteem me a virtuous man above you a vicious man, then you deny the moral life to be God's life in man.

How will you extricate yourself from this dilemma?

There is but one way. You will say that it was not your intention to represent God as holding one man intrinsically superior, or superior in himself, to another, but relatively or socially superior only; superior, that is, with reference to the purposes of society. There is consequently no further quarrel between us. Moral distinctions belong purely to our earthly genesis and history. They do not attach to us as the creatures of God. As the creature of society, I am either good or evil. I am good as keeping my natural gratification within the limits of social prescription, or evil as allowing it to transcend those limits. But as the creature of God, or in my most vital and final selfhood, I am positively good; good without any oppugnancy of evil; good, not by any stinted angelic mediation, but by the direct and unstinted indwelling of the Godhead.

I have now expressed my thought with more detail than befits a popular Lecture. But as I conceive the subject to be of especial interest to all thoughtful minds, I am anxious to commend it to your perfect apprehension. With this view, let me still further ask your indulgent attention, while I discuss an objection which may possibly arise in the minds of some of my audience.

It was alleged, on the delivery of the preceding Lecture, that I deny moral distinctions. The allegation is vaguely worded, but it is doubtless worthy of respectful investigation. If it mean, then, that I deny any difference between good and evil actions; that I call murder, adultery, theft, and so forth, good actions, of course the charge is silly, and not worth refuting.

In this sense no man ever denied moral distinctions. No man—not even the unfortunate subject of them—ever justified adultery, theft, murder, or falsehood. No man ever did one of these things spontaneously, or at the instance of his taste. I have indeed heard of persons who had a *mania* for theft; who, from some exceptional cerebral organization, could omit no opportunity to enrich themselves at the expense of others. But these cases are regarded, of course, as exceptions to the ordinary tenor of human nature, and as putting the subject beyond the pale of responsibility. Because, if there be a constitutional aptitude to this offense in the party, you manifestly acquit the party himself of it. You would no more hold him personally responsible, under these circumstances, than you would hold him personally liable for a hare-lip or any other morbid development. No man, then, I repeat, ever injured another from taste or spontaneity. Hence no man ever justified a moral delinquency, ever supposed himself acting worthily in taking his neighbor's life, property, or good name, or in seducing the affections of his wife.

The objector consequently does not mean to say that I confound good and evil actions, since the constitution of the human mind makes that impossible.

He means, then, doubtless, that I do not regard the man who does good actions as intrinsically better than the man who does evil actions. He means, doubtless, that I do not regard the morally good man as possessing any superior claims upon the divine favor to the morally evil man, but view them both as heirs of the same eventual and glorious destiny. If the objector means this by his charge, then let me suggest an amendment of its form. Let him say to me: you deny, not the existence or importance of moral distinctions among men, but simply their divinity. You deny that God is in any measure privy to these distinctions. To the charge, thus amended, I freely plead guilty. I am persuaded that God's eyes, however universal their empire, have never yet been astounded by the appearance of evil in His creatures. Whence should that evil come? It can not come from Himself, who is essentially good. Whence, then, should it have come? For the supposition, you perceive, makes it a phenomenon of God's creation; it is the possibility of evil in God's creature that we are discussing. How could evil be possible in that creature? You may say that it came from the Devil. Very well; let that answer stand.

If evil came from the Devil, then the Devil, in infusing evil into God's creature, acted either with God's consent, or without it. If he acted with it, then of course God saw that it would not injure the creature, since He had methods of turning it all to the creature's superior profit, and so proving the Devil a fool for his pains. If he acted without God's consent, then of course you give the Devil not only a superior power to God, but a superior power over God's own work, or in the sphere of God's own activity. That is to say, you make the absolute creature of infinite Good confess himself the offspring of a deeper paternity—the paternity of infinite Evil.

But take either branch you choose of this hideous dilemma, you manifestly absolve the creature himself of all defilement. For whether the Devil infuse evil into him with or without the consent of Deity, it is clearly an operation under which the creature himself is passive, and I fancy that even the Devil is too good a logician to hold one responsible for his passions, but only for his actions. Any child might otherwise refute him. My passional nature means my various susceptibility of enjoyment and suffering from nature and man; my passions are merely the concrete forms of this various susceptibility. You would not therefore hold me responsible for my passions, unless you at the same time ascribed to me the paternity of nature and man—unless you at the same time held me to have created this universal frame of nature and society, to which these passions owe all their existence.

Thus the Devil turns out an unprofitable hypothesis. He is an infinite lie. No one can trust in him without being confounded. He looms portentously large in all infant cosmologies—in all those theories of creation which are constructed by the sensuous imagination of the race; but you have only to prick him with the smallest pin of science, and he fairly roars you a confession of egregious imbecility.

The entire traditional doctrine of the origin of evil is irrational and abhorrent. In one phase it asperses the divine goodness; in another the divine power. One hypothesis represents God as allowing evil to appear in the creature only that He might display His sovereignty, not in reconciling it with good, and so affording a basis for His own manifestation in nature, but in afflicting it with ceaseless torments. Surely this is a puerile conception of God which makes him capable of ostentation, capable of enjoying a mere empty parade of his power. The conception converts Him, in fact, into an aggravated bully, intent upon the display of his physical prowess. It is groveling and disgusting beyond every other product of our sensuous imagination. It degrades Deity below the brute even. For the tiger makes no sacrifice to ostentation. He inflicts no suffering in demonstration of his power and the consequent gratification of his vanity, but only in satisfaction of an honest natural appetite. If accordingly, this hypothesis of creation were just, moral distinctions would be seen to claim a basis in God's want of love, in his inferiority to tigers.

The other hypothesis attributes evil to a defect, not of the divine goodness, but of the divine power. It represents God as designing to make man morally good. But as moral good is in its very nature finite or conditional, as it is conditioned upon the inseparable co-existence of moral evil, so God, however much He may desire it, is practically unable to keep evil out of the universe. From the nature of the case, from the nature of the good He designs to bestow, He can not make one man good without making another evil. Hence you perceive that evil stalks into creation in spite of God, being involved in the good He would create. The only way, consequently, in which He might exclude it, would be to forego His creative design altogether. For His design being to create moral good, and moral good standing in the inseparable antagonism of moral evil, in effect or practically His design is to create the one as much as the other.

We may, indeed, represent the evil man as so much

inevitable chips, or waste material; but we gain nothing by this notion. For is not he always esteemed an imperfect workman who leaves chips behind him, who can not work without a shocking waste of material? Our divines see fit, indeed, to blink all these monstrous contradictions, and doubtless they have a reward. But is it not gratuitous in them to go further than this, and represent the Deity not merely as making chips, but also as vindictively bestowing an everlasting vitality on these chips in order to their never-ending combustion?

According to this hypothesis, then, you perceive that moral distinctions among men grow out of a defect in the divine power. The former hypothesis attributes them to a defect of God's goodness, or an inferiority of His internal endowments. The latter attributes them to a defect of his power, or an inferiority of his external endowments. Each proceeds upon an implication of His imperfection, and hence they are both alike intrinsically absurd and blasphemous."

You ask, "If this doctrine of evil does not also imply *some defect* in the original plan?" Does it not involve the attributes of the Creator? Could He not have made creation perfect at once, and set man on the path of happiness, preventing all the misery and trouble in the world? These questions, my friends, are wholly unanswerable on the church theory of God and his method of creating. But the Harmonial Philosophy finds no inconsistence or perplexity in these questions; because it does not admit any such a thing as "creation" in the popular definition of the term. The Deity, considered in the creative capacity, is a divine HEART in the universe; two PRINCIPLES of *love* and *wisdom*, which are immutable and invariable. He is himself *controlled* by those principles which spontaneously flow from his inexhaustible being into and through infinitude. He does not create worlds, and then day by day labor with his hands, or by a prodigious exercise of spiritual volition, make trees, birds, animals, and man; but, on the contrary, just as the blood flows through the human body, forming bone and muscle in the system at all points and extremities, so the unchangeable principles of Association, Progression, and Development flow forth from the deific HEART of the Universe, unfolding worlds, like flowers, and progressively developing the various forms which animate their surfaces.

If the All-pervading Spirit were merely a sovereign, somewhere outside of the material and spiritual universe, then it would become a troublesome question to reconcile imperfection with perfection, as all Christian scholars invariably discover and acknowledge.

But when we come to see, by investigating the works and ways of the Actuating Principle, that Progress is a law of existence, and that development follows it as a natural sequence, then we easily recognize that the Moving Spirit is as much under the regulations of certain principles as the brain, the organ of man's mind, and even the mind itself, are controlled by laws that are "without variableness, neither shadow of turning."

But you ask me another question: "If the All-pervadnig Spirit is intrinsically good and perfect, how became man, the effect, so inclined to create and perpetuate evil?" The reply is manifestly very simple and self-evident. Evil is not substance; it is Ignorance. What is termed "evil" disappears in proportion as *knowledge* increases. Barbarism is supplanted by civilization. Wild animals become extinct as humanity spreads its wings over the territories of nature. I deny, therefore, that positive "evil" exists anywhere in the universe. A *good* thing, *through ignorance*, may be improperly used. The law of combustion, by which fire is produced, is a source of great comfort and immense advantages to the human family. But the first man who came in contact with the element *was burned*, and thus he cursed and vilified the fire; because, merely, he was *ignorant* of the organic laws of his being, and ignorant also of the science of controlling and converting fire into a useful agent.

Suppose, to continue illustrating, an engineer should construct a machine for some wise and beneficial purpose. If judiciously managed, it will produce exceedingly good results. But an *ignorant* man, not comprehending the nature and use of the mechanism, sets it in motion, gets involved in the wheels, and is sadly wounded or crushed to death. What shall we say? Shall we condemn the invention? Shall we execrate the engineer, and hold him morally responsible? Shall we *blame* any thing or anybody? God forbid. If we are reasonable, we must say, It was owing to the *ignorance* of the man which caused the good mechanism to do a disastrous work.

Now, the laws which control the moral world are just as perfect and positive as the laws of the physical world. Truth, love, friendship, ambition, &c., are each capable, under wrong development and management, of developing discords of various kinds and degrees.* Each man carries in his heart the elements of an angel; these life-principles are intrinsically good and perfect; but we see the vicious habitudes thereof only when, from *ignorance* or causes growing directly or indirectly out of ignorance and defective moral sensibilities, those indwelling principles are *subverted* and misdirected in their manifestation upon relative personalities and contiguous interests. Anger, cupidity, malice, revenge, licentiousness, hypocrisy, &c., are not immanent or residing in the constitution of mind. They are the *wrong* development, the wrong management and exercise of intrinsically *good* and, ultimately to be, angelic principles. Look at intemperance. It would not require much insight to trace the *origin* of this evil. It frequently occurs that a working-man, chained from day to day to a repugnant and monotonous labor, seeks distraction and alleviation in various ways. Lest his life should be a continuous burden and punishment, he seeks alcohol; because he finds in drunkenness a temporary relief from his cares, accompanied with an agreeable excitement. Soon it becomes his master, and he has no individual power to resist the temptation. A different social construction, making, as a general principle, every man's life happy, his future certain, his labors agreeable and various, would successfully sweep intemperance and licentiousness from the earth.

Every man, as I read the human heart, has an indwelling disposition toward *ease and luxury;* which, when the individual is on the sensuous plane of exist-

* See chapter on Moral Cultivation, in Great Harmonia, vol. II.

ence—having perhaps *much knowing* power or intellect, but *little restraining* power or moral sensibilities —is almost certain, in this transitional state of civilization, to manifest itself in *theft or burglary.* Betrayed love begets or originates *jealousy*, which may lead to *murder;* disappointed ambition and love of power originate *war;* a wounded feeling originates *anger.*

The origin of evil, my friends, is not an historical and theological question; but a present and practical problem to solve, with an eye to its successful prevention.

Hark! Do you hear that multitude of voices? Do you see those prayers ascending? There are arising, from no less than thirty thousand American pulpits, these words—or words which imply their signification: "Our Father, who art in heaven—thy kingdom come: *thy will be done on earth* as it is in heaven!" Now does the Church do any thing toward establishing this kingdom on earth? Does it institute *practical measures* to bring happiness among men? Does it do any thing conspicuously toward the banishment of oppression and crime? No! But it sends forth wordy invocations to heaven—long and loud prayers to God, that his harmonious kingdom might come on earth.

What was it that refreshed all New York City? What saved the inhabitants from fearful fevers and epidemics? What introduced the greatest blessings into and through that extensive city? Was it prayers? Was it invocations to the *living* God? It was *the energy, and enterprise, and intelligence of her citizens* that "smote the desert rock," and caused to flow, into the darkest recesses and loftiest dwellings, the pure and healthy WATER. So likewise, this human world will come to see that praying and sermonizing will never refresh and cleanse the moral condition of man, and unfold the "kingdom of heaven" on earth; but it will come to be seen that all this, and more than this, will be yet accomplished through the progressive development and well-directed energy of the human soul.

The Church, I repeat, is constantly praying for the will of God to be "done on earth as it is in heaven,"—that is to say, that the *laws* of God be as much obeyed in this sphere as they are in the spheres above. But, friends, I am impressed to say that we should come here to organize ourselves into a form, or body, which shall tend to develop this harmonious condition in ourselves and in human society. We should come here to develop into form and order the great fundamental and essential principles of Christianity—to make every man a law unto himself, and a doer of righteous deeds. By a living fact, as an illustration, the reader will obtain the import of this personal doing of good.

In an obscure street in the city of B——, there lives an honest, simple-hearted mechanic. He belongs to no organization, no moral reform association, or temperance society. He has no President to "call him to order," no Secretary to "record his movements," no Treasurer to "collect and preserve" his funds; and yet that one man has alone and mainly unassisted, defended, bailed out of prison, and procured healthy employment for about seven hundred criminals and licentious men and women. I have met this unpretending man on his mission of love to the haunts of vice—to the cell of the prisoner, and have asked him, "Who sends you, my friend, on this blessed mission? who directs you how to proceed? who supplies you with the necessary means to accomplish all this good?" Said he: "Something here (pointing to his breast) tells me when to go and what to do; and when I need money, I ask the first apparently rich man I meet for it—and then another, and another, and so on; and I soon get all I need."*

Now, this is the divine principle upon which we should come together—the principle which should actuate and control all our thoughts, our deeds, and movements. *Think of it!* SEVEN HUNDRED vicious and criminal individuals saved from a life of bondage and personal degradation, and furnished with useful and healthy employment—all by one poor, honest-hearted mechanic. And I have heard this man say, that, in all his familiarity with these so-called "depraved characters," he has not yet met with one single instance of absolute ingratitude, or positive indisposition to personal reformation. This is *very significant.* What, think you, is this man's opinion of the human heart? What view does he entertain of man? My friends, I have heard him say, in substance, that he believed the human heart to be pure, and man to be capable of endless development in goodness! Who, then, believes in "total depravity?" The answer is too plain! It is believed and

* My impressions now embrace two individuals in the city of Boston, veritable brothers in the field of human suffering—John M. Spear and John Augustus—who, in their efforts to be and to do good, are truly examples of what I mean by being a law unto ourselves. In this relation Mr. Pease of the "Five Points Mission," New York, should be remembered.

inculcated by the multitude of clergymen—by those who never make it their business to bail out of prison, and procure employment for, seven hundred criminals.

Most of the evils that afflict the world to-day did not *originate* in the fabled garden of Eden; nor yet among the youthful types of mankind; but they spring *out of ignorance*, out of defective social and religious institutions. For example: one evil in this world, is disease. How did it originate? Shall we go to Genesis to inquire? Shall we seek the information from the pulpit? Nay; because we find the *origin of this evil* in our very midst. Ignorance leads the individual to violate the laws of his being, by the injudicious use of food, of sleep, of air, of occupations, &c.; or, in this state of social isolation and unorganized industry, many persons are constrained to engage in labors which daily violate nature and generate disease. Licentiousness, or inconstancy, is another evil in present society. How does it originate? Is it a supernatural sin? Is it an evil? According to my impressions, the domestic discords, arising from this cause, could—and in the future *will*—all be prevented by congenial marriage relations. But why not prevent the evil which grows out of these relations to-day? Do you hesitate because you are all totally depraved? Far from it. Every man who has progressed to the moral scale of feeling, yearns to eradicate it at once. But ignorance of human nature—ignorance of the principles and attractions of the human mind—stand between you and the institution of a proper marriage. But *inconstancy*, or love of change, when properly and philosophically understood, does not at all apply to the institution of marriage, or to the conjugal affections; in this sphere it is seen in its *subversive* or misdirected attitude—giving results, like the wrongly used mechanism, which seem evil and disastrous to human happiness. Every man has a disposition to *alternate* the exercise of his physical and mental faculties. This is a wise and good inclination; because it maintains health and a proper equilibrium in both body and mind; and this is the proper sphere for the manifestation of inconstancy by alternating employments. Hence the evil of licentiousness is easily traced to its origin. To my mind *all excesses* are vicious—that is, injurious and hurtful to man and society—whether in individuals or institutions. It is an easy thing to sit in judgment upon our neighbors, as clergymen presumptuously preach against and vilify mankind; but it is quite another thing to be *on the throne of wisdom*, and to judge with a righteous judgment—not from appearances, but from truths!

You ask: "Does not this philosophy of evil relieve the individual of moral responsibility?" Mankind, I reply, are as a family, in which diverse inclinations and opinions are constantly manifested—one against the other. *All discords are traceable to society;* because, without association, there could not be any *war*, any *theft*, or *cupidity*, as now evidently flow from the contact of relative tastes and situations. If association is the *cause* of individual disturbances, association must furnish the *cure*. The individual finds himself, after attaining to the years or period of discretion (?) placed between two antagonistic forces: the discordant laws of society, and the harmoniously imperative Laws of Nature! The former constrain him; the latter yield him liberty, ease, and happiness. As to the extent to which the individual should be held morally responsible by society for his deeds, is an arbitrary question, which the highest wisdom and benevolence of every Age will and must decide for its own special regulation or government. Our duty surely is to study man. This is the commencement of wisdom, and the vestibule of a temple of truth, whose vast interior and divine possessions may occupy your spirits for countless ages. The more we study man, the more certain will it become that *there is no positive evil in existence;* only the local disturbances and social imperfections which are consequent upon a progressive system of human development in minds and morals. "Then," you inquire, "if this be true, how shall we rebuke evils and remove misdirections?" Plainly; you who have *outgrown* the causes of discord should teach others how to follow your example, and help them to do so. This effort to remove evil, however, when confined to the individual power of accomplishment, will not work out one-tenth of the good which would be an easy result of organization. One individual can not vote influentially unless he belongs to a combination. Hence, on this principle, all merely individual efforts to *cure great evils* will be little; while an associative movement, or a combination of individual forces, is certain to achieve greater and more permanent results. These are common-place aphorisms; but clergymen, in their sermons, generally neglect them, and denounce the *individual* as willfully sinful and degenerate!

Those who have progressed above the present semi-civilized and transitional stage of human society—

which produces or nourishes the *fungus* productions, termed orthodox theology and supernaturalistic Christianity—should openly avow the new truths manifested to their vision, and teach the people also how to ascend the glorious eminence of religious and spiritual freedom. Among the numerous reasons why we are moved to free our minds of the existing forms and institutions of supernaturalistic theology, are the following:—

It assumes to be—or to possess within its organization and cardinal doctrines—the medium or totality of inspiration; and arrogantly proclaims itself to be the supreme and sovereign authority. It arbitrarily determines what book, or what peculiar combination of books, we shall revere as the "Word of God;" and then denies to us the right of exercising the same amount of intellectual, moral, and religious liberty. It describes the circle in which we shall move, and think, and reason; and then authoritatively and dogmatically denies to us the moral and religious freedom to advance beyond it. It thus imposes what we conceive to be improper and demoralizing restrictions upon our thoughts and investigations—trammels the progressive development of our minds, and peremptorily denies to us the divine privilege of free discussion and a free expression of our inward sentiments.

It unites with society in its unphilosophical and unbrotherly treatment of the criminal, and of the unfortunate victim of crime; and it (that is, popular Theology) sanctions the old barbarian or Mosaic law of Capital Punishment.

It justifies society in the perpetuation of personal and national animosities and antagonisms. It permits war confiscation of property, and carnage; and it assists to promote successful military chieftains—without regard either to merit or demerit—to the responsible position of emperors and governors.

It sanctions the monarchical despotism of *monopolies.* It smiles, with silent approbation, upon the conflict between Labor and Capital. It permits the present unjust remuneration of the toiling millions.* It permits them to live from day to day without the least guaranty of a *home* in case of pecuniary adversity or ill health; and, more than all, it openly and emphatically sanctions, by Scripture arguments, the dark and fearful sin of *human slavery!*

It deforms and enslaves, but it does not reform and emancipate the human mind, from the confinements and mournful influences of Sectarianism. Its influence is not positive and reformatory; but it is merely negatively restraining. It opposes almost every measure or movement which originates with the people. It engenders melancholy and erroneous conceptions of the nature and destiny of man. It keeps up a perpetual warfare between the *head* and the *heart.* It encourages a gladiatorial struggle against liberty of speech and freedom of action. It even opposes temperance reformation, unless it originates in the church; and uniformly exerts its multiform influences, to restrain the progress of social and prison reforms, upon identical grounds.

It generates cupidity and hypocrisy, by teaching our children to regard certain doctrines as truths, which

* These charges apply to no particular section of this country, but, generally, to all Christendom.

(because those doctrines are not true) can not be felt; but which, nevertheless, are frequently manifested with all the show of confidence in their validity. This leads directly to practical dissimulation and deceit. Many persons are in the constant practice of *exhibiting* piety, who, at the same time, do not (because they can not) *feel* such piety to be sacred truth; and this apparently willful hypocrisy on the part of some individuals, leads directly to the theological assumption—an assumption which has retarded human progress for ages—that the heart of man is desperately wicked and depraved by nature.

It instills dark and unwholesome thoughts into the minds of our children. It teaches them to believe in the most soul-revolting doctrines. They are educated to consider themselves as "totally depraved"—and as being under the "curse" of the living God. It teaches them to regard themselves as evil, and "sinners" by nature; and as incapable of being good and heaven-worthy, independent of the Bible and the Church. They are taught to believe in a "God of Love," who, at the same time, encourages hate; and in a "God of Heaven," who, at the same time, permits the everlasting duration of Hell! Thus our youth become intellectually contaminated by the existing methods of religious education; and, when they advance in years, and become men and women, either they become bigots and sectarians, or else skeptics and misanthropes. A sadness and gloom are consequently thrown over our minds; and we deprive ourselves and our children of a large proportion of that enjoyment and progressive happiness which are the inalienable rights of man!

It asserts this whole world of human beings to be under an Adamic curse or condemnation. It has most dogmatically pronounced, and still continues to assert it, that all the sorrows, and perplexities, and vicissitudes, and trials, and discords, and diseases, and all the afflictions of this mundane state, are expressly sent by the living God to punish man for his alleged manifold transgressions! And it has openly opposed every medical reform, every social improvement, every benevolent design, upon the fabulous ground that such mortal attempts were wicked, and would prove unavailing, because they were in opposition to the "will" and punishment of God. It trammels the progress and advancement of mankind, by teaching our children and our communities to believe the erroneous and baneful doctrine, that no improvement or reformation can be permanently accomplished, except through the so-called "divine" instrumentalities and multifarious restrictions and principles of the established Church.

It strives to awaken in our minds what we consider to be imaginary compunctions of conscience. It imposes what we conceive to be unnecessary and deforming "trials" upon us; and causes us to "crucify" ourselves, and "bear crosses" that are wholly unnatural and wrong. We therefore feel that it has defrauded us, and the generations that are gone, of two-thirds of the real happiness and mental consolations which we solemnly believe to be ours, according to the laws of the human constitution and the universal Providence of God!

It dogmatically asserts Nature, and Reason, and Conscience even, to be *subordinate* to ecclesiastical authority! It inculcates the baneful doctrine that our very heart-impulses are naturally sinful and opposed to the "will of God." Here again it creates a false issue between the heart and the head; and thus it has been the sole cause of impelling many minds into sad and hopeless insanity. It sheds a melancholy, dismal gloom over our families, our homes, and the nations of the civilized world. It renders this life a dark, and toilsome, and uncertain gift of God; and, with its clouds of ignorance and superstition, it darkens our thoughts and anticipations of the other life. When our friends resign their material forms to the grave, then this supernaturalistic Theology fills our hearts with sadness, and our minds with distressing doubts, concerning their future welfare and eternal happiness. And thus it spreads gloom, and disconsolation, and suicidal melancholy, and insane despair, and mental misery, where joy, and cheerfulness, and righteousness, and happiness, should and might exist in abundance.

I have affirmed that there is no Positive Evil in existence. Now, what evidence have we that this statement is true? The evidence, I reply, is universal. There is more harmony than discord; more heat than cold; more light than darkness; more peace than war; more order than confusion. Of this I shall speak hereafter. But the fact, that there is *nothing absolutely devoid of goodness*—that every thing is overruled for good in the end—stands as a pyramidal demonstration of the negational or temporary nature of what we term sin or evil. According to the light which I receive on these questions, every thing that ever occurred has accomplished some good end—yea, always *more good* than evil. Death is a terrible visitation, that is, to all external appearance; but the individual is truly born again. Just above a sharp thorn, the bud bursts open, and a flower unfolds. So every sorrow embosoms a joy—every grief is accompanied by some beneficent provision to mitigate its intensity, and secure a good result. Wars have at last turned in favor of human freedom. Family or local troubles have been greatly diminished by the art of war. But now, these vestiges of a protracted night of barbarian ignorance and patriarchal error, are, one by one, melting, like the ice that fetters the spring-time rivulets, and all will soon be converted into a mighty ocean of never-ebbing peace. The morning sun shines out over the kindling skies of the horizon; the millennial era is imperceptibly stealing over the world. The night has been eventful. Men have groped their way in darkness. Horrid dreams have flitted across the sleeper's mind; and moral shepherds have hailed them as the reflections of some disturbed and offended Divinity. But the chilliness and darkness of the night gradually subside, and a *new dispensation* sheds its celestial rays, kindling with richness and wisdom, over the slumbering millions; and, lo! as the spring day dissipates the mists and gloom of winter, so "old things pass away, and all things become NEW." Errors, like the shadows of escaping clouds, will disappear when the "Sun of Righteousness"—of wisdom, truth, and brotherly love—shall send its all-searching light and healing warmth into their midst. Will you not, then, take a higher position in the moral grades of the spiritual universe? I know you will. Like the eccentric comets, men primarily pursue strange paths in their revolutions around the Central Source of Right. But all truth is analogous—all principles immutable. Therefore, just as certain as the comet finally becomes a beautiful planet, and rolls harmoniously in the orbit of order; so certainly will humanity eventually glide into the sphere of harmony and into the paths of eternal rectitude.

Humanity may be viewed from two positions: one affords pleasure, the other confusion; one yields us a true estimate of the whole human family; the other, distracts our sympathies and seems to substantiate the theological theory of man's fallen nature.

The best Christian scholars obtain their worst impressions of man by constantly viewing him from unfavorable positions and in the most incongruous lights; while the rationalistic philosophers, having obtained more expanded and reasonable conceptions of things, contemplate the human family with increasing satisfaction. It may be illustrated by supposing two individuals going forth to examine a landscape. One takes his position at a point of observation from which the eye can survey the entire combination of objects, trees, rocks, flowers, mounds, mountains, lights, and shades, which serve to constitute the most captivating exhibition of beautiful scenery. The other places himself in immediate contact with the constituents of the scene. We may now suppose that these individuals enter into conversation, through the agency of speaking trumpets, and commence describing what each actually observes and enjoys. The man from the distance, hailing the other who is in direct connection with the scene, asks: "What do you see?" He replies, "Oh, such discord and trouble! I wish myself away!" "What, from that charming prospect?" exclaims the man in the distance. "Indeed, I do," responds the other. "I can not advance a single step without wounding my limbs and lacerating my feet. Insurmountable rocks present themselves; and the narrow pass is overgrown with poisonous weeds and thorny vines. Rough and angular shapes are visible all around. When I look up, I can scarcely see the sunlight—so dense and gloomy is the foliage. Even the birds have forsaken this dismal retreat. And the ravines seem so dark and miry, I think the serpents brood therein."

The other observer, not appreciating the troubles his friend thus enumerates, asks: "Do you not see any beautiful flowers growing along the path, and musical streamlets leaping through the thicket?"

"Oh, now that you speak of them, I confess I do," responds the friend; "but I can not enjoy any thing—my flesh is wounded, and my spirit is fatigued and repelled, by the constant effort to surmount craggy acclivities and thorny promontories. I will seat myself in this gloomy place—though I much tremble to remain—while you describe this repulsive scene as it appears to you from your stand-point."

We may now suppose the man in the distance replying thus: "Taking, as I do, a free and comprehensive view of the whole—made up, as it undoubtedly is, of the *parts* which you have just described—I must confess that I never beheld a more perfect exhibition of harmonious beauty. The *parts* may be exceedingly *roughly hewn*; but, to the over-seeing eye, the *whole* displays design, order, proportion, and variety. The dense foliage seems like swelling waves of green, about to burst from surplus life. The craggy rocks lend a variation and strength to the scene; while the topmost boughs of the stalwart oaks, just catching the rays of the rising sun, shed forth a subdued light over the surrounding objects, which no pencil can impart to canvas, or language describe. Do not—I pray thee—do not condemn *the parts* when they are so manifestly essential to the final development of an harmonious *Whole!*"

So the case stands to-day between rationalists and supernaturalists. The former view humanity from a position which enables them to tolerate, to love, to protect, yea, to admire, the parts or the *Individuals*, for the sake of the variety and grandeur of the whole; while the latter—the clergymen of Christendom and their followers—knowing comparatively nothing of the grand scheme of existence, devote themselves to the defamation and classical execration of the minor particulars as the only method of *altering* the entire body to suit the expression they think it should wear. What would you think of an intelligent merchant tailor who had come to the popular clerical conclusion, that *one* pattern was truly orthodox; and insists that *everybody should wear the established size and shaped garment* and no other? What would you say? Would you alter your body to suit the pattern? Or, the pattern to suit your body? "The latter, of course," you reply. Now, the supernaturalists say, that *all should and shall wear their pattern.* And all the *trouble* there is, between the pulpit and the people, arises from the theological *cutting* and *carving* of individuals in order to make the *one orthodox pattern* suit all degrees and shades of mind.

But Humanity is a Tree. Its roots begin far down in the constitution of Nature, where the *Germ* was originally deposited. It commenced its upward growth many ages since. It grew onward in straight lines, until the period arrived for the putting forth of diverse branches. The lowest limbs were gigantic, replete with thorny projections, reaching far out into the air, casting deep shades on the earth. But the branches become smaller, and more beautiful, as the progression of refinement increases. The tree is not yet fully developed. But already the birds of heaven alight on its highest boughs, and the beams of the rising Sun—the bright herald of the approaching crisis—illuminate those tiny leaves which tremblingly unfold their receptive vessels and lay their faces against the firmament.

CHAPTER V.

FOURTH REVIEW.

The theological fabric.—Liberties with an infallible Word.—The paradoxical compound.—Points of agreement with Swedenborg.—The devil improved.—Things and Powers.—Evidences of the existence of sin.—No Law of Right established.—Propositions analyzed.—The doctrine of blaming.—Governments; their object.—The false issues of theology.

In the present discussion, it is deemed proper to define the *position* which I at present occupy respecting it. My posture is that of a reviewer and spectator. A master-builder is now engaged in constructing a theological fabric. My business is to observe the process; to see whether any new principles of ethnological architecture are truly developed; to observe the timbers of thought as they are one by one adjusted; to see whether the materials are sound and skillfully prepared; and to ascertain what the structure is good for when completed. You will, therefore, perceive that I am not now at liberty to turn away, as my soul truly yearns to do, and unfold, to your mental vision and appreciation, the "house not made with hands," wherein reside the immortal truths and eternal revelations of the living God. But I must, as in the capacity of humanity's advocate, devote my present moments to a critical inspection of the somewhat *new* form of Conservatism which Dr. Bushnell is now giving birth to—or the new theologic fabric which he is now erecting—on the *old* supernatural foundation.

> "Know thyself, presume not God to scan;
> The proper study of mankind is man."

On the broad, democratic, and rationalistic principle that "*all* scripture is given by inspiration," I am moved to select the foregoing passage according to the inspiration of Alexander Pope.

This text requires no expounding; only a practical application. It comes to me, on this occasion, as being highly applicable to you all in general, and to the champions of Supernaturalism in particular. It is not necessary for me to undertake to convince you of the immense value of personal knowledge; to persuade you that moral and intellectual powers are proportionate to education; or, that *ignorance* is the parent of what men term "sin" and misery. These are familiar facts; requiring no argument; suggesting no controversy. I will, therefore, proceed presently to show why this text is particularly applicable to supernaturalists.

The fourth lecture of the course, on supernaturalism, as opposed to naturalism, was delivered by Dr. B—— on last Sabbath evening. His text was taken from the twentieth verse of the eighth chapter of Romans—as follows: "For the creature was made subject to vanity, not willingly, but by reason of him who hath subjected the same in hope."

The Lecturer considered this passage, when taken in connection with the brace of verses on either side of it, to embody the *whole statement* of man's relations and abandonment to the various kinds and degrees of sin, and also to the supernatural system of redemption, which God had introduced into this world for man's especial benefit and salvation.

The Lecturer shows himself to be quite at home in his profession *as Doctor of Divinity.* Because, on announcing the text, he referred to the fact, that the passage had puzzled nearly all the English commentators as to its *true* signification. In his opinion, the three or four verses in that department of Paul's epistle to the Romans, had not as yet been properly apprehended or rendered. Consequently, although he presumed not to give the true interior and infallible import, yet he doctored the passages to *suit* his own preconceived impressions of truth, and made them read as follows.*

For mutual meditation and enlightenment, I am again moved to solicit your attention to an inconsistency. Inconsistencies or contradictions should be studiously avoided as evils that injure the tone and health of the understanding. I allude to the strange idea that *fallible* texts, or imperfect rendering of texts, can be found to exist in a book which is recommended, and dogmatically forced upon us, as an *infallible* revelation. I must repeat, and pray for an answer to, these questions: If the Bible is the *perfect* Word of God, how came the above text to be *imperfectly* translated? Or, if it be admitted that *Dr. Bushnell* rendered the passage for the first time correctly, then, I ask, How

* It is regarded as non-essential to an understanding of what succeeds, as the sequel develops the Lecturer's meaning.

can we place our faith, our hopes, and eternal destiny upon the statements of a book which is proved thus to have been giving mankind wrong impressions for eighteen centuries?

The alteration of meaning is very important. The positive or imperative tense, "shall," is removed by a single sweep of the pen, and the mere word "may" is substituted, which so exceedingly weakens the *possibility* of man's final redemption from sin, that hundreds of human souls—who have been long sustained by the supposed positive *promise* of God that *sin* shall be ultimately subdued and destroyed—have now nothing left to think of but disappointment and moral despair? Again, I ask, can a *fallible* translation of a text be consistent with an infallible Word?

By way of criticism, I am compelled by truth to pronounce Dr. B——'s last discourse a splendid tirade against, and a learned defamation or vilification of, the human character. It portrayed the supposed iniquities of the heart of the creature-man; and emitted, at several junctions, multitudes of dark, dismal, and denunciatory thoughts. The Lecturer is truly a bold advocate of theological horrors and dogmatism. He thinks man is endowed with the will-power to be an eternal enemy (if he so desires and determines) to the living God, and to his moral government. Man, he affirms, is *supernatural*, because he can overcome mechanical force, and act outside of, or superior to, the natural system of cause and effect. From the mythologic eminence of supernaturalism, he vociferated the church cries against those who dare openly prefer the authoritative promptings of NATURE to the dicta of dogmatic creeds. It is now manifest what description of conservatism this modern LUTHER is at present destined to generate, and possibly to establish. It is composed of the following ingredients: Calvinism and Arminianism in equal parts; a small portion of the conciliatory system of Richard Baxter, who had the celebrated Drs. WATTS and DODDRIDGE for disciples; a very little originality of thought; a slight proportion of Swedenborgianism; and about the same quantity of Rationalism, which, being literally interpreted, signifies an understanding of things as they are.

The paradoxical character of this compound renders some explanation necessary. Although it is truly believed, that when the various forms and shades of human credulity, in supernatural mysteries are carefully weighed, contrasted, and compared, the existing differences between popular creeds will greatly recede from view; the principal troubles and disputes among the clergy, concerning what creed, or particular shade of faith, is the most orthodox and infallible, will then appear as confounding and astounding only to those who can not readily comprehend the undeviating action of psychological principles upon human beings.* The resemblance of Dr. B——'s philosophico-supernaturalism to the chief doctrines of Calvinism and Arminianism, is visible only in the original modification of the old church *formulas*, which is occasionally attempted at various points of the discussion. Very

* The subject here alluded to, receives very particular attention in the Great Harmonia, vol. III., entitled "The Seer," uniform with this work. See the chapters, showing the action of psychological laws among religious chieftains.

many Protestants will find their condition typified by the mental exhibitions of the mind under present review. He indicates a strange independence. Socinus, himself, never attempted the reformation of church dogmas with more ardor, or never so conspicuously failed to accomplish a reconciliation of differences among his own people. He evidently has tasted of the fruit of the knowledge-tree, and feels disposed to reject the cardinal mysteries of the Christian faith, as held by other denominations; but he places new incomprehensibilities before the people, in his rationalistic effort to manifest the doctrine, that the mission of Christ was designed only to introduce a new moral law, distinguished from all preceding laws by its superior sanctity and perfection. There is all the time a manifest proclivity to trace out some hypothetical coincidence between the dictations of Reason and the dogmas of supernaturalism. Now the mind, thus striving to act natural and unnatural at the same time, one moment affirms its determination to subject all religious doctrines to the test of Nature and judgment; but, even before the sentence, containing this affirmation, is concluded, there comes forth the confounding ideal statement, that in Jesus dwelt the fullness of the Father—enjoying universal power of the Church in heaven and in earth; that, with logical propriety, the Incarnation being thus perfect, may be termed "God in Christ;" and yet, a mental reaction succeeds this, and a peculiar combination of words changes all the foregoing into something like the doctrines of Unitarianism —implying, that Jesus was a certain modified impersonation of the divine spirit of love and energy—which considers a similitude or assimilation of the human character to that unfolded by Jesus as equivalent to the all-important Salvation, which other denominations hold to, but with far more startling interpretations attached to the term.

The desire to develop a *reasonable* basis for the everlasting support of supernaturalistic doctrines, urged Dr. B—— somewhat unconsciously, I think, into the Swedenborgian method of interpreting the Word. The spiritual relations of Christ to God and to man, appear also slightly tinged by the New Church Doctrines. On this point the New Jerusalem creed, article second, is explicit. It states that—" Jehovah God himself descended from Heaven, as Divine Truth, which is the Word, and took upon him Human Nature for the purpose of removing from man the powers of hell, and restoring to order all things in the spiritual world, and all things in the church: that he removed from man the powers of hell, by combats against and victories over them; in which consisted the great work of Redemption: that by the same acts, which were his temptations, the last of which was the passion of the cross, he united, in his Humanity, Divine Truth to Divine Good, or Divine Wisdom to Divine Love, and so returned into his Divinity in which he was from eternity, together with, and in, his Glorified Humanity; whence he forever keeps the infernal powers in subjection to himself: and that all who believe in him, with the understanding, from the heart, and live accordingly, will be saved."

The affirmations of the Lecturer concerning the possibility of evil, as incident to the creation of man, and as beyond the power of God to prevent in a realm of free moral powers, may be found, differently stated, in the following Swedenborgian article of faith: "That the government of the Lord's Divine Love and Wisdom is the Divine Providence; which is universal, exercised according to certain fixed laws of Order, and extending to the minutest particulars of the life of all men, both of the good and of the evil: that in all its operations it has respect to what is infinite and eternal, and makes no account of things transitory, but as they are subservient to eternal ends; thus that it mainly consists, with man, in the connection of things temporal with things eternal; for that the continual aim of the Lord, by his Divine Providence, is to join man to himself and himself to man, that he may be able to give him the felicities of eternal life: and that the laws of permission are also laws of the Divine Providence; since evil can not be prevented without destroying the nature of man as an accountable agent; and because, also, it can not be removed unless it be known, and can not be known unless it appear; thus that no evil is permitted but to prevent a greater; and all is overruled, by the Lord's Divine Providence, for the greatest possible good."

The resemblance of Dr. B——'s assertions, respecting the visitation of good and evil spirits to man, is very well established in Swedenborg's affirmations, "that man, during his abode in the world, is, as to his spirit, in the midst between heaven and hell, acted upon by influences from both; and thus is kept in a state of spiritual equilibrium between good and evil; in consequence of which he enjoys free will, or freedom of choice, in spiritual things as well as in natural, and possesses the capacity of either turning himself to the Lord and his kingdom, or turning himself away from the Lord, and connecting himself with the kingdom of darkness; and that, unless man had such freedom of choice, the Word would be of no use, the church would be a mere name, man would possess nothing by virtue of which he could be enjoined to the Lord, and the cause of evil would be chargeable on God himself."

Nor does the similitude cease here. Swedenborg also *generalized* the evils of the world—all the sins against God and all the infernal spirits; which, when combined and estimated in the aggregate, he termed "the devil." This, as we have seen, is Dr. B——'s latest improvement in this oriental myth. But the doctrine is capable of still further amendment.

On another head, as to the future good and evil consequences of the character, which men establish for themselves in this life, Dr. B——, in substance, stated the Swedenborgian doctrine, "that immediately after death, which is only a putting off of the material body, never to be resumed, man rises again in a spiritual or substantial body, in which he continues to live to eternity; in heaven, if his ruling affections, and thence his life, have been good; and in hell, if his ruling affections, and thence his life, have been evil."

The similar appearance of the quantity of Rationalism, referred to as entering into his conservatism, is discoverable only in the very equivocal use which Dr. B—— makes of the faculty of Reason, as a power through which to obtain and establish a philosophical basis upon which to rest the doctrines of supernaturalism. Such are the signs of the times. The waters are disturbed, and the storm is hovering nigh. The old church is dying—dying from the internal convulsions accompanying the approaching crisis of a chronic disorder, slumbering in the vitals of ecclesiasticism—a disease which I am impressed to term "Error!" The result is certain as the approach of spring.

That Dr. B—— has a perfect right to alter and transpose passages of Scripture to suit the foregone conclusions of his own mind, is indisputable. All reasonable and educated persons—that is to say, all Naturalists and skeptics, so-called—take the same dignified liberties with the Bible. But what we object to is this: that such liberties should be taken by clergymen with a Book, which is universally believed and recommended by them to be the *perfect and unalterable* Revelation of God's will and promises. The Lecturer paraphrased the already specified text, and then proceeded to say, that in his "previous discourse he had drawn out or sketched the supernatural system of God; which was shown to be a realm of powers not governed by mere cause and effect, not by mechanical force, but by the free will and consent of the inhabitants of that realm." He thought that *that* lecture was a proper stepping-stone to the general subject of "evil" or "sin," as bodied forth in the present comprehensive text. His last discourse, therefore, was devoted principally to a demonstration of the positive existence of sin; to prove that *man*, by the exercise of his supernatural power, is the chief source of its origin.

Now, availing myself of the example and conceded liberty of paraphrasing a text of Scripture, in order to render the meaning more transparent, I will transfer the passage in Paul to an expression of Dr. B——'s extraordinary theory.

God, in creating "*powers*," or free moral agents, was environed, not willingly, but as a necessary *incident* to man's creation, with the tremendous "possibility" of evil. Therefore, although God did not will or desire it, yet he was compelled, by the exigencies of the case, to subject all mankind to vanity and to the disciplining vicissitudes of evil. This possibility of having trouble in his moral government God could not prevent, and at the same time *secure* to man the uncontrolled exercise of his will or moral freedom. Consequently, the Deity unwillingly submitted the whole human family to the trials and temptations of sin, *indulging* the forlorn "*hope*" the while that man would see fit to exercise his supernatural will-power in the right direction; and thus be ultimately delivered from the bondage of corruption into the glorious liberty of the children of God! Behold! how emphatically and demonstratively the revelations of St. Paul prove that Dr. B—— is a *true* exponent of the great doctrine of supernaturalism!

The Lecturer said it might appear unnecessary to undertake to prove the existence of evil; but he deemed it indispensable to his argument to demonstrate that sin *is* really in the world. Rationalists, he said, generally denied the existence of sin; and, therefore, as this subject was an open question, he would proceed to prove that sin is a tremendous and fearful reality.

In this connection it may be remarked, that the Lecturer did not *prove*—which he logically and historically endeavored to do—the positive existence of evil. Nor did he give any very definite or understandable explanation of the nature of sin, as a *thing* in the world; except this oft-repeated assertion, *that sin is a supernatural and tremendous reality*. You will observe, my friends, that there is a vast difference between an assertion and a demonstration; a difference between stating a proposition and proving its utter truthfulness. In justice to the Lecturer, however, it should be remarked, that he did undertake to prove the existence of sin by mere negatives; by inferences and implication. As this effort was the *vital* principle of his whole discourse, I will proceed to examine his several positions, which may be summed up as follows: He asserted that sin exists—first, because we Blame; second, because we Forgive; third, because we have Government; fourth, because we use Sarcasm; fifth, because men write and love Tragedy. That is to say, men instinctively acknowledge the existence of *sin* by *blaming*, *forgiving*, and *governing*. These things, Dr. B—— thought, sufficiently proved the tremendous reality of sin. The prison, the rack, the gallows, the laws, the municipal regulation of societies, and cities, &c., he regarded as so many lofty and invulnerable demonstrations of the universal existence of the reality of supernatural evil. We blame, he said, because there is something which we know *deserves* to be blamed; we *forgive* because there is wrong which *needs* forgiveness; we govern the family and society because individuals are disposed to do *wrong* from their nature; all government proves, he said, that mankind instinctively confess to the existence of a law of right and a tremendous wrong in the world. These were the positions assumed by the Lecturer. To a brief examination of these theologic propositions, in addition to what I have already said, I now solicit your particular attention.

Question.—"*Is sin a supernatural reality?*" What a thought is this! Dogmatism never suggested a more dismal idea; neither mythology a more pernicious doctrine! How came such a thought in the world? Was it introduced by the friends and students of humanity? Is it the faith of the noble, the creed of the generous, the theory of the wise? Nay! Dr. B—— quoted Theodore Parker, Fourier, Dr. Strauss, the author of Festus, and Alexander Pope, as so many rationalistic voices in favor of a more benevolent and generous doctrine—not a more generous doctrine to Dr. B——'s definitions. Far from it. He denounced it as sophistry —as the foolishness of rationalism; while *his faith* he esteemed as given of God and worthy of all acceptation!

Where, then, did Dr. B—— obtain this idea of sin? From a careful analysis of man's nature and motives? Did he draw it from the deep wells of human experience? The reply is negative. He obtained it all from a book; from the *dicta* of old writers; from the Egyptian darkness of the old theology! He talks learnedly of what God could and could not do; how the Divine Mind was environed with the "*possibility* of evil" before the world began; how God wills, hopes, and executes; but, of human nature, the Lecturer manifested the general ignorance which is characteristic of the clergy everywhere. Surely, upon the walls of the modern Zion, an angel should be permitted to stand; there to proclaim to the clergy of Christendom the text which I have selected from Pope.

The Lecturer obtained his extraordinary notions of sin from the decaying catacombs of oriental theology; and, having systematized the suggestions, he labors diligently to bend, to force, and interpret Nature into confirmatory proof of his marvelous assertions. This is his method, as it now appears, of accomplishing the promised *reconciliation* between supernaturalism and rationalistic theories of religion! He says, "sin is supernatural." We ask for demonstration. He replies, because man, the free-power, *can act independent of all* cause and effect—superior *to all* mechanical force. Again, we ask for proof. He says, Nature is bound by the laws of necessity. All Things, he asserts, are compelled to exist according to the mechanism of cause and effect, and must, therefore, move as they are acted upon or instigated; while the Powers—which are human beings, endowed with a free-will or self-determining force—are capable of acting superior to or against the laws of nature, and are, therefore, legitimately supernatural. Again—I ask, what can man do contrary to the unchangeable laws of Nature? He replies, man can build ships, procure powder, load a pistol, and shoot his neighbor; also, he can overcome the law of gravitation by raising a book, &c., all of which phenomena are supernatural. Here, then, on this foundation, Dr. B—— rests his ideas of the supernaturalness of sin.

But in the second review, I adduced several illustrations from Nature, showing that volcanoes and coal-mines sometimes do shoot and destroy people; showing, also, that nature, through the instrumentality and mediation of man's mind, plans and constructs ships; and that a *tornado*, in its mighty strength, overcomes the law of gravitation more extensively and perfectly than any human being, notwithstanding the doctrine of free agency. What, then, is sin? Dr. B—— replies: Man can lie, and cheat, and steal, and murder; but Nature, which is bound by laws of cause and effect, can not do any thing of this kind. To this I answer, that Nature, according to this definition, does *murder* through her animals and volcanoes. And it seems that *insane* or irresponsible and irrational men will *lie*, and *cheat*, and *steal* at times, by following out certain mental caprices and hereditary proclivities. Now, I ask: Are these human beings commiting supernatural sin? "No," replies Dr. B——, "the supernatural sin is committed only when a human being acts, *knowingly*, against the law of Right, or contrary to the moral law of God, as was illustrated in the *voluntary* transgression of the first man." Here, then, is the point to settle:—Does man voluntarily, from the perversity of his own nature and will, without any sufficient extraneous cause, violate the transparent and known law of Right? I assert that no man does or can do this; for which assertion I am moved to assign the following potential reasons:—

There is no universally recognized law of God—no universally received *standard* of measurement by which to determine right from wrong. This is an *important fact*, which Dr. B—— has utterly overlooked in the pending discussion. It is because the race has not yet grown to the discovery of this universal law, that the world is so exceedingly unsettled and discordant as to what Right is. Man, I am impressed to say, does not *hate* the law of Right. He feels its silent workings in his undeveloped being, without *knowing* how to interpret and apply it to his life. This universal fact, that all men have, or desire to possess, some fixed system of Right, is a living *protest* against the doctrine of total depravity, and the Lecturer's definition of sin. The heathen nations have moral codes which they hold sacred as the laws of God, although these laws may be unjust and barbarous in the extreme.

Before the champion of supernaturalism proves the whole race of man to be subjected to vanity and sin, it is first absolutely necessary to prove, beyond all controversy, that all mankind have a fixed standard of RIGHT —a true law of God, by which to measure the nature and extent of sin—and by which, also, *every man* shall in his conscience, in all states and circumstances, unerringly KNOW that he is doing either right or wrong.

But I ask, Is there any universal knowledge as to Right and Wrong? Moses says—"an eye for an eye." This he recommends as the *law of right*. But Jesus preaches quite a different doctrine, and teaches us, as the law of right, "to love one another."

Now, both Moses and Jesus have faithful, conscientious followers, whose honest convictions of *right* are thus antagonistic. In this case—although the disciple might, by the exercise of his will-power, violate the *moral law* laid down by the master,—I ask, Where is the sin? In a case of jealousy and revenge, the involved disciple of Jesus might violate the *law of love;* but he would, at the same time, if he *murdered his enemy,* be acting in harmony with the moral law of Moses! Thus, according to the Bible standard of right, the man who might *violate* the law of God at one end, would in the same proportion, be *obeying* it at the other. Now, Where is his sin? Dr. B—— would reply, doubtless, that the old law of God is now repealed; that the present *law of right*, under which sin is punishable, is divulged in the Christian dispensation. If this position be assumed, then—I ask, How can we *know* perfectly, that, when we violate *the law of love*, we are doing something positively *against* the law of God? How can we be perfectly certain that the New Testament is the word of God? Surely, the doctors of divinity openly confess it to be sick, out of order, and wrongly translated in places! Under this new dispensation, Dr. B—— says, that *murder* is contrary to the moral government of God. Hence, on man's part, when committed, it is a supernatural sin. But here let me inquire: Is it a sin when a man acts from the conviction that he is doing right? Certainly not. Why? Because, if it were *in all cases* a supernatural and punishable sin to commit murder, how many *clergymen*, according to this rule, would suffer the eternal consequences thereof for the deliberate method, which they almost everywhere sanction and adopt, of *murdering the criminal*, immediately after prayers, by the barbarous process of strangulation! Do they forgive their enemies? Do, they, when the assassin's knife enters the heart, breathe forth—"Father, forgive him?" If one man murders another, with the presiding conviction that he is doing right; then, in this instance,—I ask, Is the murderer *knowingly* acting against the moral law of God? Nay; because he would be acting from the motive or *love of right* at the moment; although the deed, in fact, may be unequivocally and manifestly wrong. I urge these points in order to demonstrate *the fact*, which has been confessed, that mankind can not be universally subjected in sin or wrong *because there exists no universally recognized principle of right* whereby to judge the world.

Dr. B—— affirms mankind to be naturally *prone* to go against the law of right. Now, on the ground of educational bias—on the presumption that he is theologically prejudiced and darkened as to the real nature and psychological organization of man—we may let this defamation of humanity pass, with the exhortation, uttered in all deference, that he forthwith sets to the music of practice the text quoted from Pope. Because, to say that man *naturally* exerts his will-power against the moral law of God, is to assert that which all the race proves to be exceedingly erroneous and pernicious. One man thinks it is *right* to hold slaves; another, that it is wrong. One feels justified in *hanging* the criminal; another, only when he *opposes* the custom with all his might. One thinks the Sabbath to be a divine institution, which must be devoted exclusively to church-going purposes; another, conscientiously, does not believe any thing of the kind. The Jew is as conscientious in selling merchandise, when Christians are going to church, as the Christian is justified, in his educational conscience, in trading on Saturday, when the Jew reverently retires to the synagogue. Of the universal disagreement as to the nature of sin, Dr. B—— has, in the work heretofore alluded to (page 47), acknowledged himself perfectly aware. In speaking of the indeterminate use of language, he says:—"The word *sin* is of this description, and most persons seem to imagine that it names a given act or state, about which there is no diversity of understanding. Contrary to this, no two minds ever had the same impression of it. The whole personal history of every man, his acts, temptations, wants, and repentances; his opinions of God, of law, and of personal freedom; his theory of virtue, his decisions of the question, whether sin is an act, or a state; of the will, or of the heart: in fact, his whole theology and life will enter into his impression of this word *sin*, to change the quality and modify the relations of that which it signifies. It will also be found, as a matter of fact, that the interminable disputes of the theologians on this particular subject, originate in fundamental differences of view concerning the nature of sin, and are themselves incontestible proofs that, simple as the word is, and on the lips of everybody (as we know it to be), there is yet no virtual agreement of meaning connected with the word." This is a very *rational* confession. All the different governments, different laws, different religious sects, and systems of managing the bodies and souls of men, are so many evidences that mankind are striving, yearning after the RIGHT; that they are not yet progressed to that point of unity where a *universal standard* of justice and equity can be perceived and adopted, coextensive with the human family.

Second proposition: "That sin is proved to exist, because we instinctively blame mankind." It is my impression that blame is a complete proof of man's *ignorance* of man. The wise and noble mind is lenient; the foolish man is always blaming. Jesus, Galileo, Columbus, everybody, have been the victims of blame.

Does Dr. B—— remember how the pious and Christian inhabitants of London rose up in holy horror against HEMING, who had the audacity to invent street-lamps? The sun had gone down, and the moon shed none of her accustomed radiance; and so the genius of Heming, in the exercise of his supernatural will, constructed and substituted *lights* at proper intervals throughout the city. But he was *blamed* for sinning *against* God. Impious, self-determining man! But why was he blamed? Why, because he was usurping the prerogatives of the Creator! Does not the Bible distinctly affirm that the Lord had made two lights; one to rule the day, the other the night? And did not Heming act, in exercising his freedom, *against* the consummate omniscience of Deity? Puny, presumptive, audacious man! how richly he deserved *blame* for such a manifest commission of the supernatural sin!

Dr. Bushnell said that the people were so perfectly conscious of being personally sinful, and of *deserving blame*, that they would come to the church every Sunday to have it preached to them, *and would pay for it too!* This was "the unkindest cut of all." But let us think of the statement. The priests bear rule, and the people love to have it so. If Dr. B—— were a careful student of human nature, he would discover quite different reasons for human actions. The people go to church because they need diversion; because they wish to be popular in business; because they desire to see and to be seen. It is true that, now and then, a person attends the sanctuary for instruction; not so particularly for the purposes of being blamed. But they become accustomed, however, to the perpetual defamation of the human character, and think there is no remedy for the evil. When Baxter first preached "infant damnation" to the English mothers, they rose up *en masse* against him; but he was a "doctor of divinity," and hence, soon succeeded, by quoting Greek and Hebrew passages and eminent commentators, in quelling the rebellious congregation. The mothers finally became tranquil, and ultimately consented to *pay* quite cheerfully "to be blamed," and to hear preached the diabolical and imaginative dogma.

The Lecturer said he would like to see how a rationalist, who believed that all things and men were controlled by the laws of cause and effect, would bear the malicious taunts of an urchin who might be supposed to be thrusting a pin in the skeptic's back. That would be a case of "manifest misdirection," as the rationalist defines sin. Would the rationalist regard it in the same light as he would the pricking of a splinter from the back of the pew? "No," said he, "the rationalist would *blame* the boy," as the self-determining cause of the disturbance, and disturb the congregation by his cries. To this I can only offer my own method of practicing the principles of a generous rationalism. In the first place, I should pity the urchin for being sufficiently unfortunate in his phrenological character to be capable of feeling like thus tormenting and disturbing another individual. In the second place, I should, without harboring any revengeful feeling, break up the immediate relations subsisting between the youth and myself, either by removing myself from the locality, or else the youth, as the *cause* of the supposed uneasiness.

To this matter the doctrine of supernatural blame does not apply; it is all cause and effect.

As another department of this inferential effort to prove the existence of evil, Dr. B—— referred to the hypothetical fact, that everybody is out of friendship with themselves—perpetually self-accusing and self-blaming; which was considered sufficient evidence of their internal guiltiness and moral obliquity. A little real knowledge of the teachings of phrenology would have solved this problem. In nearly all cases of extreme *self-condemnation* or blame, it will be found that the individuals thus affected, either have received, through hereditary descent, a defective mental constitution, or else are the victims of some atrocious system of ethics and theology. Daily walking about the streets, there is a man who believes he has committed the *unpardonable sin!* Of course, he is under constant *self-accusation*—as a being eternally condemned of God. Now, I ask, where did he obtain so horrid an idea? Surely, not from his own sinful, depraved nature. Quite the contrary. He is a victim of *Churchianity*—a mysterious and incomprehensible system, which Dr. B—— is laboring to rescue from the approaching flood of intelligence and republicanism, which is hourly rising higher and higher against the combined forces of Christendom.

In the thirteenth century, there sprang up in Italy, and was thence propagated throughout almost all the countries of Europe, a denomination of Christians, called the WHIPPERS. Their theology (like Dr. Bushnell's supernaturalism) taught them to spurn and dislike themselves, and to defame the human character in every conceivable manner. Persons of both sexes, and all ranks and ages, ran through the public streets with *whips* in their hands, lashing their bodies with the most astonishing zeal and severity, with the hope of obtaining, by their voluntary mortification and outward penance, the divine mercy and salvation for themselves and others. This sect taught, among other Christian doctrines, that *flagellation* was a virtue of equal magnitude with the *baptismal* ceremony and the other sacramental proceedings, and was called the baptism of blood! Now will Dr. B—— assert that this *flagellation* was a proof that the people were internally conscious of deserving blame? My impression is, that he must assume this psychological position; because his last discourse, which I am now examining, was as clear an instance of premeditated theological *flagellation* of the human soul as was ever instituted or practiced by the religious Whippers themselves.

The long pilgrimages, made by the pagan and early religious sects, were regarded by the Lecturer, as another evidence of instinctive sense of wrong or evil to be atoned for, through sacrificial agency. How superficial is this conclusion! Let us see. Mohammed, for example, esteemed Mecca as the horizon of his spiritual experience. He recommended it as such to his disciples. He loved the city and its beautiful retreats. It was his sacramental altar; the *table* upon which he first broke the bread and gave the wine to his conscientious followers. He did not command his people to make a pilgrimage to the city once a year. But those who lived in the days of Mohammed were first led to the sacred cave from their affection for its religious associations. The next generation considered it an established *custom*, forever to be observed; the next, a *duty*, to be discharged at all hazards; the next, a *penance*, analogous to all religious ceremonies, quite indispensable to the eternal salvation and beatification of the soul! Thus, Dr. B—— should have been *more* philosophical, and discovered a better explanation of the causes of *self-condemnation* and of self-imposed afflictions; except in those cases where an enlightened conscience in reality feels offended.

I come now to another proposition: *That sin exists because we forgive.* All the impressions which I have received on that head, amount to this conclusion: that revenge and forgiveness are almost *twin brothers;* born of the prolific parent, Ignorance. There is no such a thing, philosophically and properly considered, as *forgiveness.* A revengeful person is one who, from his peculiar temperament and organization, can not easily control his passions; he gives blow for blow—takes an eye for an eye—and thus feels that the ends of justice, according to his definition, are at once fully and per fectly satisfied. But a *forgiving* person is one who feels injured; he feels offended, he feels you to be decidedly in his debt, and will long remember it; but he controls his passions, easily, and in a commendable degree, and says, "no matter, I will not hurt you in return, my friend—oh, no! I forgive you—I can speak words of kindness to you and feel them, too." Now, this is all the forgiveness which is at yet known or developed in this world. The forgiving person smiles and stabs. We are told to speak kind words to those we consider our enemies; because, forsooth, those mild sentences "heap coals of fire upon the offender's head." This is highly gratifying to the forgiving individual! He forgives in order to be all the more revenged. Now I am impressed to consider *blame*, *revenge*, and such *forgiveness*, as the legitimate children of Ignorance. "Forgive your enemies; love them that curse you," &c.; but I thank God that I can behold, in the approaching era, a more transcendent state of morals—a state, in which the pure and wise, and high-minded man *can not be injured or offended!* Nothing to forgive; for there is no offense! The *noble parent* does not feel offended at the little infant; though it might cause some dreadful accident or injury. Men and crimes are quite different things. The little bee makes honey; but, if molested, it will also sting.

I pass on to another proposition: *That all government presupposes the existence of sin in the world.* Here, again, I am moved to pronounce Dr. B—— in transparent error. For governments manifestly presuppose the existence of ignorance, imbecility, and diversity of inclinations on the part of the people. An intelligent man, as already shown, *is a law unto himself!* A moral and well situated man needs no constables, no prisons, no gallows, to keep him in the paths of rectitude and righteousness. Dr. B—— thought, that, granting the doctrine of cause and effect be true and applicable to man, children should be left to unfold in the family like flowers in the garden; giving forth their native odors, without the farce of family governments. But the fact, he thought, was quite to the contrary. He asserted that man was a self-determining power; that the family arrangements were made as a proof of the expectation of evil as a consequence or necessity of such freedom. This point I will not now dispute. For I behold mountains of ignorance in families and states as to the most effectual and salutary methods of developing and governing the individual. But I will simply remark, that, in a family where rationalistic spiritualism or the harmonial philosophy has displaced the church theology, and it is truly practiced by the parents; the household regulations are arranged so harmoniously, and with so much liberty for the play of diverse individual inclinations, that the children can have an opportunity to be cultured like the flowers, and to unfold the sweeter elements of their being, without being molested by the horrid dreams of supernaturalism. A judicious and philosophical husbandman will *fence* in his gardens, that no cattle or swine may disturb the growing vegetation; even so the philosophical parent would put a family government for the purpose of protecting the inward harmony from unnecessary and unnatural molestation.

The other evidences of sin in the world, which Dr. B—— considered under the head of *Sarcasm* and *Tragedy*, I am moved to pass by as requiring no special comment. In alluding to the passage in Shakespeare, the Lecturer asked, whether "Lady Macbeth would have exclaimed, in the agonies of a stricken conscience, 'Out, damned spot!' if there were no 'damned spot' which existed to smite her for her voluntary transgressions?" This question would appear in its true importance and legitimate force if I should ask:—When a man, afflicted with a bad circulation of blood, retires, and falling asleep, is heard to labor with the idea that a *vulture* is upon his breast—commonly called the night-mare or incubus—would that man be thus troubled if there were no vulture there? The reader, I think, will apprehend my meaning. Dr. B—— affirmed that Tragedy is a manifestation of, and contention between, right and wrong! while all natural intellects regard this description or species of theatrical representation as the impersonation of bad dreams and savage cruelties, characteristic of a low and barbarous stage of civilization. "All tragedies are of kings and princes." Dr. B—— affirmed, in substance, "men write and love tragedies, because it is a terrific display of, and combat between, sin and goodness." But I think, men write and love tragedies, because, to the revengeful mind, they are sublime, and to the undeveloped imagination, exciting. Again, let it be repeated, if the Lecturer would but receive the exhortation of Pope to "study man," and leave the high truths pertaining to the "Lord of Hosts" for subsequent investigation, he would certainly become less theological and more rationalistic. The cause of truth would be thus advanced.

This discussion was commenced, apparently, with a perfect, though carefully expressed, assurance of personal competency to philosophically prove the supernaturalness of sin, and the necessity for a supernatural plan of redemption. But the effort thus far has utterly failed. He can not intelligibly and decisively determine what sin is; because there exists *no universally recognized standard of goodness.* Surely, the decalogue, and the Christian Bible, do not constitute a universally recognized standard; for *every clergyman* in Christendom entertains different conceptions of Right, obtained by reading the same identical book and commandments. Until, therefore, Dr. B—— ascertains, beyond all dispute, what the law of God absolutely and eternally is; and until that law is acknowledged all over the world as the only admissible and everlasting criterion of Right; it will remain unqualifiedly impossible for him to supernaturally define what sin is, or to convict the whole creation as being made subject to vanity, and men as voluntary aliens to the Lord of Hosts.

In conclusion, Dr. B—— urged, quite logically from his premises, the people to avail themselves forthwith of the redemptive plan of salvation. They were, he affirmed, all convicted of the tremendous reality of sin, and should, therefore, immediately set about—— [something of which, I venture to affirm, not ten of the entire congregation had the least adequate conception]. His theology is not only time-sanctified, but measurably popular. It acknowledges no necessary connection with, or dependence upon, either nature or common sense. It professes to be established upon a basis entirely supernatural. It takes no practical and beneficial cognizance of the social and natural wants of mankind; but merely enjoins faith in certain abstract dogmas and incomprehensibilities, which have already divided the world into petty sects, and spread hostility and discord throughout the land. Whereas, if Dr. B—— would but study mankind more, I know he would "blame" less, and become of far greater service to the rising generations. By an adequate knowledge of phrenological science, and the law of hereditary transmission of qualities, he would be enabled to judge mankind with a righteous judgment, and to teach the people how to avoid entailing unhealthy and vicious constitutions upon their offspring.* But trembling for the safety of doctrines based upon a supernatural foundation, the Lecturer discourages the investigation of Nature and her laws; and frowns, dogmatically and sarcastically, upon nearly all the splendid and valuable discoveries which *rationalists* and researchers have exhumed from the deep vaults of universal nature. In reply to the Lecturer's concluding earnest and prayerful appeal to the people, that they should forthwith *avail themselves of the redemptive scheme*, and turn all their love and attention to the Lord, I am impressed to partially neutralize it in the reader's mind, by quoting the following impressive parable, written by Leigh Hunt:—

Abou Ben-Adhem—may his tribe increase!—
Awoke one night from a sweet dream of peace,
And saw, within the moonlight of his room,
Making it rich, and like a lily bloom,
An angel writing in a book of gold.
Exceeding peace had made Ben-Adhem bold,
And to the vision in the room he said:
"What writest thou?" The vision raised its head,
And, with a look, made all of sweet accord,
Answered, "The names of those who love the Lord."

---

* See chapters on the action of psychological laws, as applicable to the generation and improvement of the human type, in Great Harmonia, vol. III.; also in the Edinburgh Journal, edited by Combe; also in the Educational System of A. Bronson Alcott, of Boston, Massachusetts. This mind is most worthy of the attention which has been bestowed upon more popular personages. His spirituality of character render him a natural exponent of the psychological laws of Education, which the shepherds of the land should more fully comprehend.

"And is mine one?" said Abou. "Nay, not so,"
Replied the angel. Abou spoke more low,
But cheerly still, and said: "I pray thee, then,
Write me as one who loves his fellow-men."
The angel wrote and vanished. The next night
It came again, with a great wakening light,
And showed the names which love of God had blest,
And lo! BEN-ADHEM'S NAME LED ALL THE REST.

CHAPTER VI.

FIFTH REVIEW.

Reconciliation impossible.—The end of controversy.—The effort to prove the text.—Mankind vilified.—Necessity for the medicine of redemption.—Patent remedies and Dr. Bushnell's conclusions.—No universally recognized standard of Right and Wrong.—Nature as it is.

Dr. Bushnell has now attained the summit of the philosophical argument, in favor of supernaturalism, and against the rationalistic theories of religion. In the progress of the effort, man and nature have been constantly referred to as living witnesses and demonstrations of the supernatural faith and theory. The young minds of the congregation, and the skeptical members of all professions, were to receive, from this naturalistic argument, ample satisfaction, that nothing but supernaturalism can be the truth. The Rationalist was, in the commencement, promised a philosophical demonstration of the practicability of God in Christ, of the atonement, of the redemptive plan of salvation, of special providences, and prayer. To accomplish this desirable end, this modern Luther has relieved his mind of five discourses, the last of which number I design to review on this occasion.

The apex of the rational or philosophical argument

is now reached by this independent champion of popular theology. During the eccentric march, nothing has been neglected which could, in any conceivable manner, *impeach* the character of man, and bring the entire human family into direct confliction with the nature and will of God, and with the ineffable harmonies of the moral universe. The Lecturer has labored diligently to *convict* mankind of the most diabolical sins and abominations. He has said very much calculated to weaken the individual in his private efforts to be and to do good; and has somewhat discouraged those who would strive, by the aid of science and spiritual rationalism, to live righteous lives in strict obedience to the moral and physical laws of their being. He has, in his intellectual gyrations, raised the theological telescope, its lens deeply colored in the dyes of orthodoxy, and bade his hearers look through that beclouded medium, at the "system of nature," as differing from the system of God, and then at the spiritual "realm of powers"—causing the people to observe in either direction the illustrations and confirmations of the supernatural creed. And then he *inverted* the instrument, and bade his skeptical hearers to gaze in the opposite direction, at mankind in their multifarious spiritual relations to the wide expanse of created things. After the Lecturer had succeeded, as he supposed, in utterly demolishing man's faith in the divinity of man, and converting the whole system of nature into a perfect pandemonium of wretched antagonisms to God, then he mounted the ruins—ascended the falling and crumbling fabric—and said: "Here, then, I stand—feeling assured that nothing can shake me from my position—and now I offer to mankind, as a sovereign remedy for all sin, the redemptive plan of salvation."

The Lecturer said, in concluding his last discourse, that he left the subject at a point where the Christian plan of redemption was seen to be essential to individual regeneration. The presumption is, therefore, that the *philosophical* department of the argument for supernaturalism is now completed. And, of course, we, who desire to be reasonable and rational beings—and professedly candid in our recognitions and valuations of an argument, *pro* or *con*, on any subject—should now ask ourselves the questions:—

First. *Has Dr. B—— proved Rationalism to be erroneous?*

Second. *Or, the Bible scheme of redemption to be indispensable to peace on earth and good will among men?*

My impression is, that these essentially important points have not been proved—nay, not even apparently so; and, therefore, I am moved to present you with the following considerations.

Before the Lecturer can build a spiritual Zion on the scriptural foundation, or before he can repaint and re-embellish the old superstructure, and invite the whole human family to take possession, and satisfy them that they can live therein in safety and concord forever, it is first necessary to test and ascertain the condition of the premises. The ground-plan should have been far removed from the neighborhood of earthquakes. It should be firm as a rock; capable of withstanding the surging billows of time; and impregnable to the army of sciences which promise to march steadily onward, regardless of popular superstitions and error. As you probably all know, Dr. B——'s foundation is neither Nature, nor Reason, nor Intuition, nor any thing else which is accepted by the Rationalistic school of philosophers; but his avowed basis is the Bible—the present recognized sacred canon. Do you not see, then, what he should have done for the rising generations? Do you not see what all skeptics, infidels, atheists, lukewarm believers, and harmonial philosophers, very properly, and hence emphatically, demand? My friends, if he could not have accomplished it in forty lectures, and yet believed such a consummation possible, in the sphere of historical proof and spiritual and inferential demonstration; nevertheless, he should have *first* given us the plain unanswerable evidence that the *Bible* is the veritable word of God! But has he done this? Has he proved to our satisfaction that he stands upon a sure foundation, which can never be shaken? Far from it. He began his lectures by taking a text as bodying forth a great truth; yet he *altered it* to fit still closer the preconceived and prearranged convictions of his own mind. Thus making, as it were, assurance doubly sure, that man's Reason, after all, on the ultimate analysis, is the master or umpire of the Bible and its teachings. This was the most essential point to determine for the rationalist. The Lecturer should have known that the principal cause of skepticism in religious matters is the self-evident fact, that the Bible, which is the only foundation of the supernaturalistic system, is the creation of human heads and hands; that it contains historical and chronological errors and contradictions; that it bears the impress of human imperfections in its codes and inculcations.* These are points which required attention in the commencement. But these important matters were passed over; hence, all his arguments and special pleadings for the truth of supernaturalism, fall lifeless to the ground; and his superstructure is as the house built on the sandy foundation. The frame-work is completed; doors and windows are made and adjusted; and the whole house is put in readiness for the entrance and use of the proprietor. But the tempest sweeps o'er the hills; old ocean proclaims the speedy approach of the destroyer; the distant forests break forth in dismal lamentations; the rains descend; and the proprietor is driven out, amid the ruins of his newly-constructed residence, to do battle with the prevailing storm! The prevention of such a disaster, evidently is a sound foundation and a firm construction. But does Dr. B—— not see that he has gone on in the work of constructing a theological fabric, without ever giving the least satisfactory assurance that the premises are tenable? Yea; whether he perceives it or not, it is nevertheless true, that he has totally neglected to do away with the chief cause of skepticism in Christendom. He employed his REASON, I am happy to say, throughout the discussion. But it was not a free reason. This I regret. It was manifestly engaged (before the trial commenced) to discharge the duties of an attorney or counselor for the system of supernaturalism, to which he stands before the world fully committed. He assumed the premises, and then applied a small amount of philosophical argument in

---

* See contradictions detailed in "The Arabula."

order to convince the people that the Rationalistic system is essentially erroneous. This, I repeat, has not been done; because the ground-plan of supernaturalism is not *proved* to be immutable; the Bible was not shown to be a supernatural revelation of God's will. More particularly, I come now to examine the lecture in question, delivered on last Sabbath evening. This text was again taken from the eighth chapter of Paul's Epistle to the Romans, twenty-second verse—reading as fol lows: "For we know that the whole creation *groaneth* and *travaileth* in pain together until now."

When a modern son of Hippocrates or Galen, discovered a prescription for the chemical preparation of some *blood-detergent* or purifying compound, forthwith he sets himself to enumerating the number and variety of diseases for which his remedy is to be confidently recommended as a panacea. He thinks over the five hundred different "ills which flesh is heir to," and comes to the conclusion that his compound is not only a "perfect cure" for the great leading diseases—asthma, rheumatism, consumption, scrofula, and gout—but that it is in fine a "universal panacea" for all known and conceivable disorders. But here arises a question. How shall he make the people believe that "the blood-purifying compound" is THE unfailing remedy for all diseases? His course is very plain. He must develop a "New Theory" of disease, culled from the writings of learned authors upon pathology and therapeutics. The theory must be constructed in such a manner as to make the final conclusion very logical and self-evident, that the "Blood-purifier" is the only invaluable sovereign remedy and infallible cure for the sick to get and use, no matter what the disorder may be, or how originated. In the first place, the Esculapian makes it appear, from certain argumentations, that all diseases originate in the blood. He writes emphatically on this affirmation. He elaborates long columns of argument with the special design of creating a general faith in this one-idea theory of disease and physical distress. Every thing must originate in the vascular system. The respiratory and circulating departments give rise to many maladies; but the impurities, and impoverished condition, of the blood, he asserts, are the *primary causes* of all human physical and considerable mental suffering. Now, I ask, why does the proprietor of the "blood-purifier" publish this philosophy of disease to the world as the truth? The answer is distinct. Because he believes he possesses a remedy *for all* blood-diseases. Hence he advertises that his "universal panacea" is an infallible and sovereign remedy for all diseases which originate in the blood; among which, he enumerates, are the following: consumption, scrofula, cancer, *broken bones*, sick head-ache, measles, *squinting*, rheumatism, fevers, and *clump feet!*

Now, does Dr. B—— not see that his *recent effort* to prove supernaturalism is perfectly represented in the foregoing illustration? He has found, as he believes with commendable integrity, a soul-purifying and world-lubricating medicine—a certain and unmistakable remedy for all the disorders and consequences of sin. He, therefore, commences a learned and argumentative diagnostication of the moral constitution of man, and finds it sadly in need of the balm in Gilead.

He discovers and affirms that this "universal panacea" can be made available and effective only in cases where the individual is actually guilty of the supernatural sin. Lest, however, he should fail to convict all mankind (which he can not do by any known standard of righteousness), of the high sin, for which the *medicine* is particularly designed and administered by clergymen, he prudentially quotes a text from Paul to prove that the whole family of man, together with a large portion of the productions of nature, are charged, by the recording angel in the courts of heaven, with the commission of supernatural crime. This is just the universal disease which the redemptive plan is recommended to eradicate! Thus, it is manifest, that Dr. B—— has, under the avowed intention of removing doubt and skepticism, put his mental energies to the work of creating a fresh demand for the ecclesiastical medicine which he scientifically compounds, and in the curative properties of which, I doubt not, he places the utmost hope and confidence. Hence, with all conceivable honesty of purpose and true zeal for the universal acceptance and administration of his infallible compound, Dr. B—— proceeds to show that all "disorders originate in the supernatural sin; among which he enumerates the following:—murder; theft; dissimulation; duplicity; wars; famine; diseases; storms; fogs, which bedim nature; pestilential miasm, which generates death; deformed fish and vegetation; abortions; snakes; and malformed saurians. All these disorders, he thinks, are caused by the existence in this world of supernatural sin; and he presents his "compound" of *atonement*, *redemption*, *forgiveness*, *special providence*, and *prayer*—as the sovereign remedy for the regeneration and reformation of all. The Lecturer, also, recommended the redemptive medicine as the most perfect "fire annihilator" in the world! For he said; when a house was set on fire, it was evident that nothing in nature could do it, except self-causing and self-determining man. [Parenthetically, I will here remark, that houses, hay-stacks, volcanoes, and coal mines, are frequently *fired* by the chemical action and combustion of nature's own ingredients. Query: Is this one of creation's disorders?] He said, "there was free will at one end of the line and a house on fire at the other." This burning house was a dissolving exhibition of the consequences of the supernatural sin. And the redemptive compound was recommended, in effect, as the best annihilator of these fiery trials through which the travailing and groaning creation is compelled to pass.

The last discourse, under review, was a continuation of the arguments and theologic evidences in favor of the utter depravity and moral viciousness of man. The premeditation and words with which the Lecturer studied how to defame, vilify, and characterize man's imperfect nature, is not a little surprising in view of the fact, that he considers *himself* a member of the same human family. What is man? Dr. B—— thinks that the "*serpent*" is man's true representative; an animal, which was said to be an abortion, shaken from the lap of nature, and condemned to crawl in the dust all the days of its life. How can an animal be condemned for moral wrong? Again, What is man? Dr. B—— characterized him as the "sinning substance;"

a being or free power "doing as he was not made to do;" an enemy to God's universe, and a destroyer of nature's primeval harmony. Yes; nothing can exceed the contempt and pity which Dr. B—— professed to feel toward and for the race of man. Every true philanthropist must regret this. According to the Lecturer, man is as a foreign substance under the shell of the egg; that is, a sinning power in the fields of nature. By this Dr. B—— evidently means to imply, either that man has very nearly converted all creation into a defective egg, or else, by the process of incubation being allowed to go on to its final issue, the whole creation, owing to man's voluntary sins, turns out, at last, to be a deformed chicken, having one wing, or three wings, as the sequence.

On opening his discourse, the Lecturer asserted that the whole creation is groaning and travailing in sin, "*concomitantly* or by implication with man;" and then, referred to the third chapter of Genesis, seventeenth, eighteenth, and nineteenth verses, wherein it is said—"Because thou hast hearkened unto the voice of thy wife, and hast eaten of the tree, *cursed* is the ground for thy sake: in sorrow shalt thou eat of it all the days of thy life. Thorns and thistles shall it bring forth to thee; and thou shalt eat of the herb of the field, * * * for dust thou art and unto dust shalt thou return." To this matter I have presented several objections. In this connection, however, it is deemed proper to first direct your attention to the Lecturer's definition of man as a "sinning substance;" a being "doing as he was not made to do." You remember, I presume, how the Lecturer supposed that he had satisfactorily shown the whole family or fraternity of man to be buried in supernatural sins. He said, in substance, as you remember, "that his whole subject depended upon the establishment of the existence of positive sin in the world." This fact was clearly demonstrated, he thought, in the previous lecture; and so, he felt at liberty to go on with his theme, and demonstrate that Nature is suffering concomitantly and by implication with man.

The system of supernaturalism, then, is not proved to be a truth. Why? For the manifest reason, already urged, that there exists no universal standard of judgment as to what sin or evil really is. It makes *no difference*, in a discussion of this nature, what opinion you or I may entertain on the great question of Right and Wrong. The whole family of man, most certainly, can not be tried and condemned, for certain thoughts and acts, according to mere *individual* opinions of merit and demerit. Minds can be adjudged only by what they individually conceive to be right and wrong. This is the church theory. But it can not be altogether true. Because it would convert all ideas of a divine and unchangeable government into a world of anarchy and ill-constructed comedy. I will give an illustration.

For example: suppose a man in Christendom should commit the crime which is termed murder. Prior to the act, however, he had read the injunction, "Thou shalt not kill." He had received this as his standard of right, and shaped his conscience to it. Now this, therefore, becomes *the law*, according to theology, by which that man is to be tried in the court of heaven. In the moment and paroxysm of anger he destroys the outer life of a fellow-being. A few months subsequently he is executed by the sheriff. He is straightway arraigned before the King of worlds, for the purpose of being then and there judged according to deeds done in the body.

The Judge accordingly asks: "Of what sins are you guilty?"

"I am guilty of murder," replies the prisoner, sorrowfully.

At this moment, he who had officially sent the prisoner to that awful court by strangulation on earth—the sheriff—arrived, and is, also, placed in the prisoner's box.

The Judge next addresses him: "Of what supernatural sins are you guilty?"

"I am guilty," says the sheriff, "of envy, and, occasionally, of perjury."

"Is that all?" asks the Judge.

"Yes, so far as I can remember."

Judge: "Why do you consider yourself guilty *only* of these sins?"

Prisoner: "Because I have followed, as nearly as possible, the precious commandments and word of God in all other respects."

Judge: "Do you know the prisoner who was occupying the stand when you arrived?"

Prisoner: "Yes; he was guilty of murder. I knew him well."

Judge: "Can you inform me what occasioned his sudden departure from earth?"

Prisoner: "In obedience, my blessed Lord, to your expressed command, as given to Moses, and in accordance also with the combined moral and legal sanctions of both the church and state, I, my Lord, in the capacity of a sheriff, was that man's *executioner!*"

Judge: "You say, then, that the first prisoner is guilty of murder; that you are guilty only of envy and perjury; and yet you confess, as I understand you, that you were *the real cause* of that man's physical death."

Prisoner (somewhat alarmed, but resolved on self-extrication): "Yes, my Lord, *he* committed murder voluntarily, and therefore *against* thy law, which says—'Thou shalt not kill.' But I was an officer under a government that employ thy ministers of the gospel, who believe and teach thy word with becoming integrity. Thy vicegerents convinced me that capital punishment 'IS RIGHT!' They quoted thy words, saying: 'Whosoever sheddeth man's blood, by man shall his blood be shed.' Then they prayed for thy ever-enduring mercy to fall upon the soul of the murderer. Thus, my Lord, I am not guilty of the *voluntary crime* of murder; for I conscientiously discharged my duties as sheriff, and hung the prisoner up as an *example* to the vicious, and as a terror to evil-doers."

Now, I inquire, in view of Dr. B——'s theory of sin and punishment, how can the Great Judge dispense justice, to redress the wrongs and punish the crimes of these prisoners? Both committed murder; that is, both destroyed external or physical life; one in the heat of passion, the other from a conviction of duty. Where, then, is the law of justice? Shall the sheriff go into heaven, and take a seat in the midst of glory and goodness, simply because he did not *intend* any sin in strangling the prisoner—his brother? And is the victim, who was thus sent legally to the heavenly court of eternal justice, to be forever *consigned to a burning hell*, simply because he had the *misfortune*, yea, the terrible misfortune, to *believe* the Mosaic commandment to be true? Verily, according to this theory, the imperishable law of right and wrong, by which a man's soul is theologically asserted to be judged in heaven, is a mere inveiglement--a fantastic drama—I might truly add, a "comedy of errors." How much better for the human race, according to this doctrine, were they all, like the untutored heathen or beasts of the fields, ignorant of the means of condemnation! The brute and the idolatrous heathen are exempt, through their ignorance of the Bible, from all future punishment; but the civilized races—unfortunate beings as they are—must almost all suffer, for the same acts or sins, the eternal consequences of knowledge. In all this, I again ask, Where is the universal and unchangeable law of distributive Justice?

Another point is essential. That is, supernaturalists must *first* show that there exists a universally admitted standard of *Right* before they can logically condemn a single individual of "blamable wrong" in the sight of God. Unless they can do this, how do they know but that all theologic judgment and condemnation are merely arbitrary? Dr. B—— may think it is "blamable wrong" for me to preach the harmonial doctrines; but I do not think so. I hold it to be a plain duty. The church is divided, according to his own acknowledgment, on the question of Right and Wrong. He thinks, and very properly, too, that *lying* is blamable wrong. But there are Christian sects who conscientiously believe that any thing is good—even pious frauds—so long as "the end justifies the means." But, enough of such superficiality. It has been shown you, that, although there is "blamable wrong" in this world of relative individual dependencies—merely local disturbances, confined to the common level of individual affairs and interests; yet, there is no LAW by which all mankind can be proved to be guilty of the supernatural sin; which crime is theologically defined to be the voluntary action of man, *knowingly*, against the moral law of God. Every man, it is true, has an indwelling and indefinite conception of right and wrong. But the sense of right, which most persons feel the strongest, is almost wholly educational. You all know this to be true. You know that there are as many different ideas and laws of "RIGHT" in the world as there are races of men, or sects of religion; yea, these educational views of sin and goodness are as numerous as individuals on the earth. If, therefore, Dr. B—— depends upon his success in convicting the race of sin, in order to create a demand in the world for the saving and cleansing "compound" of supernaturalistic redemption, then he has reasons for discouragement, because he has signally failed in the premises. In the succeeding discourse, I am impressed to show, that, in the philosophy of "free will," the Lecturer has derived many deductions or inferences from untenable and groundless propositions.

But now I must solicit your attention to another point. I allude to the *origin* of supernatural sin. It was asserted in the first text to Dr. B——'s course of lectures, that "God was before all things, and in him all things consist." In reply to this, I said that Dr. B——, in order to harmonize Rationalism with Supernaturalism, and all things with the text, was logically under the necessity of charging the existence and subsistence of all things, evil as well as good, to God. If all "things consist" in God, it follows that the origin of sin, the disastrous deluge, the horrible experiences of man from generation to generation, the formation of a devil, and hell itself; all must be traced and referred to the creative, Omnipotent, and Omniscient Mind. And thus, as it seems, Dr. B—— has finally made the case appear! He affirms that God was surrounded with the possibility of evil before he created man. The creation of man was, consequently, a hazardous experiment! The simple plan opened a door for the entrance and existence of evil, which the Lord could not shut, consistently and logically, with the creation of free moral powers! Hence, Dr. B—— has openly acknowledged sin to be, in the aggregate estimate, a tremendous and supernatural reality. He has conceded, in the development of his theologic philosophy, that sin is truly a mighty antagonist to God; who could not but have permitted its existence and absolute enthronement about him, even *before* the population of the earth by human beings. Thus, by the power of church-logic, sin is deified. It is a tremendous reality in God's universe. Nay, it is not so! Evil is a transient shadow; a fleeting meteor. It is but the *dust* of mankind's progression. All things have *dark sides*—cast deep shadows upon the earth; but they do so, because the effulgent sun *shines* upon them. My interior meaning is, my friends, that *sin* is but the name which men give to contrasts or contrarieties in minds and morals. The towering oak receives great quantities of heat and light from the sun: and, when thus illuminated, it looks grandly above all other vegetation as the lord of that kingdom; but, at the same time, that magnificent tree casts a dark, deep *shade* over a large piece of ground. It may obscure the brilliancy of many flowers and beautiful trees. Thus lights and shades exist; because the all-controlling luminary shines out over the fields of creation. Now, shall we term the light, goodness; and the shade, evil? Which, I ask, is the *positive* fact; which the most conspicuous reality? Is it the darkness? Or the light? There is but one answer. The sun is the tremendous reality; it is the *great positive fact*, which illuminates Nature, and causes lights and shades amid the vast contrariety of things of which the world is constituted. So it is with what men term Evil. Evil is but the result of a universal Goodness; the *shade* cast by the *moral character* of man when his character is *illuminated* by a higher conception of Good—measured by a higher standard of Right. Solomon continued to be a wise man, until there appears a man of higher wisdom; then the illumination of the latter casts a dark shade over the former, who then gradually recedes from view. So was Moses a great and brilliant character, until he was thrown into the *shade* by the Prince of Peace! Like shadows, all sin is local, and, when compared with the soul's immortality, it is altogether negational and evanescent.

According to Dr. B——, the creation was groaning and travailing in pain previous to man's creation. In the great geological epoch, which preceded the human species, the Lecturer affirmed that there were races of "malformed creatures"—snakes, fish, &c.—running parallel in their development with the regularly developed types of the same general class. Thus, Dr. B—— proves himself an *infidel* to the Mosaic account; which asserts, that after the Lord had created fish, and all creeping things, and fowls, and vines, the heavens and earth, and all that in them is—then "He saw every thing that he had made, and, behold, *it was very good.*" It seems by this, that the Lord entertained not the least suspicion that he was environed by the tremendous possibility of evil. According to Moses, the Lord did not regard the *creation of man* as a wonderful and stupendous experiment. He created *Adam* with as much pleasure as he did any thing else, and blessed him. The Lord pronounced frequently, that all things he had made were "good." This was uniformly the *all-sealing* word, spoken and declared, according to the account, as *earnestly* subsequent to man's creation as previous to that event. It seems, therefore, that Dr. B—— is far more learned and proficient in the mysteries of godliness than Moses appears to have been. After the Lord had made the house, and furnished it, then he very naturally desired some one to live in it to keep it in order. He had unfolded the earth; sent the waters into their various divisions; made fish, and birds, and animals; festooned the mountains with evergreen; and decorated and essentialized the world with blessings and goodnesses; then, as a natural want, the Lord desired some intelligent and *rationalistic* being to enjoy the creation. Hence, he says: "Let us [that is, Brahma and Vishnu] make man in our image." This important resolution, you will perceive, was made in the vast consilium of the other world, the Lord not betraying the slightest particle of apprehensiveness that the creation of man would *involve* the tremendous possibility of evil. But why (according to the Bible) was man created? Plainly enough, it is said, to "have dominion over the fish of the sea, over the fowls of the air, and over every creeping thing." And subsequently to the creation of male and female [*i. e.*, free moral powers], the Lord "blessed them, and said, Be fruitful, and multiply, and replenish the earth, and subdue it." Does this appear like the theory so earnestly propounded by the Lecturer? Assuredly the Lord did not anticipate, as has been shown, any great *misfortune*, even as "possibly" growing out of man's creation. It appears, also, that the human creation was merely *an after-thought;* a spontaneous suggestion and requirement of nature. Every herb was growing with unbounded luxuriance, the fields were teeming with the ripened harvest; although "the Lord God," it is said, "had not caused it to rain upon the earth." Well, what then? It is written—"There was not a man to *till* the ground." * * * And so, "the Lord formed man of the dust of the ground." This shows, very simply and conclusively, that the Bible doctrine of supernaturalism is vastly *different* from, and more *superior* than Dr. B——'s incomprehensible theory.

The Lecturer considered fogs and vapors as blemishes in nature, caused by the supernatural sin! But from Genesis we learn, that, before the creation of man—and, hence, *prior* to any supernatural transgressions in the world—the rain was not caused to descend upon the earth; nevertheless, as it reads, "there *went up a mist* from the earth, and watered the whole of the ground." It manifestly appears from this, that man—"the sinning substance"—did not originally cause vapors and fogs to rise up between Dr. B—— or any other man, and the contemplation of some beautiful scene in nature.

How explicitly the Mosaic account of creation contradicts the positions taken by the Lecturer! True, it is exceedingly difficult to anticipate what a *doctor of divinity* might do with the passages in Genesis, should he undertake to *doctor* and *improve* them; but, one thing is absolutely certain, the Bible account of man's creation makes that event a matter of ordinary importance and suggestion. The Lord did not work timidly, as one would who was perfectly conscious of being environed with the black clouds and portentous shadows of some possibly stupendous and eternal disaster. On the contrary, he labored in quite a different state of feeling. He made man, according to the relation, on the suggestion of the moment, with the greatest conceivable cheerfulness, dispatch, and skill. And when the Lord saw the man alone, in the great temple of nature—so completely furnished with all things, as it was, and adapted to all the conveniences and happiness of housekeeping, he concluded that it was "not good that man should be alone." Upon this discovery and suggestion the Lord acted promptly and energetically, and forthwith "made a woman" to assist Adam to till the ground, to keep house—to multiply and replenish the earth.

Nor did the "curse" drive man out of luxury into active employment; because it is distinctly asserted or implied, that, before the first pair was placed in the garden, man was made expressly "to till the ground" —"to subdue the earth"—"to have dominion over every creeping thing." Now, it is manifestly unreasonable to suppose that man could engage in so much manual labor without "sweat on his brow." Nay. Man had the earth to "subdue"—implying that there were existing, even then, "thorns and thistles," and many rough places to smooth, in the vast dominion over which *man* was made the princely sovereign! There are other points of interest connected with this particular question, but I leave them for the present, and pass on to another consideration.

Dr. B—— asserted that Nature represents both man and God. All the disorder, groaning, and travailing in the world must be attributed to man; while God must be praised for all the existing harmony, perfection, and tranquillity. According to this, the works of God are inter-penetrated and *inverted* by the voluntary or supernatural sins of man! Think, my friends, of the unutterable *absurdity* of this doctrine. I ask—Can the wisdom and omnipotence of the Living Spirit be *counteracted* and *transcended* by weak and ignorant mortals? Can the finite *overthrow* the Infinite? Nay! The Lord God omnipotent reigneth; he is *before* all things, and *in him* all things consist; the measure whereof is *longer* than the earth, and *broader* than the sea. Who hath resisted his will? It is not of him that *willeth*, nor of him that *runneth*, but of God that showeth mercy. Can man *resist* the universal Will of the

Supreme Being? Dr. B—— said, that man is a sinning substance—a power, confusing and disordering nature; because "he does as he was not made to do." This is truly a bold assertion. How does he *know* whether he tells the truth or not, in this matter? He takes his text from PAUL as a sufficient guaranty or indorsement of his theory. Here, then, I will quote from the *same authority*, to prove (if it be thus valid) that *Man* does not and *can not act* contrary to the wise designs and ordinations of Jehovah (see Romans, ix. 10): "Is there unrighteousness with God? God forbid. For he saith to Moses, I will have mercy on whom I will have mercy, and I will have compassion on whom I will have compassion." Further on it is asserted by Paul, in substance, that Pharaoh had not committed the so-called supernatural sin: "For unto Pharaoh the Scripture saith, for this purpose have *I raised thee up.*" Now what are the reasons assigned by the Lord for creating the tyrannical and murderous Egyptian king? Was he made to be good, and happy, and to assist others to the acquisition of wisdom? Far from it. The Lord says: "I raised thee up, that *I might show* my power in thee, and that *my name* might be declared *throughout* all the earth." Now, I ask, if Dr. B—— believes that Pharaoh was thus designed to perform a mission—confessedly to subserve the purpose of displaying God's sovereign prowess and will, and to publish his name throughout the earth—how does he know but that every living *king*, and *tyrant*, and *pirate* on earth, is to-day doing, by express providential design, the sovereign will of God? *This is not my impression.* But I am now answering the supernaturalist on *his own* ground. We have Bible assurance that evil is overruled for good. As plain as Dr. B——'s text are the following passages from Paul: "Who hath resisted HIS WILL? Nay, but, O man, who *art thou* that repliest against God? Shall the thing say to Him that *formed* it, *why hast thou made me thus?* Hath not the potter power over the clay, of the *same lump* to make one vessel unto *honor*, and another unto *dishonor?*" What shall we say, then, to all the wickedness and disorder in the world? "Is there unrighteousness with God? God forbid." In view, then, of all this plain Bible language, how can Dr. B—— assert, with so much scriptural assurance and professional dogmatism, that man "does as he was not made to do?" Or, that Nature undertakes to accomplish more than she is able to perform? How does he know that "the *apple-tree* puts on more *buds* than it is capable of developing" properly into healthy fruit? Surely, every thing which grows has a *residuum* — some refuse materials — to the labor. And why may not the falling apple-blossoms be considered—like the expenditure of muscular strength which is consequent upon our bodily exercise—as the result of the tree's effort to produce (what it succeeds in to perfection), viz.: the precious *fruit* which decorates its bending boughs and delights our taste.

I pass on to another point: Dr. B—— considered at length, but in a very unsatisfactory manner, the effect or consequences of sin—first, upon the Soul—second, upon the Body—third, upon Society—fourth, upon Nature. What was said under these respective heads, I am impressed, needs no elaborate review.

In the SOUL, it was said, sin laid waste the moral nature—desolated the creature man; his feelings, passions, and their multifarious dependencies. This was only another way—a theological way—of saying, *that all voluntary or other infringements* upon the *indwelling* conviction of *Right*, are succeeded by appropriate results and legitimate consequences, from which there was no possible escape, except, by taking *internally* and eternally the redemptive "compound" which, as you remember, is Dr. B——'s universal *panacea* for all mental, physical, social, and natural disorders.

In the body, it was said, that sin brought *wrong things* together—a man and alcohol, &c.—developing pain, contagion, discords, diseases of all kinds, and death. It was distinctly asserted, moreover, that death and disturbance were in the world before man; seemingly in anticipation of the horrid catastrophes which *supernatural sin* was certainly destined to develop! Friends, do you see the *deformity* of such an assertion! Do you not see that all the "malformed creatures" and universal "abortions," which Dr. B—— alluded to, exist nowhere but in his own darkened affections and beclouded reason? Theology has lamentably distorted his vision, circumscribed his affections, crippled his understanding, and deformed his naturally good powers of judgment. Theology has laid waste his *love for man;* and his admiration of nature, also, is contracted exceedingly. His conceptions of the harmony and unutterable progressive perfectibility of God's works, are exceedingly angular, and hugely-fashioned; and, when he looks out upon Nature, from the *blistered* and *stained* windows of his theological Zion, he sees only his own *malformed* cogitations; but he very honestly takes them to be *deformed fish*, *grotesque disorders*, and the innumerable "*abortions*," caused by the workings of supernatural sin upon the physical creation! And as if his mind had not been beclouded and desolated enough by the theology of supernaturalism, he summons to his side *no less* equivocal teachings and testimony of another clergyman, Hugh Miller, who *unblushingly*, and, to some extent classically, gives in his evidence, that the works of God are, in very truth, interpenetrated and *inverted* or subverted by the free-will crimes of man! What Dr. B—— said concerning *bodily pain and death*, may be found, much better stated in Combe's book on Man; or, in the phrenological publications of the day, associated with the philosophical exposition of their obvious causes and important uses in the providence of things, and with valuable suggestions as to their final extermination.

Of society, it was said, that sin had laid it nearly in ruins—causing, by its power and propagative tendency, *wars*, *cheating*, *murder*, *massacres*, *ease*, *power*, *luxury*, and *licentiousness*—all to be considered as the furniture of sin. In replying briefly to this statement, I would *first* call attention to the fact, that the most gigantic cruelties, the bloodiest wars, the highest spoliations, and the deepest licentiousness, and the other crimes and vices supposed, are *sanctioned* in the Old Testament by a "Thus saith the Lord." Does Dr. B—— remember how the *Lord* commanded Moses to "war" against the Midianites? Does he remember the spoliations that were recommended? Does he remember the revolting crimes which the Lord permitted the children of Israel to commit? In view of this—I ask, did man, according to Dr. B——'s theory, create and perpetuate these sins? Assuredly not. Man is the victim of an oriental and demoralizing theology; which originally sanctioned war and all the other sins enumerated. What occasioned that stupendous *war*, known as the Crusades? Did the people generate that war by exercising the prerogative of free-will?—By doing as they were not made to do? Nay; the thirty years' war was a "holy war,"—that is to say an honest and conscientious war—as most all wars are—in which the defenders of the faith signalized themselves as valiant "soldiers of the cross!" Dr. B—— should not, therefore, "blame" man for the existence of war, and for analogous evils; because, according to the writers of his theology, there were times when the Lord himself *commanded bloodshed*, and gave us particular directions, through his holy prophets, as to the localities and methods of its accomplishment.

With regard to theft and licentiousness, I can, for the present, only say, that had Dr. B—— studied mankind, like a rational philosopher, he would have found, that badly-constructed and wrongly-situated minds give rise to these transient and transitional evils. *Fourier* has elaborately considered the social causes of these evils, and has mathematically shown, that a certain organization of *Labor*, *Capital*, and *Talent*, will effect the desired cure. If Fourier's positions be true (which no church-disciple has as yet been able successfully to controvert), then we have the plain solution of the problem of evil. Ignorance, improper social alliances, and immoral situations—giving rise to antagonisms of individual interests—these are the simple and self-evident explanations of sin's existence. Dr. B——'s medicine—the redemptive compound—has been tried for many long, eventful centuries, and has *failed* to remedy the evils complained of; why not, then, be humanitary and charitable, and let the combined *wisdom of this century* use a new panacea in the great work of human amelioration?

In *Nature*, it was said, that evil had wrought sad results. The so-called facts he adduced on this head I will not stop to review. They are not considered of sufficient importance to the thinking world. But in regard to the allusion to the existence of snakes, fish, and the "abortive flounder," I have some impressions which I will presently express. In this place, however, I will merely utter my present regret that Dr. B—— had not familiarized his mind more with Nature. It seems that he has studied, or rather observed, an enormous and destructive *battle* among some exasperated *ants* in this city! The battle-field—a yard square of earth—was strewed with the *dead*, *wounded*, and *dying!* They finally "fought for *halves*, after many of them were bitten into pieces." "Thus" (concluded Dr. B——), "it is with society." Supernatural sin operates even upon the little ants! Now, how much more reasonable would the Lecturer have been, had he said, that the *lower* we descend in the kingdoms of Nature the more cruel and revengeful the creature; the higher we go, the nearer we approach the angels.

In conclusion, allow me to give you a concise view of *Nature as it is.*

As you remember, Dr. B—— complained of Christian

poets and moralists skipping over the fields of Nature. "They think it is Beautiful." In doing this, he thought that they were *unfaithful* to the Scripture doctrine. He, it would seem, is ready to *sacrifice* every thing upon the altar of supernaturalism—so degrading to the mind are the fossil vestiges of old opinions!

Progress, my friends, is a law of Nature. "That *was not* first which is spiritual, but natural, and *afterward* the spiritual." The fair and beautiful always unfold from from the rudest beginnings. The first developments of minerals, of vegetables, and animals, are universally low and imperfect. The *angular* form is first; then succeeds the circular; then the ascending circular, which is the spiral; and this form merges gently into the spiritual. For example, the child is first, which is angular; then the youth, which is hasty and impetuous, because changing from the angular to the circular in character; then comes manhood, which is the perfect circular; then the period of maturity, which is the ascending circular, but which soon becomes a spiral, and glides away into the spiritual realm of life! And so all brutes, and birds, and fish are developed, *primarily* upon the lowest possible plane of being. There is a regular chain of beings from the little insect to the *highest* form of matter. The supernatural idea that malformations or abortions exist, is derived from a perverted and *superficial* view of the progressive gradations of Nature's unceasing developments. It was first necessary to invert and misinterpret the true line of progress among animals, before a *case* could be made out to substantiate the text: that "the creation *groaneth* and *travaileth* together in pain until now"—all, it was asserted, in consequence of man's voluntary sins.! Such are the logical disclosures of an erroneous theology.

But I am impressed to consider *True Theology* as the holiest and sublimest form of knowledge. It conveys our thoughts far away into the peopled realms of infinitude: speaks to us of the harmonies and sublimities of eternity; and leads our affections onward and upward to the Supernal Mind. True theology teaches, that *every thing* is forever progressing in goodness and perfection—is eternally *growing* more and more lovely, more harmonious, more wise, more happy.

The time hath been when this planet was but a dark and barren desert. Frequent convulsions and earthquakes sent into the air black and grotesque rocks—creating, in a moment of time, channels for the roll of oceans—and forming deep valleys and ravines, dark and dismal as the fabled dominions of Pluto. No bird of song broke the silence; no creeping thing animated the dust. Thus was it once with our earth.

But the eternal-principle of Progression continued still to exert its mighty power upon the physical elements; and soon, there came forth green leaves from the mountain cliffs, lofty palms from the valleys, and sea-mosses quickly gathered, in rich profusion, upon the craggy acclivities.

Another long era passed, and the ocean was peopled with living forms—even the earth became animated with mighty saurians; and so, in due order of progression, animals came forth—improving, in their type and character, in harmony with the advancement and refinement of the elements of food, light, air, and the surrounding geographical conditions. And finally, as the crowning issue of all—as a coronation of the mineral, vegetable, and animal kingdoms—there came forth Man! And Man, physically and spiritually, has steadily advanced from the *earliest dawn* of human life to the present day. Still his course is eternally onward. And the once barren and dismal earth is rapidly becoming an incipient paradise.

Old theology complains, through its popular devotee, "that Nature is too much praised!" Indeed! Nature too much praised? Nay, it can not be. He who would study the works and ways of God, must contemplate nature; and the creation can not be examined without inspiring the true mind with gratitude, delight, and religion. Nature teaches that low and imperfect forms always precede high and beautiful creations. But Nature, my friends, *is not limited to this little planet;* neither to the myriads of earths and systems in space; nor to the infinite system of suns in the upper skies; it is the boundless universe, and "beautiful" as the Living God!

Love-streams break forth from the deep depths of Deity like the impetuous gushings of a mighty fountain. In its deep harmonious workings, it sends its startling energies through myriads of planets at the same moment—arousing the little germs, which lie hidden and slumbering in the earth, into the joy of being —yet, there is no discord; for WISDOM describes the method of the vast accomplishments. As progress is the law; so the development of every thing is graduated upon an infinite scale. Trees grow from the earth upward. And there is a harmony more or less perfect in every thing. The coral worm works with harmonious skill, and builds the mighty reefs; against which the ponderous waves of old ocean may perpetually roll; and upon these islands cities might stand secure for ages. The song of birds, too, and the waving willow, blend together in harmonious motion. Sweet fountains gush forth musically; melodies break forth from rippling lakes; the summer winds breathe joyfully over the green fields; and the distant valleys murmur forth a peaceful hymn! But this *natural harmony* is more and more perfected as we ascend the spiritual scale of being. The songs of birds foreshadow the perfections of the human voice. The sweet harmonies of the midsummer season faintly typify the diversified beauties of the Summer Land! The Universe is beautiful as the Living God: because it is his TEMPLE.

CHAPTER VII.

THE DYING DOGMAS.

A prophecy.—Freedom of the will.—The unreliability of consciousness. —The doctrine of moral freedom considered.—The spirit and the father.—The case of Dr. Parkman and Professor Webster.

THE antagonisms existing between the popular dogmas of theology and the plainest declarations of Reason are hourly becoming more and more distinct and visible. All efforts to harmonize them must ultimate in disappointment and defeat. Because there exists no essential affinity between them, no indwelling principle of common sympathy, around which a unitary organization of reason and theology could only be permanently established. Of this there can be but one explanation. The dogmas of theology originated at a period when the human mind had not yet put forth its energetic faculties of understanding. Reason is a recent development. It has not yet appeared in its true ministry and glory; but, slowly as unfolds the spring vegetation, reason is appearing in the broad horizon of the moral world—darting its penetrative illuminations far away into the abysses of ignorance, and most powerfully into the gloomy retreats of long-fostered dogmas. These bequeathments of the past, these *idols* of the sacerdotal orders of men, must now be uncovered and examined. A lifeless and godless form may be draped in the holiest garments; and, to all external seeming, the worshiped idol may present evidences of possessing a divine energy and spirit; but the devotee, should he allow the reason-principle to perform its functions, will instantly become sufficiently clairvoyant to perceive the emptiness of the dogma, and its utter inapplicability to the present wants of the age.

Now it can not be denied that the current churches are the legitimate children of the Catholic organization; which is the most extraordinary religious institution on the face of the earth, considered either as a political or as a moral combination of educated men and spiritual forces. However, there is a manifest difference between the progenitor and the children. This consists, simply, in the seemingly spiritual character of Protestant churches, also in the mental liberties which give rise to democratic institutions of education, and to the still greater blessing of free, representative governments. Nevertheless, there are points of analogy between the parent and the offspring; which, as honest investigators, we should not fail to recognize and reveal.

As educated Protestants, we stand in open hostility to the graven images and idolatrous ceremonials of the Catholic institution. Wherefore? Because we hold image-worship to be utterly incompatible with true religion; and irreconcilable with all reverence due the one only and eternal God. Very well. We, therefore, divest our churches of all idols; and in the same proportion, we abandon many forms, and leave ceremonial-worship to the poor, benighted, imbecile devotees of the

Catholic religion. How is this? Do we truly, as Protestants, destroy all idols, and worship God only in spirit and in truth? Let us see. As logical and orthodox Protestants, we still adhere to certain cardinal principles in theology, as unequivocally essential to the soul's eternal salvation; also, as the divine doctrines destined to be universally recognized and potentialized, under the direct descension of the Divine energy—the Holy Ghost—to the final destruction of all heathenism, and the reconciliation of all things to the glorious liberty of the children of God.

These cardinal doctrines we have carefully examined, harmonized, pronounced them "good;" and deposited them in the theological armory, as our beloved [idols] dogmas or sacredized essentials. The first essential is "original sin," recently defined as being supernatural. The Protestant church assigns to *this idol* a conspicuous position. It is necessary that the people should behold it frequently. Hence it is placed in *demi-relievo*, and learnedly described, at regular intervals, as the foundation of all troubles in this terrestrial sphere—as the grand cause of the unspeakable manifestations of divine mercy detailed in Scripture. But here a question appears. Clergymen dwell devoutly on the glorious attributes of the Creator. They can not enough express their glowing gratitude for the "Revelation" of the Divine will and promises. The advent of the only begotten Son, too; this is the grand consummation of all deific love and wisdom—the *ne plus ultra* of all conceivable mercy and providential manifestation. But is it so? Strange thought! The realms of spiritual existence contain no such de formed conception of the deific nature and attributes. Ponder the supposition! Think you that man could ascertain nothing of the Divine Mind through this universe of life and animation? Was it necessary to plunge the human family into the depths of discord and degeneration, in order to reveal the Divine attributes to the human affections and reason? Was it first necessary to allow the race to generate every description of iniquity, and become dead in trespasses and sins, before the attributes of *mercy*, *love*, and *wisdom* could be manifested to the earth-children? If clergymen eulogize the effects, they certainly can not but condemn the cause and the occasion. It is no better than the oft-uttered assertion, that poverty and squalid wretchedness are expressly designed as means to develop and exercise the Christian virtues termed kindness, brotherly love, and charity; while, in real truth, poverty and want are the symptoms of a defective social condition, which symptoms, well-organized talents and industry will effectually remove; and then the virtues may be normally exercised in the higher spheres of human life and interests. Nevertheless, the church idol—"original sin"—must be kept before the people. The devotee must first *examine* (for this is a glorious attribute or privilege of Protestantism), then *believe*; then, to be truly orthodox, he must *worship*. "In time of peace prepare for war;" which, in this supernatural department of human interest, signifies the preparation and formidable array of clerical talents and cogent argumentations, against the approach of the vast army of modern sciences and discoveries, whose leader and commander is REASON.

The second essential is "the Atonement," which is now undergoing extensive repairs. Several very distinguished and adequately qualified *sculptors* in theology, are now laboring, with a commendable zeal and integrity of motive, being actuated by the desire and design of elaborating a certain rationalistic, "atonement;" which they confidently believe will meet the reasonable demands of the most intelligent and logical mind in Protestant Christendom. This religious reformation has not escaped the attention of Dr. Bushnell. He has himself done something toward giving the Christian world a more comprehensible theory of "God in Christ;" though it can not but be regretted, that, in his effort to be both classical and natural, independent and truly faithful to the old masters, he has too deeply buried this beautiful and energetic work of art. Several Unitarians are now preparing to repair the idol of Protestantism. Unfortunately, however, they have resolved to copy too accurately many things from the prevailing orthodox pattern. The New Churchmen* are entirely settled as to the perfect and eternal interpretation of this supernatural problem. The interior import of all visible idols in the primitive history, is clear as the blue vault of heaven to their unfolded faculties; and so, like the Second Advent people, they devoutly and confidently await the "time" when the New Jerusalem, the Holy City, will come down, from God, out of heaven, adorned as a bride for her husband.

---

* "The Seer," contains several impressions and elucidations concerning this form of theology.

Nor is this all. The third essential is "faith," which is also undergoing the most astounding alterations. This idol is situated, in the Protestant church, directly opposite to the other just considered. The recent efforts put forth to place this graven image upon a philosophical pedestal—to establish it upon the everlasting foundation of nature and reason—may be regarded as the premonitory indications of the *interregnum* which is about to appear in the religious world. Men formerly received all spiritual nourishment, like infants, through the vessels of the affections; which is the primary or rudimental process; it is invariably characteristic of the most incipient and uncultivated stage of mental development. But having spiritually become men, like Paul, they very naturally "put away childish things;" and, among those things, numerous minds have been amazed to discover their creeds—the cherished idols of childhood. Dr. Bushnell is not alone in the field of altering the theologic faith. It is a precious idol to abandon; especially, when the mind has not attained to "the fullness of the stature" of passional and judgmental harmony. Hence, very many individuals have chiseled out a new form of religious faith. But when the deeper analysis comes, the same deformed and decrepit idol is revealed, which was first worshiped through the medium of the unenlightened affections. The exact truth is spoken when I say, that Christendom is now as a slumbering volcano! The conflicting elements lie underneath all this fair exterior. The thunders of a stupendous reformation are sure to issue from the now open mouth of the Protestant church. The supernatural faith will be shaken as a reed in the tempest. New channels will be formed for the inflowing of new truths; and then, a long-promised Era will steal upon the religious and political world. It will come forth like the hurricane; but its action will be gentle as the breathing of flowers. It will sound like the thunderings of the mountainous water-fall; but its influence upon the world will be as the music of "many waters" to the ear of the care-worn and thirsty pilgrim. It will appear as a moral pestilence, breeding internal agonies and mental despair; but it will be as the *spirit* of a glorious divinity, floating unseen among us, "creeping, like the summer winds, from flower to flower." Such are the impressions which I receive concerning the approaching crisis. "Faith," the present idol of Protestantism, will be essentially altered, modified, and transformed into a milestone to indicate the highway and progression of humanity. Like the pyramids, it will stand as a monument of what the ages have erected in the human world; and, as such, it will forever possess interest to the historian, to the antiquarian, and the spiritual philosopher.

The fourth essential is "free agency;" which is being re-examined and logically prepared for exhibition. This is the greatest dogma in the orthodox church. It is an idol of the utmost importance. All theology would be flying in the wind, like the tempest-torn sails of a ship, if it were not for the potent presence of this graven image. It is a strange work of art! Blocked out by the old masters, subsequently chiseled by the professional artists in theology, and placed upon the pedestal of mere *assertion*, it has become the most favorite Idol in the Protestant institution. Should any rationalistic disorder or epidemic prevail, the "doctors of divinity" forthwith diagnosticate the pathognomonic symptoms of Free Agency, to ascertain conclusively whether the contagion really extends to the cardinal dogma, or to the others. If not; then nothing is said. If so; then comes a period of theological fumigation. That is, the clergy attempt to produce a kind of intellectual blindness among the people, by decomposing, apparently, a few rationalistic arguments with the flame of their *burning* eloquence. Such an effort has been recently made; as we have seen by the discourses "on supernaturalism," under review.

How, then, does the matter really stand? Are Protestants not idolaters? The Catholic has his "holy virgin" in the form of a female statue; but we also have a "holy virgin" in the form of a man-made book. The Catholic has sacred saints; but we have sacred dogmas. You perceive, then, my friends, that Catholics and Protestants are alike idolatrous: the latter being so, intellectually; and the former, sensually. The two forms of religious faith and culture are not essentially distinct; only antagonistic in regard to the ways and means of worship. The logical accuracy of this will appear in the sequel. Can we, then, continue to worship these theologic idols? Can we still cherish them as the only beings that have brought life and immortality to light? Children play with balls; but men amuse themselves with the rolling planets. Young intellects cherish every thing through an exercise of the sightless affections; but matured minds love all things which flow easily through the understanding. Such are truly harmonial philosophers.

We, then, as *Protestants* in Protestantism — being moved to address Protestants as they formerly decried the heresies of the Catholic church—must faithfully ignore those *dogmas* which pertain to the popular theology.

The position of the clergy, amid these sacerdotal idols, is potent to sustain error. The most charitable interpretation which an enlightened mind can indulge in, is the probable *honesty* of all men who continue to preach the antiquated doctrines. This conclusion, however, must be mainly grounded in benevolence; for "how," many ask, "can a man remodel and perpetually interpret an idea in theology as truth, when the plainest declarations of science demonstrate it to be an error?" The only answer is, "Men love darkness rather than light," when they have not sufficient independence and integrity of soul to cast aside all forms, and worship God in *spirit* and in truth." The friends of true freedom have had occasion to regret a recent manifestation of this mental condition.

Dr. B—— has labored to infuse new vitality into the old dogmas; but the process seems like the action of the galvanic force upon the lifeless body. The muscles contract violently; the arms fly up against the silent breast; the mouth opens; the eyes glare like angry lions upon the people; and the strange phenomena immediately disappear. So will all efforts terminate which are designed to add new luster to the dogmas of Christendom. You who do not believe so, may engage in the godless task; for *experience* is still the best schoolmaster to those who can not discern the signs of the times.

The advocate of supernaturalism, as he unfolded his method, appeared, to the reviewer, in the midst of church doctrines, which he was about to impregnate with new theologic animation. Behind stood the idol called "Original Sin;" on the right, the idol called "The Atonement;" on the left, the idol called "Faith;" and before him, higher than all the others, stood the idol termed "Free Agency." This idol was considered vastly superior to the others in the discussion; because, in the opinion of the Lecturer, it was *the great thing* to establish, as a basis upon which to rest the utility and essentiality of the pre-arranged dogmas. The doctrine of "moral freedom," therefore, will be more particularly reviewed on this occasion. In this connection, however, it should be understood that the Lecturer did not present what we would consider cogent reasons to sustain the affirmative. He depended mainly upon the superficial reasons already given; and placed himself too confidently upon his *consciousness*, and upon his prevailing sensations of freedom, to establish the favorite doctrine. This cognitional source of our present being, he considered the "self-evident" demonstration. I will, therefore, first proceed to reveal the fallacy of this conclusion; and then I will consider the question as it is in nature.

It was repeatedly affirmed, as you remember, that "moral freedom is a matter of consciousness"—"everybody feels and knows his liberty," and so forth; which, compared with the evidences heretofore considered, was the principal proof presented to substantiate a doctrine so essentially important to the consistence of the other dogmas. The witness, then, which is called to appear and impart testimony in the pending trial, is *consciousness*. You will observe, that this term has a signification quite distinct from the word *conscience*. Conscience means the internal faculty of knowing; a self-knowledge of what constitutes Right and Wrong. But consciousness, on the other hand, signifies something more sensuous; a knowledge of operations and sensations passing in one's own mind; or, the mental phenomenon termed, a cognition of external objects through the medium of the senses. Now the question is: Can the character of this witness be shown to be above impeachment? Was it never known to impart, to the court of the human understanding, any false and contradictory impressions? If this witness never deceived the judgment, then it is, indeed and truly, the most complete demonstration of the dogma under present analysis. But if, on the contrary, it can be shown to be a very treacherous and imperfect delineator of truth; then the testimony deposed by this witness can have no important weight in a case of such momentous interest. Let this witness, therefore, be cross-questioned, in order to arrive at the actual pro and con in the premises.

Metaphysicians have divided all the consciousness of our mental being into five distinct compartments, termed the five senses. The sensation of existence is consciousness. The windows and doors, through which this sensation goes out from and re-enters the sensorium, are the eyes, the ears, the smell, the taste, and the more general sense of feeling by the nervous mechanism. All ideas of the contrariety of objects and influences, constituting the material world, are derived through our *conscious* existence, as defined by the senses. The senses, then, may be regarded as the divisions of consciousness; the different channels through which the nerve-spirit of our present life receives influences and imparts impressions to the understanding.

I hope it will not be considered presumption, should I here affirm, that Dr. Bushnell is organized in these respects precisely like every other man; that, therefore, his *personal* declarations, concerning the consciousness of the utter freedom of the soul, are worth, in the present investigation, as much, to say the least, as the assertions of any other intelligent individual.

Now I am moved to affirm, that human consciousness is a very equivocal and unreliable source of knowledge. Wherefore? Because we are constantly *deceived* by our sensations. The senses frequently fail to impart accurate impressions to the mind. According to all human consciousness, this earth is neither globular nor revolving. Aside from the opposition founded upon the so-called heresy of asserting the revolution of our planet, Galileo was opposed and confronted by the universal *consciousness* of the race, that the earth was a vast permanent surface, whose edge had not yet been discovered. The same thing is believed to-day by thousands of minds. Our senses declare to us, very distinctly, that the Sun and Moon roll round the earth—rising uniformly in the east, and disappearing behind the western hills. The diurnal motion of the earth is against every man's consciousness; that is, this witness does not impart a truthful impression to the understanding.

Two years since, while on a visit in the State of New Jersey, a very industrious although uneducated farmer, confessed to me his utter inability to believe in the revolution of this orb every twenty-four hours. "Why," he exclaimed, "it is against my consciousness; against the positive testimony of my senses. Don't I *see* the sun going from east to west? On the earth, as you know, there are millions of movable things, and great bodies of water. If my house was turned bottomside up once a day, wouldn't the chairs, and the crockery, and every thing movable therein, fall from their places, and be dashed into pieces? A pail filled with water, you very well know, being turned upside down, would necessarily be immediately emptied of its contents; and so, if this earth turned upside down, as people say, wouldn't all things be thrown out of order, and the lakes and rivers be emptied of their waters?" This man's honest argument, fallacious as it was, very accurately and forcibly represents Dr. Bushnell's dogmatic assertion, that his consciousness was a plain demonstration of the freedom of the will.

Again: this witness is not reliable, or sufficiently unwavering to be received as proper evidence; because it is known to be extremely susceptible to morbid developments and tendencies. Many present are confounded by the strange operation of internal sensations, as derived from external sources. A morbid brain is conscious of various inconsistencies. Insane minds imagine—that is, believe the concurrent testimony of their consciousness—that they are certain great distinguished characters: Napoleon, Paul, Alexander, and so forth; and with as much calmness of pretension, too, as would befit the most sane Christian. An intoxicated mind, with the blood whirling in the cerebral recesses and vessels, is conscious of strange motions among the objects about him. Should he declare his *consciousness*, on going forth from the brothel into the street, he would affirm he saw the street revolving like the wings of a windmill, and the lofty steeples toppling from their foundations. I would inquire: Which is in motion? The external objects; or, the *morbid* consciousness? Now, it is by no means an impossible or unnatural thing to suppose a clergyman's mind to be somewhat intoxicated with the spirit of certain dying dogmas, even to imagining himself a perfectly free moral being on the testimony of his morbid consciousness.

Enough has been adduced to invalidate the evidence of Dr. B——'s principal witness. Its character for prevarication and waywardness is sufficiently made to appear. It is not even reliable on the greatest astronomical fact ever revealed to man. Consequently, the rationalistic mind is absolutely forced to seek for evidence in other directions. The enlightened judgment, independent of the ordinary plane of consciousness, is forced to consult well-ascertained data, before it can arrive at clear and satisfactory conclusions on any given subject.

I come now to the negative consideration of moral freedom; which is, that there is no such a fact in existence as *absolute* independence of the human will.

In the first place, let me describe to you the conditions upon which alone man could be a perfectly free moral being. The pre-consultations considered as essential to the moral freedom of the first man, Adam, in the great experiment of life, are still necessary to every individual. The Christian Church has always had some vague doctrines concerning the pre-existence of the soul. Indeed, when we except the speculations of Thomas Dick and the universal analogies of Swedenborg, Christians have cherished the most mystical and unsatisfactory opinions of the other life—more vague, even, than the traditional myths and beliefs of the North American Indians. For present purposes, however, we will suppose the pre-existence of every human spirit. On this hypothesis, I will now state the conditions which are required in order to establish the dogma of man's moral freedom.

The parent should have a conversation with the soul of his child, previous to the bestowment of a physical body. The language should convey to the unterrestrialized spirit this unmistakable information: "This material world is a valley of trials and misfortunes. It is replete with hard substances which the soul can use only through the mediation of physical agents. The external world is now—indeed, it always has been—undergoing slow and gradual changes; and philosophers say, these unceasing alterations will in time render this world a serener and more spiritual field of existence." The spirit here asks: "Will you inform me how the inhabitants appear?" "The present human race," replies the parent, "is rude, impulsive, and imperfect. It is known to consist of different tribes or nations, manifesting considerable varieties of external appearance, and employing diverse kinds of languages. These nations have not outgrown war; nor the causes of discord and wretchedness. Poverty and wealth, indolence and industry, ignorance and wisdom, present the strangest contrasts; and the world makes in the issue a strange dream, which the human mind hereafter cherishes as the daguerreotype impression and history of its earth-life. But notwithstanding all this, there is more than enough to compensate man for his strange eventful passage from birth to the final result. We have love, and friendship, and consequent joys: each twining around the family circle, wreathing the plowman's heart, and inspiring the merchant's mind with dreams of wealth and enterprise. We have rolling seas, beautiful rivers, mountains swelling with life and loveliness, a sun of ineffable brilliancy, and an earth filled with countless stores of luxurious wealth; and all for man! Now," continues the parent, "I desire you to become my son, clothed in a physical vesture. But we have a religion that teaches the moral freedom of every man; because this doctrine is alone compatible with the *plan of redemption*, which is said to have been instituted expressly for our future salvation, but which can prove availing only when accepted in the freedom of the human will. God can not save, they say, unless man is entirely willing. Therefore, I desire you to exercise your freedom in becoming the offspring of an earthly parent."

"What is the position of a son?" inquires the spirit.

"To learn some particular trade or profession; and to do battle with the world of free but conflicting powers about him."

"What is the position of a daughter?"

"A daughter has a different sphere. The home, the family, and the social circle, are her proper fields of action."

"Then," says the spirit, "if I come to earth I prefer

being a daughter. But tell me further: what are the nations called?"

We may now suppose the parent informing the spirit of the names of the different nations, with their colors, declaring himself to be a European.

"From what you say," replies the spirit, "I will not be born into a physical body, unless I can be a Caucasian or an American. Nor will I *consent* to become a Christian; for, according to your relations, it would be better for my eternal welfare if I should be born where the Christian religion is not known or preached; hence, I will only be born on the planet Jupiter or Saturn. Neither will I *consent* to be born with any physical or mental defect. I require perfection in every particular; thus to be all the more capable of exercising my moral freedom. I will not *consent* to accept any derangement in my temperaments; neither in my powers of comprehension. If, therefore, you can impart to me all I now demand, physically and mentally, I will consent to be born into the material world, and take the eternal salvation of my soul upon my own responsibility."

Such a final decision would certainly be made by every well-informed spirit, should it be enlightened, and thus *consulted*, as to the liberty of choice, *prior* to its advent upon this or any other planet. And the dogma of moral freedom can not exist, rationally and intelligibly explained, upon any other conceivable basis. As the doctrine now stands interpreted, it assuredly has nothing to recommend it to the intelligent mind. The assumptions of divines on this head can have no important bearing; when every individual is known to be forced, *uninformed and unconsulted*, into this breathing world, frequently "deformed, half-made up," and with a "nationality," and complexion, too, which may prove a blessing or a *curse*, just as the tide of human prejudice may chance to flow at the time. Think you, that any being would *consent* to be born with a black skin, or with a defective organization? Would any free moral being *consent*, on the supposition of possessing all due information, to be introduced into this life with one leg shorter than the other?—With an imbecile brain?—With a hare-lip?—With a predisposition to consumption and scrofula?—Or, with any other disorder, physical or mental, which children are compelled to accept with their birth? The utter absurdity of the idea breaks upon the mind with a redoubled force, when suggested by the monstrous assertions of the clergy, that "we are created free moral powers!" The very fact of beginning to be, implies a *primary dependence* of the creature upon the Creative Principle.

All intelligent mechanics know, that a human invention of "perpetual motion" would be possible were it not for the *primary necessity* of employing perishable materials, and driving home the *last* screw—implying, thus, that the "motion" would have a beginning, and, consequently, a certain termination. Even so, when considered as to its derivation, the human soul is the result of the harmonious action of a Creative Principle of Nature; and it *depends* as much upon the eternal existence of the divine Creator for its everlasting being as the heart *depends* upon the presence of the human spirit for life and energy.

If you should study the science of man, my friends, you will observe that all liberty or freedom is *comparative;* not absolute. All will is *consequent;* not primary. The soul does not will itself into being; but after its existence and organization are determined, then the inherited force, through will, sets the mechanism in motion. If the physical arrangements are not from birth harmonious, the *will* can not render them so. Because the *will-faculty is an effect* of the mental combinations; not a cause of them. A child has the will, or the desire, to play in the fields; but the determining power can accomplish nothing, unless the body is well and the limbs free from paralysis. Will, moreover, can not exist as an independent faculty of mind; because it is a *conditional* and interfixed power—receiving promptings from the passions, and admonitions from the judgment. If the will acts by the instigations of the reason, then it is merely the lever of the *directing* power. Or, if will acts by impulses proceeding from the passions; then, as before, it is executing the impetuous suggestions of a cause upon which it (the will), as an effect, must necessarily depend. Will, therefore, is not a self-causing and self-determining power; but it is, when carefully defined, the *focus* of the mind.

The human spirit, as I see it, is composed of actuating springs, which are LOVE; and regulating faculties, which are WISDOM. These, combined and organized, constitute a THINKING SUN. This spiritual sun, like its representative in the heavens, sends off rays in all directions. These rays are inclinations. The reflection or refraction of these inclinations upon the countless external objects which develop and attract them, forms a *focus* in the mind. At this point all the rays converge, and, when all external and contiguous conditions are favorable, the *full force* of the internal sun (the mind) is manifested at this focus. This focus is the will. It is no more independent of the powers which contain the inclinations, and which emit them, than the focal point in a lens is independent of the rays of the sun.

The metaphysical nature of the subject prevents a clearer illustration; which, taken in connection with the fact that no human mind can perfectly analyze and comprehend itself, must serve to explain away all ambiguity in the description. The peculiar nature of this review, moreover, does not encourage any elaborate considerations of this kind. They are deferred to a more requisite occasion; when another, but more carefully prepared, criticism may be called forth from the author. Till then, we will let this point rest; and proceed to consider man in relation to the world.

You ask: "Are you not mistaken in affirming the partial freedom of man? Do we not behold examples of moral liberty in every man?" To this I reply briefly. As you recollect, Kossuth, the brilliant Hungarian Governor, was referred to as a fine example of a Man in the exercise of his freedom. Now it seems to me the merest insight into the true philosophy of human existence and events, would have prevented the reference altogether. Development is a transparent principle of nature; and mankind is the coronation of *all* the nature which pertains to this earth. It is self-evident that great events develop great men. A Washington appears when the occasion requires. Giants are slumbering: because there is no temple to overthrow. Should this people be suddenly oppressed by the invasion of a foreign army, the pressure would develop a Washington as naturally as the spring unfolds the flower. So Kossuth is a development of the times and events of his country. His love of Liberty was born with him, by the direct action of psychological laws upon his unfolding nature. Several of his relations were the victims of Tyranny, to which, very naturally, his mother became an ardent but speechless foe! If the external circumstances did not exist, the great "centerstance," Kossuth, would not be to-day known as the influential Angel of Liberty. To believe that he is self-determining and self-directing is to believe contrary to truth; for he is, like the head upon the human body, the sensorium and mouthpiece of the Hungarian body, to which, by the most endearing ties, he is firmly attached. He is, therefore, acting out his paramount impulses as spontaneously as (but no more so than) the rose breathes forth its native fragrance. True, his liberty is greater than the rose; hence he does more, enjoys more, has greater privileges; in exact proportion to which are his responsibilities—not to the supernatural sphere, remember, but to the events and people by which he is supported. Thus, if the Hungarian is an example of moral freedom, he is also an *illustration* of moral *dependence*, as growing out of the universal relationship of all created things. If you will but study his very emotional organization, in connection with the power of circumstances to develop man, I am quite certain your legitimate conclusions will be analogous.

Methinks there now arises another question: "Is

not man free to go where and do what he wills? Can he not journey from city to city, and steal, and murder, when he desires?"

The problem of "blamable wrong" now begins to appear. From the theological presentation of the question, it may be difficult for many minds to turn away, as they should, in order to study the nature of man with an eye single to the acquisition of truthful conclusions. If you divest your minds of all supernaturalistic notions, and analyze the individual relations which subsist between every man and the external world of effects, the truth will surely break upon you in all its beautiful connections and simplicity.

As already shown, every man's freedom is *comparative* and conditional; not absolute or uncaused. It is, in other words, the *result* of certain conspiring causes; hence, it is not self-subsisting, but dependent. Suppose, for example, you Will to visit the city of Boston. Now this *will* can have no external manifestation or accomplishment, unless all the outer contingencies, over which you individually can have no absolute control, are conspiring to aid you. You depend upon bodily health, upon the existence of safe and certain means of conveyance, and so forth; which must all be in full operation before you can accomplish the end of the will. These are common-sense affirmations which every one of my audience fully comprehends.

But let us look at this matter, as the clergy do, from a *moral* posture. Suppose an individual had high duties, as personal responsibilities are termed, in Boston, which require his immediate presence and attention. And there being no physical hinderances to prevent him from going directly among them, upon which an excuse might be properly based; still he does not, or *will* not, go forthwith and discharge those duties; the question is: "Is not that man doing, in some sense, a blamable wrong?" Or, let us again suppose, a man is a partner in business. He plans with the utmost subtilty and care, the impoverishment of his companion; and, having accomplished his designs, he leaves the country, with all his partner's earnings and his own; the question is: "Is not that man doing a blamable wrong?" Or, to suppose still further, one man assassinates another, committing the double crime of murder and robbing; the question is: "Is not that man doing a blamable wrong?" I think the question of "blamable wrong," in connection with the problem of moral freedom, is here stated in full force; and my answer, in order to be adequately apprehended, must commence with the consideration of a few principles, to which I now solicit your attention.

Man, as we have seen, is introduced into existence without any previous consultations as to his desires or choice. This is, to commence with, a total violation of the conditions of moral freedom. Because, if the theologic assumptions be true, the individual is in danger of ultimating in everlasting woe—his chances being, according to the calculations of some divines, one to seventy-five. All this is irreconcilable with the workings of a divine Perfection. A free moral power should have its choice consulted as to the nature it will accept, and the laws to regulate it. Contrary to this, no man creates the laws of his finite being; they are made for him; and he, as an inevitable sequence, is compelled to obey them. Man, therefore, in the consciousness of his being, is not self-causing or self-determining in any sense; but is the *issue* of certain creative principles, which he can no more break or subvert than a planet can leave the orbit in which the laws of condensation and gravitation have fixed it, and take independent voyages through the firmament.

Man, I repeat, is not the creator of the inexorable laws of his being; hence, he is their everlasting subject; hence, too, he obeys. The paramount law of his nature, which he can not alter, is Attraction. He obeys this law every instant of time; true as the needle to the positive magnet. For present purposes, I will denominate this law, Interest; because your minds will more readily apprehend the signification of the term. Interest, I say, then, is the ruling principle of every human being; no one can act without it, nor feel the disposition to act. It operates in all degrees or spheres of existences, with the same philosophical precision and determination. No man has *a will* superior to his attractive or moving principle; he can not have; his will is merely the agent, *or fulcrum*, whereby this law, like a lever, moves the individual from point to point, from attraction to attraction, among the countless contrarieties which make up existence. Perhaps, my friends, you think me too abstract; but I know I am not so to the over-seeing and comprehensive intellect. However, let me bring the subject home to the individual.

Suppose you now WILL to walk into the street: the question is—"How came you to feel that will?" There is surely an *antecedent* somewhere, and generated by something. You can not *will* to walk hence, unless the attraction here *diminishes*, permitting *another* attraction to obtain the ascendency in your minds. The paramount or chief attraction you are under the necessity of obeying. But in this you may become confused, like a flock of sheep whose leader is lost in hesitation; or, like the tides which, while changing from one point of attraction to another, form *eddies* and contrary currents. These eddies and *contrary* currents, in human affairs and deeds, are the very matters about which the clergy are perpetually preaching. Upon them the priesthood predicate all their theories of man's moral freedom; and I fear it will be long ere the doctors of divinity can be prevailed upon to study man, and the profound philosophy of existence. Men would move in the paths of rectitude as naturally and spontaneously as the planets roll in their respective orbits, without manifesting disorder, if they were, like those planets, subject only to a single unchangeable law of attraction, always developing uniform results. But with man the case is different. He possesses within himself innumerable affinities, and, hence, is subject to the influence of countless attractions. These set in upon him from all directions, at the same time causing him to *hesitate*, to *deliberate*, to *decide*, and finally to *act* in accordance with the paramount attraction. This is all the moral freedom there is in the constitution of things. I will verify this on another occasion.

Now comes the solution of the questions propounded. But first let me direct your attention to the fact, that all the trouble, discords, and abominations in this world arise from the conflict between the laws of nature and the government of society. The laws of nature are implanted in the constitution of every man; but he does not and can not so truly feel the laws of society. These are the creations of ignorant and finite man; and they are at war with the laws of nature, because they are wrong and unjust. The individual, therefore, is situated between two contending forces—the imperative laws of nature and the restrictive laws of society—and the confliction generates all the evils in the world. Society says to the man, "Your *duties*, sir, lie in Boston—you must proceed there immediately." But the law of nature in him does not affirm the same thing. This law is superior in its influence upon his Will; indeed, he feels *only* this law, accompanied with its attractions or interests, and can only happily obey it: yet the social law he may *fear* exceedingly; and, this gaining the ascendency in his mind, he proceeds to obey it, with certain internal conflicts which he is theologically taught to term, "compunctions of conscience." His mind may be so undeveloped that only ordinary desires and attractions can affect him. Hence, while my mind might esteem his attractions of character as low and demoralizing, he, on the other hand, might consider my attractions as imaginary and poetical. Hence, too, each being ignorant of the other's integrity to the laws of nature, we would commence *blaming* one another. I, considered as an orthodox clergyman, might call him "a poor miserable sinner;" and he would call me a penurious shepherd, determined to shear all the wool from the flock. So the compliments might be reciprocated; until, by my superior ability to use language and arguments, I may finally subdue his voice, overcome all his inordinate attractions, place *my attractions* in the ascendency before him, and, lo! I have achieved the conversion of a fellow-sinner. Very well: when this method can be philosophically practiced, instilling high and humanitary sentiments in the undeveloped mind, I will become a co-worker in all religious revivals. This is the practical and logical tendency of the Harmonial Philosophy.

But what shall we say concerning the "moral freedom and blamable wrong" of the dexterous and faithless partner in business. The practical conclusion of the case is, my friends, that society is, to a considerable extent, accountable for his actions. I affirm this under the strongest impression of its entire accuracy. If a suit be instituted for damages, it would be far more just should the individual bring it against society than society against the individual. Society had no right to be so defective as to permit such a disaster. If the fire burns a city to the earth, what do you say? Do you blame the fire? or, the defective use made of it, and the combustible nature of the dwellings? Surely, a fire-proof house is the best preventive against a fire.

So with our social organization. If it is not murder-proof, theft-proof, and proof against the evils complained of, it assuredly should not *curse* the low, misdirected, or undeveloped powers which very naturally obey the laws proper to their nature, to the disturbance and derangement of the general organism. It is true, thousands obey the laws of society by violating the inward principle; but such are not happy, because they are actuated or kept in bondage by *fear*, which regulates all their external interests and actions. But such are esteemed by the clergy as examples of free moral powers in the loyal exercise of their liberty to do right or wrong—so *superficial* are all theological theories and conclusions.

Methinks you inquire: "But is not the delinquent partner also deserving blame?" To this I am impressed to reply: "*He that is without sin among you, let him cast the first stone.*" That is to say, there is blamable wrong in this world; but let us denounce *deeds*, not men. Let us not vilify and crucify the individual; but the social organization by which the individual is used and molded. But this, you say, is evading the question. Assuredly not. You say, the partner had the ability to *plan* the mischief, and, hence, the inward power of unoerstanding exactly what he was doing, &c., and should have not done the deed. This is precisely what I say; only I affirm that he was a *misdirected* man—acting from what you would pronounce the *lowest* motive of his nature: but at the same time, the fact should not be overlooked that the lowest motive was the *strongest* in his mind. It was his prevailing and psychologizing Interest to do the mischief; to which all his plans and deliberations were playing the parts of agents and attorneys. The *client* was the all-absorbing Interest. But you ask: "Where did that *low* and miserable motive originate?" Divines affirm it was generated in his own will. This I deny, and ask: Where did that man obtain his conscious being and its laws? Did he determine his organization? Certainly not. But why did not the other partner commit the same theft? Because, perhaps, the other mind was endowed with a higher realization of justice, which no ordinary attractions could influence or dilute; or, he might *fear* society. He would, therefore, act out the law of his being as faithfully as the other. Still society should not be so structurally defective as to allow the least developed mind an opportunity or tendency to create disorder. This man had a right to demand, from the various dependencies, a feeling *superior* to the Interest of wealth and its supposed joys.

You now revert to the instance of the murderer. What shall we say? Is the murderer not guilty? Should we not denounce him as a "free moral power"—"doing as he was not made to do?" Yea, verily! He was doing as he was not made to do; but the primary cause *did not originate in his Will.* Whence came it, then? I answer: Society is guilty of the outrage; for it permitted the *lowest* motives of the mind to become paramount and the *strongest.* No man in his proper condition, ever committed murder from a natural preference. The thought is revolting! If he should kill from a native taste, whence came that taste? Did he create himself? Far from it. Is there unrighteousness with God? God forbid! How then came that man to destroy his brother? I answer, he acted as a strong power in the hands of a still more powerful combination of causes; for which society, not individuals, are truly responsible.

Take for example, the case of Dr. PARKMAN and Prof. WEBSTER. Did the latter murder the former from a spontaneous exercise of his so-called moral freedom? The facts are quite to the contrary. The crime grew out of a pecuniary obligation and embarrassment between the individuals. The debtor did not liquidate the debt when he promised to do so, and the impatient creditor became abnormally suspicious. This suspicion generated aggravating insinuations and constant inquiries, under which Prof. WEBSTER writhed and smarted as only a proud man could. His wounded pride overpowered his other and higher feelings, and developed a degree of anger altogether insupportable. His strongest Interest was centered in the removal of this bane to his happiness. This led to the murder. You say: "He should have restrained himself." Oh, it is exceedingly easy to say what a fellow-being should do under given circumstances, and to blame him if he acts contrary to *our* notions of right and wrong—especially when we are not organized, situated, and influenced in a similar manner; but, when *our turn comes*, we find ourselves acting perhaps no better than he; only we, being privy to all the causes, can see mitigating and modifying circumstances accompanying our crimes, which we honestly believe, or wish to believe, would justify utter forgiveness. Society held Prof. WEBSTER responsible for his moral delinquency or murderous deed. Is this exact justice? I hear a protesting voice,—"Prof. WEBSTER should have more properly instituted a suit for individual damages against society. Because the crime in this case was the legitimate effect of a social relation between debtor and creditor; of which antagonistic relation the distinguished individuals were the most unfortunate victims." The precise thought here intended can be much easier *misunderstood* than apprehended. It is quite a manifest departure from the popular definitions of Justice; and, like the traveler in a strange country, the reader may unintentionally wander astray. You exclaim: "Oh, it is all a plea for vice—relieving the individual of moral responsibility, and encouraging transgression—by charging *all* upon the structure of society." Error could not be more remote from Truth, than is this conclusion from the author's meaning. Every individual is surely doing a blamable wrong when he acts *inconsistently* with the indwelling Law of Right. But who shall say what that Law is? Who shall sit in judgment against his neighbor? According to my impression, this Law is Harmony. Any thing, therefore, which develops discord is wrong; as a *cause*, it must receive an unqualified condemnation. Now the reader will apprehend the significancy of my affirmation, if he understands me as *condemning the causes* of discord or sin, whether traceable to individuals or to our social construction. In the case of Prof. WEBSTER, there is no denying the plain fact, that the murder did not grow out of any innate taste or voluntary desire, but, primarily, out of a money-relation between the parties—to which they were unrighteously subjected. This pecuniary trouble, then, taken in connection with the inherited temperaments and mental tendencies of the criminal, was the *cause* of the premeditation and the sin. Therefore, inasmuch as the first cause of this evil is to be found in our social arrangements, so am I, in common justice to truth, compelled to charge upon society the damages and injuries done to the parties involved.

You ask, "Why does not every man destroy his creditor, when similarly embarrassed in a money relation?" For the same reason that every man is not physically and mentally organized precisely alike.

Each man would be a NEWTON or a SHAKESPEARE, were it not for this fact, that the inequalities of birth, the contrarieties of surrounding circumstances, and the different social positions which men occupy—all conspire against the possibility of every person *being* and *doing* in a corresponding manner. One man can bear fifty times more embarrassment and vexation than another, and manifest no discomposure or retaliation. It depends altogether upon individual organization, and the use which society makes of that organization, as to the good or evil issues. You inquire: "Who made society?" Society is the work of ignorant and undeveloped men. Like the *first* cotton machine, society does not properly accomplish or manufacture what the constructive minds desire. Individuals are not personally responsible for all the evils evolved from present social arrangements. For it is the human aggregate which forms society. The social mechanism can be improved, only, on the event of the masses becoming enlightened as to the actual *causes* of sin so-called, and as to the best methods of reorganization. The reader, therefore, will apprehend me as not tolerating vice, or as exculpating the individual from the commission of discordant deeds which he, as a *comparative* free power, can prevent or abstain from; but as teaching the doctrine, which can not be successfully refuted, that the greatest evils in this world arise from Ignorance as to the organization of men, and, equally, from a defective social arrangement. A different and harmonious organization of human occupations and interests would render society a better Parent to its offspring! But the individuals were not the real sufferers; because, when their physical existence terminated a better opened upon them; but they were citizens, and husbands, and fathers! From these relations sprang all the suffering which the murder developed. Society, therefore, receives back, with interest compounded, all the wrongs, the insults, and oppressions which its antagonistic relations inflict upon individuals. Society, when it strangulates the murderer, at the same time, absolutely *insults* the moral feelings of every man who has outgrown theology and the prevailing evils of an undeveloped race.

In conclusion, I will briefly reply to the almost thoughtless assertion, that "this philosophy is immoral." This assertion, my friends, is grounded in ignorance and prejudice. The logical fruits are: *personal analysis, self-development, harmony, peace, brotherly love, and a universal unity of interests.* We are taught to feel ourselves free to do Right; but we are not free to do wrong. The law of our existence is Justice or harmony; this is our highest Interest or chief attraction. Almost the last words which broke from the soul of Jesus, when he separated from his sorrow-stricken disciples, bring out in full force the practical teachings of this philosophy: "*Be ye one, even as I and my Father are one*"—a blending of interests the most intimate, wise, and divine. This state can never be developed under the teaching of supernaturalism; which tolerates social antagonisms on the fallacious theory of man's moral freedom. This doctrine which asserts that each man is a self-determining and self-regulating power, is disproved by every thing in existence. The mission of the Christ-principle is to reveal to the race the peace and unity of truth. It will unfold a Wisdom-power among men to the ultimate establishment of a sacred harmony on earth, permanent as the Eternal Mind.

I have said that man's will is an *effect*, and not a cause; that it is, therefore, not absolutely, but *comparatively* free. If a man wills to accomplish any thing, the execution thereof depends wholly upon the favorable conspiration of surrounding things. There could be no lying, no stealing, no murder, if every man was an isolated being—an independent, self-causing, self-determining, and self-sustaining power. Nay. Association *is the parent of all* discordant contrasts in men and deeds; and the Law of Progression is the parent of the countless varieties of character visible in the human world. I say, then, that man is comparatively free in his will. He can follow out, or after, his *strongest* attraction or Interest on the condition that all relative influences and circumstances, over which he can have no direct control, are friendly to his proceeding. Kossuth, in the exercise of his freedom, could do nothing, though he might *will* forever, if there were no hearts to beat sympathetically with his own. Now I regard his love of, and labors for, Liberty as the natural result of the events which developed him, and of the peculiar organization which, *without his consent*, he originally derived from his progenitors. Hence, manifestly, the reason why all men are not precisely like Kossuth, is to be found in the fact, that all are not personally organized and situated in a corresponding manner. So, therefore there is no great cause for aristocracy in feeling; for the most splendid man before the world to-day might have been, through the accident of birth, a negro delving in the earth for a livelihood.

But you ask: "If this doctrine be true, how shall we graduate the measure of personal responsibility?" This question I will more fully answer hereafter. My present reply is: from the mind of fine endowments we should expect fine results, all immediately surrounding things being favorable. I think many who now pass for good Christian citizens, have never committed theft or murder, simply because they have not been situated amid the adequate temptations. But what might constitute an irresistible temptation to one man, could form no inducement whatever to another, possessing a *different* temperament and a higher organization. This fact men are quite too apt to overlook in pronouncing judgment upon the moral delinquencies of the victims of vice. The man who would not be tempted at all to do a certain thing, which some weaker brother was influenced to accomplish in society, sits in cold judgment against the misdirected mind, and consigns him, on the ground of moral freedom, to some loathsome prison or burning hell. Such is the doctrine of supernaturalism!

Man, I repeat, is free to do right; but *he is not free to do wrong*. When he does right, he glides peacefully along with the divine life-currents of this beautiful universe, like a flower on the ocean's bosom. This is the glorious Liberty of the children of God. But to attempt to do wrong, or rather to be influenced by social laws to go in a wrong direction, is to meet with insurmountable impediments at every step; it is like an effort to ascend the impetuous tide of Niagara Falls. "According to this philosophy," you ask, "what motive have we to use our comparative freedom?" I answer: The *chief attraction* of every soul is Happiness. But there are very few who know which road to take to find it. Thousands think it is to be found in licentiousness, in gaming, in prowling through the world, like the prodigal son, in drunkenness and recklessness; but such soon discover their error; for a miserable experience teaches a different lesson.

Happiness, then, is the chief of all attractions; and all mankind would go directly to it, if they possessed sufficient wisdom. We, therefore, who have this wisdom, should impart it to those whose present proceedings are against the law of Right. This Law operates *in* us and *upon* us, whether we recognize it or not; and every movement which deviates from its imperative tendency, is attended with the legitimate consequences. These results are recorded in the book of life; not always in accordance with our educational notions of right and wrong, with our voluntary or involuntary doings; but, invariably, in proportion to the *real* deviation of the individual. Society does the most injury to individuals in this respect. You ask: "What do you mean by the book of life?" The book of life, my friends, is composed of the human body and mind. The lids are made of the body; the folios of the mental faculties. Upon these leaves are written the many deviations of the individual from the paths of rectitude.

The recording angel is the Law of Right, or the Positive Principle of nature, which is Harmony. The mark of transgression is upon the brow. The individual—the book of life—is immortal; it soon passes away to the Spirit-Land. The record of misdirection appears on the living faculties; is manifested in their deformity and decrepitude; in their inability immediately to advance, with the higher spirits, upon the eternal highway of Love and Wisdom. Such are the motives, according to this philosophy, which we have for exercising aright all the comparative freedom in our possession. One can righteously affect a Family; another a Society; another still, can affect a Community; and still another, can move a Nation with the power of Mind—if all the immediate outer conditions conspire to that end. But society must be changed. For the greatest injury which can be done an individual, is to place him, by the mere accident of birth, in a world which favors crime, and the perpetuation of mental misery.

CHAPTER VIII.

CONCLUSION.

Political and Religious causes of the coming crisis.—A struggle between Catholics and Protestants.—The triumph of Reason.—The result.

The friends of progress should always be able to read that greatest of all living chapters in Creation: the condition of the human world. It concerns everybody; because the world is composed of individuals. And if those who stand upon the summit of the hill are incapable of seeing the broad extent of humanity that surrounds them, then who shall go to the contemplation? The whole world, as a general thing, sees future events through the eyes of a very few persons. Indeed, it is almost true to say that, considered in the historical sense, the entire body of mankind has but two eyes or mediums through which to contemplate the condition of things, namely, Politics and Religion.

On this occasion let us look at the world through the medium of Religion. My impressions upon this subject may be briefly written. I, therefore, solicit your clearest discernment to the following points: It is well known by all the inhabitants of Christendom that the world is full of sectarian jargon and bitterness. And that very conspicuously before the world are arrayed, in bitter and uncompromising hostility, two powerful forces—*Protestantism* and *Catholicism.*

In order to bring these religious institutions distinctly before your minds, I will describe their leading characteristics.

Catholicism is a system of supernaturalism. It claims to be the "One, Holy, Catholic, Apostolic Church"--based upon supernatural *authority*, claiming unending infallibility. It denies the *right of individual judgment* upon religious subjects; but inculcates the virtues, charities, and hospitalities of Christianity through the agency of popes, bishops, and priests, who profess to have their authority direct from the supernatural source.

Protestantism is also a system of supernaturalism—I mean, when considered as a whole. It claims to have discovered the true import of the Sacred Scriptures. It is based upon a supernatural foundation, but encourages the right of *private judgment* upon all subjects pertaining to religion and conscience. It likewise inculcates the virtues and charities of Christianity through the medium of clergymen, schools, and colleges.

Now I am not impressed to consider the minor points of either Catholicism or Protestantism, nor the different views which one party or the other entertains concerning the truest methods of biblical interpretation. There have already been too many churches built, and too many salaries paid, to have these oriental and insignificant affairs discussed. But I have to do only with *the foundation* upon which these two very popular institutions manifestly stand. It is essential to understand here, what is very generally overlooked, that both of these gigantic religious organizations are struggling to maintain an everlasting position upon the *same* identical basis. There is one foundation; but it is not large enough to sustain two such stupendous and inharmonious superstructures. Hence it inevitably follows that both must fall forever—leaving the ground to be occupied by something more consistent. But one must decline and crumble before the other. Now the question is, which of these two religious institutions is first destined to decay?

Let us leave this question unanswered, for a few moments, and turn our thoughts in another direction.

It is well known by the clergy and people generally of the present day, that there is rapidly growing a rationalistic religion and a philosophical Spirituality. This is the Harmonial Philosophy. It stands upon the revelations of Nature, and upon the foundations of the highest form of Reason. It fully accepts the virtues, charities, truths, and liberalities of every known religion; and simply rejects every thing which claims to be intrinsically based upon the miraculous or unprofitably supernatural. It looks upon the moralisms and precepts of Christianity as a natural development of a well balanced mind—or, more properly, as a natural unfolding of *truth* in the general progress of mankind. It regards all the real miracles, prophecies, and miraculous powers, as explainable upon philosophical principles; and holds to the doctrine of human progress and universal improvement in the constitution of things.

Now, it will be perceived, the declarations and positions of this Philosophy are clear, and positively antagonistic to both Protestantism and Catholicism. It is essential that you fix your minds firmly upon this point. The rationalism of this day is positively opposed to *the two great forms* of religious belief. Because, as before said, the quarrel between Protestantism and Catholicism is sustained on the desire which one party has to supplant and transcend the other. For they stand upon the same foundation. By this I mean to say, that the Bible is the unmistakable originator of both these religious institutions. It is the ground-plan of each; and the two start from the same degree of apostolic authority; but there is a vast struggle, not now obvious, but certain to occur between these Powers—a war, destined summarily to settle the question of the ground-title, and the divine right of human government. A supernatural religion based upon and supported by miracles equally supernatural, is the basis of both superstructures. There is no denying this plain fact. I would not be understood to consider Catholicism as good in all respects as Protestantism; for it is clear that the latter has wrought many improvements in the form of religious worship, has abandoned many expensive and unnecessary ceremonies, and encouraged individual education, and private judgment in scriptural reading.

But mankind are now far more civilized and advanced in arts and sciences than in any former era. Men understand each other better now; and the great laws of nature are more easily and generally comprehended. The shackles of bigotry and intolerance drop off as the cause of Freedom advances; and all members of humanity—of Christendom especially—are becoming more thoroughly reasonable and baptized in the pure waters of wisdom.

Here, then, is the point: men are becoming *more reasonable.* The fate of Christendom depends wholly upon this one fact: men are *realizing* their manhood and becoming intelligent and strong.

Among other revolutions which await the higher portions of mankind, is a religious one, which will be more powerful than any known to history. But it will be effected principally by Reason. One party will reason philosophically, the other theologically; both will reason *correctly* from the premises assumed. You may be assured of the truth of this approaching crisis. The world must recognize it, because it will be accompanied with war; for politics are inseparably connected, all over the world, with religious systems. Religion will develop reason; but politics will impel the masses to unsheath the sword and to stain the bosom of nature with blood! Friends of progress! be not discouraged; for the final crisis must come; then the strange interregnum.

Concerning so-called revealed religion, the majority of the people will reason thus: "We believe Christianity to be a supernatural development of truth. There are truths our feeble reason could never have discovered—such as the character of God, the doctrine of immortality, and so forth; hence, a *supernatural revelation* is essential to our future safety and present enlightenment." (Remember, my friends, that thousands of Protestants will and do reason in this way.) And looking about on either side, they will say: "What means all these sects? Whence their origin? Is this the result of religious liberty? Nay; it is religious anarchy! Wherefore? Because all Protestantism is in error. We have a supernatural religion, but we have been striving to comprehend a supernatural matter, with our common, natural judgments! This is unreasonable." Thus many will say: This is unreasonable; and it is all chargeable upon Protestants. They have been very inconsistent. They believe that Christianity is a supernatural revelation of supernatural truth; and yet they have the presumption to think that every man should read this supernatural revelation to please himself. Catholicism is more consistent, and *more certain* to redeem the sinner from the mortgage which the devil holds against him; because this religion is true to all the apostolic symbols and pen and ink habiliments of the early Church, as these were supernaturally originated and organized on earth. Protestantism, on the contrary, is unsafe (on the supernatural theory) as a divine power unto salvation. Its existence is based upon the original developments of supernaturalism; but, on the score of freedom of opinion, this church has adopted a somewhat more *spiritual* method of accomplishing the new birth and the sinner's final salvation. This freedom of opinion is now the great trouble. It has opened the door to all manner of heresy, atheism, demonism, and diverse sectarian antagonisms to the claims of supernaturalism. Now I am impressed with the conviction that no natural judgment is adequate to the just understanding of supernatural things. If Christianity is a system of supernatural truth, then it requires a supernaturally illuminated mind to comprehend its import and arcanical bearings. In this matter, the Roman Catholic religion is altogether more consistent than the Protestant religion. This is undeniable.

But it may be said that Christianity is only *natural* truth, supernaturally revealed—presented to man for his acceptation or rejection in his freedom. Now, by taking this position, you clearly admit that the entire system would eventually have been unfolded by the general progression of humanity—you come upon rationalistic grounds of interpretation. If Christianity is a system of natural truth, then it would have *naturally* come forth like the sciences of Astronomy, Geology, &c., in the common course of things. But if it came through a miraculous channel, or was divulged through the agency of supernatural means, then it evidently requires the same means to enliven it and to spread it triumphantly over the earth. Do you apprehend the full bearing of this reasoning?

Let us take an example. Suppose you construct an engine: you adjust the parts, introduce the vapor, and the wheels turn. But what would you think of the mechanic who insisted upon making a steam-engine go by *water*-power. You would doubtless consider him ignorant or insane. Now, apply the same reasoning to Protestantism. Protestants believe that Christianity was introduced, and set in motion, by *supernatural* and miraculous means; and yet they reject the means by which the whole system was originally moved, and try to keep it in action by *natural* and common causes. In this matter of theoretic consistence, I affirm, Catholicism has always been, and is now, far in advance of Protestantism. For if we have a supernaturally revealed religion, we should have a class of men supernaturally endowed, or ordained, to understand it, and to impart its wonderful truths to mankind.* While Protestantism is divided and subdivided into many conflicting sects, the One, Holy, Catholic, Apostolic Church stands perfectly unmoved and unchanged! Now, why is this? The reply is plain: simply because that church is, and always has been, perfectly *consistent* with its assumed premises. It stands, like Protestantism, upon a supernatural foundation. Its doctrines are derived from the Bible, which is claimed to be a super-

---

* Protestantism founds the Church on the Bible, making the Bible prior. On the other hand, Catholicism rests the Bible on the Church, making the Church prior. Ask a Protestant which he believes first, Church or Bible? and he will say, "Bible;" which he believes *because* of the other? and he will say, "I believe in a Church, because I believe in the Bible." "You start, then, with the Bible?" "Yes." "But how do you know the Bible is the Word of God?" "Why, I know it because 'all Scripture is given by the inspiration of God.'" "But, my friend, the question is, *what* Scripture? How do you know that these sixty-six books are the Scripture? Why is 'Solomon's Song' scripture, and not the 'Book of Wisdom?' Why the 'Epistle of St. Jude,' and not the 'Epistle of St. Clement?' Where do you find in the Bible an inspired list of canonical books? and if there were such list, how could you know that that list itself was inspired? If you fall back for aid on the Holy Apostles, you find them quoting the 'Book of Enoch,' and displaying familiarity with 'Wisdom' and 'Ecclesiasticus,' and even quoting passages from the heathen poets." The Protestant has no answer, or he may take refuge in the remark that he believes the Bible on account of its evidences. "But have you ever personally examined those evidences to see if they are sound?" "No; but others have, and so, the Bible being generally accepted, I accept it." And after a series of questions, my brethren, you find it all comes to this, that he believes the Bible to be the infallible Word of God, on the testimony and assurance of fallible men. As another has expressed it, the world is put very comfortably on an elephant, and the elephant on a tortoise, but the poor tortoise rests nowhere.—*Ewer's Lecture.*

naturally derived book; hence it requires a class of regularly inspired men to divulge its great teachings, and to secure their proper acceptation by, and influence upon, the human character. This class of men should take charge of our souls; and we should not interfere with religious doctrines or political acts, only so far as the supernaturally inspired men shall desire and command. Now, be it remembered, the Catholic Church is, or claims to be, in possession of this class of inspired men. There is a great organization of Popes and Bishops who claim to have supernatural authority, from PETER the First, to the present time. The supernaturalistic chain is complete. To be consistent, then, let us leave conflicting Protestantism, and go back to the bosom of the Mother Church.

Here, my friends, you have a brief synopsis of the simple process which is likely to occur in thousands of Protestant hearts. It is now occurring, privately, all around the world. There will be a peculiar reaction in *favor* of Catholicism. The One, Holy, Catholic Church, is destined to spread throughout many of the territories of Christendom; because one party in Protestantism will see its inconsistent position in matters of religious theory. But another party has appeared—the Liberal Christians and the Harmonial Philosophers. This form of religion unqualifiedly rejects all *unnatural* supernaturalism. Hence, Protestantism and Catholicism, as religious institutions, are alike repudiated. It does not make *every man's* judgment his *only* guide in matters of importance, but asks—" Where shall we find the most truth, the highest wisdom, the noblest religion, the truest happiness? It has these desires for its *eternal magnet.* Hence it interrogates the boundless fields of Nature with an honest soul and lofty brow! This is perfect and immutable freedom. Anarchy can never invade the principles of this party; for it is based upon Reason, upon Nature, and upon Nature's God.

We have now obtained the final reply. Protestantism, as now constructed, will first decay; because it is to be divided into two parties—the smallest party will go back into Catholicism; the other will go forward into Rationalism. And then, after a succession of eventful years, a *political* revolution will hurl the Catholic superstructure to the Earth, and *the prismatic bow of promise will span the Heavens.* The nations and races will then be comparatively free and happy. For the Millennial Epoch will have arrived; and there will be something like a realization of peace on Earth and universal good will.

CHAPTER IX.

REASONS FOR THE FAILURE OF PROTESTANTISM.*

THE history of Christianity illustrates this text. Her career has been marked by crises, when men, stirred by unusual earnestness, have arisen against the quiet order of things round about them. These crises have occurred at irregular intervals. They have always been provoked by some evil that has been long and silently growing. They are periods which try men's souls, because they are periods when new men attack old and cherished prejudices. In the second century after Christ, the germs of what afterward became Arianism appeared in Lucian of Antioch. Those germs grew and spread in the Church silently, but so widely and alarmingly at last, as to lead earnest Catholics, in the subsequent century, to rise in their majesty, reassert the faith in its purity, as it had come down from the Apostles, and brand the new dogmas as deadly heresy. In the Middle Ages, Roman errors silently and slowly grew and spread, till at last, in the eleventh century, earnest Catholics in the eastern portion of the Church, enduring the evil no longer, rose in their majesty to condemn it; and that non-intercommunion with Rome

* Extracts from a Discourse delivered by Rev. Dr. F. C. Ewer, at Christ's Church, in New York, Sunday, September 27, 1868, from the text, "I came not to bring peace, but a sword."—MATT. x. 30.

was decreed by the Orthodox Eastern (or Greek) Church, which has lasted till to-day. In the Roman portion of the Church the same evils continued to grow, with new ones which broke out from time to time, until at last, in the fifteenth century, earnest men all over the West rose in their majesty against them; and we have the Reformation — so-called. Subsequently, coldness and deadness grew and spread in the Anglican portion of the Church, till at last, in the eighteenth century, those earnest souls, John and Charles Wesley, kindled the blaze of Methodism. God hath cast our lives at the opening of one of these crises.

I would not have you unalive to the fact, or undervalue its importance. For many years men have been floating calmly down the stream of Christianity. There have been petty differences and discussions between sects, it is true, but no general upheaval. Foundations have been undisturbed. But now a storm is very evidently rising, which is disturbing the bottom of affairs; and it is impossible to predict how we shall all come out of it. We may look to the warnings and advice of our former rectors, speaking, as it were, from the grave. But the leader of twenty or ten years ago could give us no general sailing directions for these new coasts and channels, these new heavens and seas. The voices of the dead may warn us concerning those things which they knew; they can not warn us concerning aspects and conditions unseen and unanticipated by them. Leaders in conservative and quiet times are rarely the leaders in revolutions. Revolutions roll them under. There are evils raising great fronts around us—evils that have been long and silently growing. And as in the fourth century, as in the eleventh, as in the fifteenth, and as in the eighteenth, earnest souls are at last roused at these evils, and men are beginning boldly to speak out. It is noteworthy that the laity are ahead of the clergy in this matter. It is the evident and disastrous failure of Protestantism, as a religious system, that is raising the mutterings of this storm. What is it that is the mother of all this infidelity? What is it that is the prolific cause of all this low grade of spirituality and character in life? What is it that hath broken up respect for old age, for parents, for authorities? What is it that hath laid Christianity open to the successful attacks of any resolute skeptic? What is it that hath dimmed the clearness of the eye of faith? What is it that hath removed the spiritual world and its dwellers far off to an astronomical distance, practically sundering the communion of the saints by the wall of death? What is it that hath substituted sentiment for principle—that standeth over the sick bed, anxious to wrest from the lips of the sufferer a cabalistic—a magical utterance that shall save him *in* his sins, but with scarce a word as to repentance, and confession, and amendment, and his salvation *from* sin? What is it that is the prolific cause of all this absence of the self-sacrificing spirit? What is that has left the masses without a religion, and that has sent us all on a course where we are at last ignorant as to how we can get at those masses? Mission chapels for the poor, with Protestant or semi-Protestant services, and with a limited attendance at each of the well-to-do poor, are amiable, but melancholy efforts of the day. God knows we are thankful for the good they do, but it is true that we no longer flatter ourselves that with them we are getting at the masses. The very pamphlets on church work that are pouring from the press are indications that we are walking in darkness; that we have been and are in the midst of some great blunder. What is it that hath set its face stubbornly, and reared stubborn prejudices against the only appliances that have ever succeeded in reaching down to the masses so as to hold them under control? It is time for us to ask how much the Protestant prejudices, which we have inherited from generations behind us by no means infallible, are worth, and how much they are costing. It is time for us to ask whether we shall longer weigh them against the Christianizing of millions of the neglected poor. What is it that hath left ministers stranded upon the high rocks of life, preaching to the select rich? What is it that hath sold the gospel to the rich in the house of God? What is it that hath hushed the voice of resounding praise throughout the great congregation, and delegated the praise of God to a salaried four? What is it that hath killed out from among us all anxiety for the salvation of God's man, as a unit of creation, extending through all time and space on earth, and that has elevated instead that selfish aspect of religion which makes it simply a process for the salvation of the given individual. Your and my salvation, my brother, are, of course, all-important to ourselves; but God, when he made His Church, made it for all time and for man, in the fullest meaning of the word. Nowadays, however, so long as a given individual of to-day can "get saved" in some human religious institution, that institution is considered as answering all the purposes of the Church;

and there is not the slightest anxiety as to whether or not that institution contain a theological disease which will kill it, and leave the individual of two centuries hence without any institution to "get saved" in.

I propose to call your attention to a few of the facts that mark the disastrous failure of Protestantism, and to ask you whether those facts are not enough of themselves—to say nothing of others—to stir to its depths any spirit that has a particle of earnestness; and I warn you beforehand, that if Protestantism has failed, we are not to look to Rome for a cure. A recent able writer has said, this would be but to fly from the effect to the cause. Justly has he said it; for Protestantism was produced by the errors of Rome; and why fly for cure from a system that has proved itself false in the nineteenth century to one that proved itself false in the fifteenth? I remark, first, that in this city there are three hundred churches, some of them large, most of them comparatively small. They will hold, when all full, say about 200,000 persons—call it 250,000. Where are the other three-quarters of a million of people in this city every Sunday? Making a liberal allowance for children too young to attend, for the sick who can not, and for all engaged in employments for the public convenience, and considering those of our vast floating population who attend as strangers, and considering, moreover, the empty seats in all the churches each Sunday, there is an enormous residue that are non-church-goers. Compare, nay, contrast the immense church attendance of the population in Roman and Greek Catholic countries with the attendance of the mere fragment of the population in Protestant lands.

My friends, have you ever thought of the fact that there are countless thousands all over this land, to say nothing of Germany and other countries, that have rejected Protestantism? I do not mean to say they have taken to Rome; but they have at any rate abandoned Protestantism as a religious system. There is scarcely a man or a woman in the land that has not a relative—shall I not say relatives—who, while they still have a kind of respect for the Christian religion, no longer believe those doctrines that all Protestant denominations preach in common. The fact is, with the most of them, dogmatic Christianity is identified with its Protestant presentment. They know no other, and, in abandoning Christianity for skepticism, it is Protestantism that they have weighed in the balances and found wanting. And there are thousands of men and women, therefore, that at last do not go to church anywhere. These men and women are rearing children; and the latter are, by example, by casual domestic remark, and by carelessness of their parents, inheriting a similar abandonment. Protestantism has been trying to meet the evil by modifying and softening some of its subordinate dogmas. But people see that its fundamental dogmas remain, and that the modified subordinate doctrines only make the whole system more thoroughly inconsistent with itself; and so the great evil of abandonment grows greater and greater. Now rise a grade above this class, and take the men and women that do attend church. How many of them are there that really believe Christianity as presented by Protestantism? Some of its dogmas they believe from habit, from early prejudice, or they scarcely know why. . But those whose minds are shaken as to the rest form a very large element of every Protestant congregation. This is a fact which the clergy may not wish to contemplate. But it is a fact. Here we see not total abandonment, but that process of abandonment in progress, which has been working for much more than a century, and which is at last very noticeable from the large proportions it has at length assumed. These two classes I have mentioned form the vast bulk of the community. Isn't that an alarming fact? What are you going to do with your prejudices under the circumstances? Now turn and look at the individuals that compose these two classes. There was a time when it was the staple remark, that men became infidels because they desired to live a wicked or careless life. Doubtless there are some even to-day who are skeptics for the above-mentioned reason. But it were sheer blindness thus to account for the present general disease of infidelity which afflicts the community.

Look around upon our relatives and friends who belong to the two great classes I have spoken of. Are they bad men? No. Are they unreasoning or unreasonable men? No. Are they unearnest men? No. Many of them are filled with the spirit of honesty, and truthfulness, and uprightness, and conscientiousness, and nobleness, and generosity, and hospitality, and kindness of heart, filled with all that which is the very basis of religion. Often they are men that stir our admiration. But they have consciously and conscientiously rejected (that is the word *rejected*), either in whole or in part, the Protestant presentment of Christianity, and deliberately remain in that condition. The grandfathers were Calvinistic Presbyterians, the fathers were Congregationalists, the sons were Unitarians, the grandsons are Parkerites and infidels.

The attempt to mend Protestantism as a religious system ends in abandoning it altogether as a hopeless case. The Rationalists have a ground to stand on; the true Catholics have a ground to stand on; but Protestantism has no *locus standi* (if I may use such a phrase), and its process of disappearing I have given above. The men I speak of either do not think of or do not care to accept Rome, and so they are left without any distinctive religion, unless we can say, indeed, that each has his own.

The two basis ideas of Protestantism are, first, "the Bible, and the Bible only, for Christians;" secondly, "each man practically his own infallible interpreter of it." Now, the consequence of this is, that Protestantism has not fostered humility, but arrogance. It has not cast over the individual mind the wholesome shadow of a distrust in its own ignorance or partial views, or unexamined prejudices; but it has spread broadcast the rampant spirit of practical individual infallibility. And so these men, nursed in that school, absorbing the spirit from the very atmosphere about them, are perfectly satisfied, unalarmed, and at peace, each in his own partial or complete infidelity.

Then, again, they see how these two basis ideas have led to the thousand conflicting sects of Protestantism, the splitting up of denominations on little petty points which their common sense tells them are unimportant; and so they gladly escape the maze in disgust, and, with a self-complacent down-looking upon the whole field of battling Protestant sects, settle down themselves into the mere religion of being good men. * * * They will take parts of the Bible and say they are true; but it is because those parts appeal to their minds as true. That is to say, Protestantism has wrecked the community on the rocks of individualism, and left each man to be a Bible to himself. Some people say, "Any good man is a Christian." But there were good men and true, and honest, before Christ came—millions of them. Ancient civilizations could not have existed, indeed no civilization can exist, without an enormous leaven of such elements. But the phrase "Any good man is a Christian," and the phrase "A true Christian is a good man," are by no means identical. * * *

Now, what is it that has led to and is responsible for the rise of these two enormous classes in the community? My friends, it is not Christianity as presented by the one Holy Catholic and Apostolic Church; for that has not yet got the ear of the people, and it is, moreover, very much hushed even in its own pulpits. Nay, it is the Protestant presentment of Christianity that has had their ear for the last two centuries. By its fruits shall ye know it. And this wholesale abandonment of it, that has been silently and steadily spreading in the last century, till it has invaded every family, is one of the indications of the failure of Protestantism as a system; and is arousing many reluctant but determined souls to the sad duty of dragging down that which has been quietly sitting on the throne as a king, too sacred to be touched, and solemnly arraigning it at the bar for trial. Protestantism, give us back our fathers, our children, our husbands, that are lost in the forests of skepticism! It is this that is arousing and banding together a broad Catholic party in the Church, which, if it will not close its eyes to the Roman failure of the fifteenth century (a failure made doubly disastrous by the Bull of 1854), is determined no longer to close its eyes to the Protestant failure of the nineteenth. A party that is determined to maintain and spread all that is truly Catholic that has come down from the past, and combine with it all of the present that has proved itself good, both in thought and in appliance—it is this that has provoked the beginnings of a second reformation, that will be a reformation indeed.

In this claim that Protestantism has failed, you will not, of course, understand me as asserting that there is nothing good in it, and that with all its evils it has been productive of no benefit whatever to the world and the Church. This would be but mere extravagance, foolish exaggeration, and not the result of that calm, attentive out-look which the seriousness of the times and its dangers demand. Catholics are not unmindful that the Methodists, for instance, have struck something that is in harmony with human nature; and that that something can be wielded on the naturally enthusiastic heart of man in a better way, and on Christian rather than rationalistic plan. Make the man one with Christ, through the sacramental system, and then bring in the lever of enthusiasm, and you have not substituted practical Immediation for Mediation, nor struck a ruinous blow at the foundation of Christianity. Catholics are not unmindful of Baptist practice or Unitarian literature. But I can not pause upon this point.

I hasten to a second indication of the failure of Protestantism as a system; and I do so by asking the question—Protestantism, where are the masses? When we run our eye over the different sects, we are struck with the fact that each is made up of a peculiar type of man. There is, for instance, the Methodist type, and the denomination vary to greater or less extent around the type; then there is the Presbyterian type, and the Baptist, and the Quaker. I am not speaking disparagingly—far be it from me to do so. The whole matter is too serious. But we all know that men are constituted differently, and have different appearances. This is so nationally. No one would mistake a Frenchman for a Scotchman, or for a German. This is so, too, inside of our people. So that, speaking generally, there are nice points by which men may be classified. Now, as a fact, Protestantism has been able, in the past, to draw to itself, at least for awhile, only certain classes of men and women. And the patent fact remains, that it has failed to attract man in all his conditions and kinds. Of course I do not mean to charge against it that it has not Christianized the whole world. What I mean to say is, that it has failed to be a religion suited to every kind of man. There are men of æsthetic tastes; its cold and mean appearance repels them. There are men who want a positive faith; its shifting dogmas disgust them. There are holy women and self-sacrificing men who would gladly live a life of self-abnegation and high spirituality, who would gladly give themselves up as laymen and laywomen to a life of prayer and charity. It frowns upon sisterhoods and brotherhoods. It says to such, "Get you gone from my doors, I have no place nor need for such as you;" and it turns them back either into the world or to Rome. Christ's cause needs vast amounts of money all the time. It has fostered selfishness toward Christ; so that when the offertory plate passes down its aisles, it is considered that the act should be tolerated as an exception; and if it passes too often, the offertory plate is considered as a positive intrusion. As a fact, after 240 years of trial with a fair field, even where, as in this country, it has been vastly, overwhelmingly in the ascendant, it has failed to reach the masses. It has failed, even though it has preached—in very loud tones, too, at times—all the terrors of hell fire, and pictured by contrast all the gross splendors of a physical heaven. And it is this, too, that is stirring earnest men. Where are the masses? Why do your appliances fail to make permanent harvests among them? * * * Where is your control over them? Politics gathers in all indiscriminately at its assemblages. How about Christianity? What is the matter with you? How long will you blindly hug your prejudices, and leave Rome to be the only one that can reach down to and control the masses? My friends, look at the Roman and the Greek branches of the Church, and contrast them with Protestantism in this respect. Why is it that the Anglican branch of the one great Catholic Church has no more succeeded with the masses than has Protestantism? Why is it that there is an Episcopal type of man? It is because we have run our Catholic and Apostolic wheels in the Protestant, Calvinistic, and Lutheran ruts, which they do not fit, never will, and never can. * * * It is not because the clergy and laity of Protestantism are unalive to the wants of the masses, or to their own duty in the premises that Protestantism has made a signal failure. They are earnest and godly men. Heaven knows, they spare no efforts; instant in season, out of season, earnest in prayer and in work. But this only makes the matter worse. The fault is not in them. *Men are often better than their systems*, and without doubt they stand acquitted, while their system stands condemned. I have mentioned but two counts in the presentment; time forbids me to go on with many others. But these alone, viz., the wholesale abandonment of Protestantism by large masses of thinking and good men; and, secondly, its failure to reach the masses, are signs of the times worthy of thought and account, in some part, for a movement among us which has not had its equal in earnestness and determination since the days of John Wesley.

CHAPTER X.

ROMAN CATHOLICISM AGAINST PROGRESSIVE SPIRITUALISM.*

My text is taken from the Scriptures, according to the inspirations of St. Ralph:—

"Every one's progress is through a succession of teachers, each of whom seems, at the time, to have a superlative influence, but it at last gives place to a new."

DISCOURSE.

Each person is organized and developed on a principle of individuality, differently from every other. Each is destined to override the physical and chemical trials of death, and gain the shining shores of a higher sphere. This latter fact is well established. The next

* A New York daily contained the following paragraph, which was handed to Mr. Davis to read, just before the time arrived for the delivery of his evening lecture at Dodworth Hall, New York, 2d May, 1863:—"Father Smarius, of the Roman Catholic Church, from St. Louis, recently delivered a lecture in the College of St. Xavier, in this city, to a large congregation, mostly women, against the doctrines and teachings of modern Spiritualism. He treated Spiritualism as the extreme results of New England Protestantism. The theory, as taught by its supposed original apostles, Judge Edmonds and Andrew Jackson Davis, is old Hindoo Pantheism, and *was exploded seventeen centuries ago!* The Witch of Endor was a medium like the class of modern times," &c., &c. The foregoing was the substance of the paragraph. After reading it, Mr. Davis delivered, in reply, the substance of this chapter.

fact, as well ascertained, is, that the individual, having gained the better shore, becomes acclimated to that better existence, forms an acquaintance with the by-laws and general principles of the divine government, as exemplified in that state of life, and, by means of association, becomes educated in common with the hundreds, and thousands, and myriads, who have long since departed from this earth, and from the other earths in the universe. They learn, among other things, that they can *return*, and thus demonstrate their individuality to those who still remain in the body.

Now, we are told that all these well-established facts were "exploded seventeen hundred years ago!" How can mankind's faith recover from the terrible wreck of that "explosion?" Seventeen hundred years before any one of us were born, the doctrine that man is a spirit, and that, as such, he continues through eternity, and that he sometimes revisits the earth—"exploded!"

What is the foundation of religion in the Roman Catholic Church? What are the fundamental doctrines taught by all the notable priests and bishops? Just this: That the human mind is a part of a great scheme "of eternal life;" that it is not instantly converted into a saint nor into a sinner, but enters an "intermediate state;" is neither perfect enough for bliss, nor utterly consigned to the cells of hopeless perdition; but, very reasonably, they say precisely what we do, that there is a place next to the event of death for the temporary residence of the departed spirit. Thus every Catholic Father opposes his own faith when he attacks the teachings of Spiritualism.

"The Witch of Endor" is brought up, by a Catholic

Father, as a type of all the modern mediums! No truthful man, who is acquainted with the great developments of Spiritualism, would ever take *that* case as a standard by which to judge the myriad forms of "manifestation" in the present day. According to the Bible account, she was a medium who was enabled to show her visitor the spirit of a departed warrior. That is but one instance, and but *one* phase. The mediums of the present epoch are classified in varieties, from five to twenty-five; and these varieties have twenty, thirty, or forty different shades of manifestation. All the varieties are, of course, regulated by the unitary facts and laws, viz.: (1) That man is a spirit; (2) that as a spirit he is eternal; (3) that he can revisit the earth.

There can be no "original" apostles of that gospel which is as old as the universe. How can a person be an "original" apostle of that which is just as eternal *behind* us as in *front?* The Catholic Father says that this doctrine is based on "Pantheism." Nay, nay. It is not based on any kind of "ism," but upon the basis of science—upon sure FACTS, well ascertained, but wonderful. Facts are the beginning and the end of Spiritualism. The verities of "eternal life" have been demonstrated in many ways by these facts.

There are everywhere persons who have not yet seen adequate evidence; not yet perfectly convinced; but there are scores and scores of others who have received the most ample evidences, and who are therefore convinced beyond the possibility of doubt. Such have knowledge! Spiritualists have no "Pantheism," nor any other "ism" as a denominational tenet. There are worthy minds among us who undoubtedly believe that "all things *are* God." Few persons are large-minded and good enough to believe so holy a thought of Nature. Certainly the heathen were not sufficiently spiritualized to believe it fully. They only saw and worshiped "blind forces," and they classified and called those forces "God." And why? Because such were the first religious yearnings—primitive up-workings of the Infinite Spirit in the soil of the human mind--the Asiatic reason grasping after something higher and better in its intuitions and conceptions of the Infinite. The most learned heathen believed in *intelligent* forces within matter. And such was the philosophy of Hindooism. Spiritualism, I repeat, is not based on any theory of matter or mind, but upon FACTS. We have the largest freedom in matters of opinion. We have persons among us who firmly believe in "a trinity." Others in our ranks believe all things with reference to a personal Deity; and with reference to good and evil spirits in the other world; and with reference to churches, and Bibles, and religions in this world. And so, indeed, do we find persons in the Summer Land still believing in multitudes of dissimilar doctrines, as I have shown during this course of lectures.*

Therefore, the Catholic Father can not justly describe Spiritualism as based on any "exploded notions," unless the spiritual *facts* and fixed *axioms* of human nature can be classed among notions. The history of man's spiritual nature and development is complete and perfect. These facts are received: (1) that there

* See a volume by the author entitled "Morning Lectures."

is *a life* within man superior to the animal; (2) that such life eventually lifts him above the lower world; (3) that it causes him to yearn for and aspire after immortality; (4) that he seeks "eternal life," not only for himself, but also in his relations to mankind—in Literature, in Arts, in Poetry, in Science, in Mechanics and Philosophy—and so looks calmly upon death, and triumphs over the grave. Such a person is a Spiritualist, no matter whether he be in the Christian or in the Heathen Church. Wherever a man intuitionally and intellectually triumphs over the idea that physical death is the end, there a Spiritualist is born. But we have, I repeat, a variety of minds among us who draw very different conclusions from the *facts* of Spiritual intercourse that come to their knowledge. We advise and encourage the largest freedom in matters of opinion.

The Catholic Father can not attack Spiritualism as he might criticise the Protestant Church—*i. e.* from a few speculative principles and premises that have not been demonstrated. He might logically trace mere speculative principles to their certain conclusions, and then say: "These conclusions are false; therefore, the premises are false." He might take a creed, a theory, and show that the miracles, and alleged facts on which it is based, are fictions and "pious frauds," and thus prove that the conclusions logically deduced from the false premises are invalid and worthless. But there are certain facts—for instance, that the two halves of a thing are equal to the whole—about which there is no chance for a dispute. The logical conclusion, like the fact itself, is immovable.

So with Spiritualism. It is not based upon philosophical disquisitions or speculative opinions of any individual, either in or out of the body. The Catholic Father traces New England Protestantism up until it is merged into Spiritualism. We, on the other hand, trace Protestantism down until it is lost in unsound Catholic roots. The whole tree is fruitful of both good and evil.

We stand at the opposite extreme of this religious controversy. The Roman Catholic Church is at one end; Protestantism is between that church and the Harmonial Dispensation; of which fact-paved Spiritualism is a part. There are about fifty-six sects of Protestants, and as many gradations of faith, based, not upon knowledge, but upon the speculative opinions of certain individuals as religious leaders, who had each a different mode of reading and interpreting the Bible. Every such religious man, who was possessed of the ability to throw from his intellectual powers the positive magnetic force of genius into his new theology, inevitably drew around him the minds that entered into the nucleus of a new sect, and such new sect, as Presbyterianism for example, in the course of years, grows strong, gathers financial power and great respect, begins to develop a literature of its own, and, by the aid of the pulpit and press, is enabled to exert an immense influence upon families, and entire communities and nations. Such is the brief history of every important sect. Each of the sects was the outgrowth of honest speculative opinions, and logical conclusions drawn from identical premises, viz., the Old and New Testaments—neither of which are authenticated as reliable disclosures from God.

We do not take any such speculative and untenable course. We do not start from the Testaments. We begin with the established scientific fact, (1) that "man is a spirit;" next, (2) from the certain discovery, or fact, that "man does not and can not die" with the dissolution of his body; that, (3) as an individual, "man goes to the Summer Land;" and, (4) as an individual, "man can and does return to earth, making palpable demonstrations of his personal identity."

On one point we need have no controversy with the "Mother Church," because we agree with her that Protestantism is "a go-between," or sort of connecting link in the progressive developments of Theology and Religion, as the zoophytes are links between submarine vegetation and early forms of animal life. Protestantism is a thelogical stratification between two great developments.

Bishop Colenso comes forth from behind the fictions of authority, and applies the reason with which the Eternal Father has endowed him. By the gravity of his analytical judgment he drops down through the Pentateuch, and lands on the granite foundations below, viz., the solid stratum of common sense, which the Father had established in mind before Genesis was written. Here is a bishop who has carved his way through the adamantine fortifications of prejudice. He has battled bravely. But when the world begins to blaze with this "War of Theology," it will be a bitter war indeed; not wholly inseparable from the conflict of swords. In the midst of it Protestantism will be cut in twain, as was the personal devil described by the gifted Milton. In the poem, you remember, it is said that, as the sword passed through the celestial rebel, the wound instantly closed up. But such recuperation will not be the experience of the divided Protestantism, because it is bitterly opposed to unity and self-restoration. And there is a large reversionary property in the religious faith of the sects of Protestantism. This portion will certainly go back to the old heirs in the Mother Church. But there also is a large portion of spiritual property in Protestantism that will as certainly expand into the broad fields of free and independent growth. Such will step upon the Harmonial platform. And then the religious world will present a new phase of development, viz., Roman Catholicism at the lower or negative end—no sects of Protestantism in the middle—and the Harmonial Philosophy at the upper or positive pole. Catholicism will believe in the ascension of the spirit after death, in the communion of saints, and in the forgiveness of sins. We will believe in the ascension of the spirit after death; in the communion of sinners as well as saints; and that sin is never forgiven, but only outgrown — as much in the next as in this world.

So, at last, Catholics and Harmonialists will be organically opposed to each other. We shall certainly stand upon a platform of facts, and upon the testimony of the natural intuitions, which have climbed up through ignorance until they touch the truths of the unfolded heavens.

When these opposites in authority shall gain an elevation sufficiently conspicuous to be seen by intelligent men and women, the result will be a rapid destruction of the present variety of sects—indeed, the entire destruction of all existing forms of sectarianism—followed by the resolution of all Protestantism into "Authority" under the Roman Catholic system, or into "Freedom" under the sway of the principles of immortal reason and progress. The Roman Catholic Church is *retrogressive* in its very instincts; the Harmonial Dispensation is *progressive* in its very instincts. The Roman Catholic Church believes in the authority of an "organization;" the Harmonial Philosophy believes in the authority of "facts" and "principles" as recognized and systematized by reason. The Roman Catholic Church takes old-time religious experiences and bottles them up, and labels them with Latin terms, and puts them on the shelves of authority, and feeds them to the hundreds of thousands within its pews. The Harmonial Dispensation, on the other hand, takes these old-time spiritual experiences, harmonizes them with modern facts, and spreads them broadcast over the people, upon whom they fall like manna from the free heavens. Thus freely and lovingly the people are fed and nourished, and unconsciously they grow higher and higher out of their creeds, out of sectarian bondage, into the glorious light, and liberty, and happiness of the sons of Progression.

I think the Catholic Father is doing the people an excellent service. He is helping to bring up a controversy which he can not put down. All such agitation is what is necessary for the onward growth of the religious world. It is said that the majority of church-goers are women. What is the significance of this fact? Why do not more men attend? Because there is a class in society who are determined to take up free thought. Most men in these days take no interest in such useless theological questions as are debated in the evangelical pulpits. Unthinking girls and their female relatives go to the churches; but real women and real men do not willingly support either clergymen or pulpits that carry on a war in opposition to the doctrines of eternal Progression. Some men have worked and lived out of doors long enough to have grown physically strong and morally independent. As a general thing, men will not be guided by the leading-strings of the old systems. But women are differently situated and differently influenced. They dwell within the inner circles of custom-bound society. Those inner circles touch them and fashion them on every side. A woman can not move without being watched and pressed by this neighbor, and criticised by that neighbor, and misrepresented by the other; and so, by and by, each female is molded into the shape of that society within which she must move and make her home. Women must dress and go to church, and sing, and pray, and do all things according to the prescribed rules of society. Children and their mothers are thus unfortunately in bondage to custom. Men, for these reasons, do not form a large portion of religious congregations. Men are free to go where they can hear an earnest discourse. They feel at liberty to go where there is something worth hearing—"food for thought." They begin, in advance of women, to cultivate the spirit of "independence." But there are noble women, happily, who are very strong and very brave in freedom. They, too, are becoming independent.

What has brought about this change among women? Why are so many of them becoming free? Nothing but this dispensation of Spiritualism can explain the fact. The Quakers started with the idea that women should be spiritually at liberty to speak. Therefore, women dared to speak in Quaker meetings whenever "the spirit moved." The spiritual position of Mother Ann Lee, whatever Protestant slander has done in the way of blackening her history, looms up in the vital part of a religious movement, as an example. Ann Lee was, of course, hounded all through the world by both Catholics and Protestants. Priests and ministers were not willing to have the people taught by a woman. In the first place, it was unfair to the man's right to the pulpit; and, in the next place, it was contrary to the opinions of Paul. She must be anathematized, and she was accordingly. She survived it, however, and is now an inhabitant of the Summer Land, hale, and hearty, and happy, because she did her duty, notwithstanding the many absurd things she may have thought or uttered. She spoke and wrought out of the fullness of her inspiration, and now experiences the peaceful satisfaction which springs from conscious honesty and unswerving integrity.

The genius of this new dispensation is calling all women to ascend the platform of free thought. The spiritual platform has expanded and deepened until it reaches humanity, and goes down into the hearts of the people. It everywhere welcomes woman to the fields of usefulness. Woman, therefore, is gradually seeing the golden rays of celestial light that are heralding her emancipation from cramping and dwarfing influences. She is to be redeemed from that tyrannical society that makes her a mere automaton, and a slave to false and foolish customs. She sees the time coming; yea, rapidly approaching. The Catholic Church dreads it. The Protestant Church dreads it. True, Protestant ministers permit their wives and daughters, and their female members, to go way down in the basement of the church and talk "out loud" in conference meetings, in Bible classes, and in prayer. Yes, women are allowed to pray! Ministers don't object to so much co-operation. But when woman is seen standing where the ministers stand, in the pulpit—thus openly infringing upon the "patent right" which the ordained clergyman is supposed to have long since received from the kingdom of heaven—they concentrate their prejudices and their words against her, and then it is that Spiritualism opens to her the free future, and declares to her the glorious possibilities of complete emancipation. Colleges and public schools are being established for her, and already she begins to take a position equal to her brother man in many if not all the spheres of private and public life. The result is, that they move harmoniously and beautifully together. The liberal religious sects—the Unitarians, the Universalists, the Quakers, and the Shakers—are friendly to woman's progression. But the other sects of Protestantism, including the old Mother Church, look down upon it all with concentrated prejudice and profound contempt.

But the "Newness" is upon us. The Summer Land has been revealed. "The winter of our discontent" in theology is certainly passing, and human existence is made a thousandfold more precious and glorious by perpetual revelations.

There is to-day an influence in the world which is moving and molding the masses. They know not exactly what it is, nor whence it comes. But thousands of people, for some impalpable reason, are believing less and less in the old doctrines of Church and State. It is because the time has come for the culmination of the faith that man is a child of the Father and Mother—of God and Nature—and that, as their child, he is to live after physical death in a sphere "*not made with hands*"—full of Mansions, Spheres, States, Districts, Territories and Provinces. All this "good news" is what has come to mankind. A genuine new gospel! Is it fanaticism? Is it pantheism? Is it something that was "exploded 1700 years ago?" No man who interiorly knows any thing of religious history—comprehending the natural workings of the human soul—could ever stand up in the presence of an intelligent congregation, and say aught against these truths. No wonder the Catholic priest had "but a sprinkling of men," and a "great congregation of women," to listen to his tirade against modern Spiritualism. Men who know the history of theology, of fanaticism, and of Roman Catholicity, have no interest in such one-sided and shallow controversies.

But yet there are ignorant men to the number of hundreds and thousands; therefore, the work must go on. The upheaval, the revolution, and the division, must take place. A great theological warfare must be waged, and it might as well commence when "the rebellion is crushed" as at any other time. It can not commence until the world's political convulsion has very nearly exhausted itself in the minds of the people.

Then the flame of religious interest will be kindled, and it will burn like wildfires on the broad prairies. Then will come a new and a higher pentecostal experience. Then the people will be singularly excited. They will not be able to repress their awakened anxiety to know definitely about the future. They will say, "Give us knowledge as well as faith." "Give us a *basis* for our hopes." Then they will accept impersonal Reason. Reason will rest and be grounded upon Nature; which is forever harmonious with intuition, and indorsed by experience and facts.

From the Summer Land this theological revolution, and this great disunion and division of the sects, has been many times announced. It was first definitely announced to me in 1851. It was then made very clear that Protestantism was to be divided; that the Roman Catholic Church was then to have a great accession of persons and of power. Distinguished Protestants will return to the old authority. Rome at one end; Reason at the other. Conservatism, in the shape of religious dogmatic authority, in one place; Progression, in the shape of enlightened experience and advancing reason, in another. The Conservatives will be friendly to Music, and Art, and Science, only so far as these divine agents administer to the advancement of Church interests. The Progressives will be favorable to and supporters of all things and of all influences that can aid in advancing the cause of civilization—the onward development of the whole people toward harmony in society, and toward justice and freedom in government. These two parties and positions will be distinctly unfolded by the on-working laws of Progress.

The atmosphere is filled with individual private experiences. These experiences are frequently reported to, and by, those who are called mediums. Private details are interesting to those only who have been the subjects of such experiences. But the finest evidences from the Summer Land, and the best things in Spiritualism, can not be divulged to a promiscuous audience. Neither can such evidences be made plausible to the reader of a newspaper, because no speaker or writer can paint all the convincing items of conditions, and the scenery which pertained to and accompanied the demonstration. Only the general fact can be given to a hearer or a reader. Because a third party can not see the minutiæ, the narration seems trite, and many times unsatisfactory. Hence we say, "Go seek for yourselves." Individuals return to relate their private experiences; to say in touching language what they think of the dear ones remaining on earth; to tell how often they have watched over their loved; to narrate how many times they have endeavored to exert an influence in the way of guardianship, and government, and protection; regretfully to inform the beloved how often they have failed, or joyfully to tell how many times they have succeeded. They tell us these things over and over again, and we have accumulated unmistakable proofs of the truth. It can not be fully described to you, nor can you impart the vividness of the truth to your neighbor—only the skeleton of the experience; but all the *internal interest* can be conceived and treasured up by no one beside yourself. Hence the basic historical facts of Spiritualism can never be spread by propagandists. You can not go about and preach the mere externals into the reason and intuitions of people. Spiritualists are believers because of the incontrovertible evidences which they have individually received or obtained by investigation.

Heretofore I have shown you that the Summer Land is filled with countless varieties of persons, and that these persons, instead of being in antagonism with each other, as sects are here, are in harmony with the great plans and design and moral government of the Divine Mind. The higher intelligences almost never return to earth. They do not find language adapted to the expression of their finest thoughts or richest experiences. Neither do they obtain the attention of those who could best appreciate their thoughts. They therefore turn their backs to the planet from which they sprang, and go onward, knowing that you and I, as we ascend the ladder of experience, will see, and feel, and know what they have felt, and seen, and known. Hence, revelations from the most frequent spirit visitors are not often high, intellectual displays. They are not manifestations of moral and intellectual archangelhood. They are, on the contrary, expressions purely social, pathetic, and unsophisticated, coming from persons who are mostly under the influence of affection; not often under the control of high forms of thought and contemplation. The old philosophers, and the men who were in this world interested in the various Sciences, and those who were influential in the formation of Literature, and Art, and Governments, are the very men who now take the *least* possible part in the special thoughts and private interests of mankind. They interest themselves chiefly in the grand movements which are carried forward by the hundreds and thousands of lesser persons, who feel that they must communicate to mankind frequently in order to enjoy the social life of the existence which is bestowed upon them.

Some of the inhabitants of the other world do not seem fully to realize that they have certainly thrown off their relations to the earth, but keep leaning and yearning earthward, facing this way, their affections pouring into the channels of their terrestrial friendships. Others are interested in mere material property left behind. Of course these persons are not comfortable. The Roman Catholic Church, in its earliest conceptions of this thing, said: "There is a purgatory." Verily, there is a state of mind that is next to the grave —just the other side of it—which faces its tenants earthward far more than skyward; which causes its inhabitants still to feel that they have not thrown off all connections with the low earth. These spirits are the ones that are affected favorably by such communications as the mediums are enabled to make; they are often lifted, through the "satisfaction" which such communications give, and, for the time, are raised to a higher and a pleasanter sphere of feeling.

Now, these are some of the facts in Spiritualism; and they are accepted as true by the Catholic Church. These religious opposites will eventually meet. When they meet, they will shake hands. I have met Catholic bishops face to face; I have talked with them. They are, generally, what the world styles "educated persons." Many of them have been more pleasant, and courteous, and agreeable to me than have the same number of Protestant ministers. They hold that Reason has nothing to do with the dogmas and discipline of the Church. The Bible itself is not so important to the Catholics as the authority and principles of the Church. Accept their Church; or individual Opinion. Reason is a part of the individual. It is also the instrumentality by which individual opinion is manufactured into practical forms. They ask: "Which will you take—the Church, *or* individual Opinion?" They take the Church, and that is a finality with them. What it teaches in religion, "is from God;" what it does not teach or permit, "is from the devil." Thus the argument is closed up forever.

On the other hand, we say that the Church is an accumulation of merely human experience, human authority, and plans of human discipline; and that experience and reason, and the inspirations of the intellectual, moral, and social faculties, are the "Latest Revelations from God;" that when a man or a woman, owning these inspirable and inspired faculties, is filled with an earnest desire to use them rightly, then comes the power to *do*, as well as to *be*, good; and with that comes progress, and from progress harmony, and out of harmony come happiness and oneness with Deity.

When there is a harmonious blending of heavenly with earthly influences—*when the spirit in man meets the Spirit of God*—then the two are indissolubly wedded; and at the nuptial ceremony of such a union Truth and Justice officiate, because they are the ordained priests of heaven and eternity.

DESCRIPTIVE LIST

OF

The Complete Works

OF

ANDREW JACKSON DAVIS,

FOR SALE BY

WM. WHITE & CO.

(PUBLISHERS OF BANNER OF LIGHT),

No. 158 Washington Street, Boston, Mass.,

AND

American News Company, New York.

THE PRINCIPLES OF NATURE:

Her Divine Revelations, and a Voice to Mankind. (In three parts.)

Thirtieth Edition, just published, with a likeness of the clairvoyant author, and containing a family record for marriages, births, and deaths. This book contains the basis and philosophy on which the whole structure of Spiritualism rests. It embodies and condenses the fundamental principles of human life and human progress up to and beyond the present, and has a steady and constant sale. Price, $3.50; postage, 48 cents.

THE GREAT HARMONIA:

Being a Philosophical Revelation of the Natural, Spiritual, and Celestial Universe, in Five Volumes.

Vol. I. THE PHYSICIAN. Contents of Vol. I.—What is Man? What is the Philosophy of Health? What is the Philosophy of Disease? What is the Philosophy of Sleep? What is the Philosophy of Death? What is the Philosophy of Psychology? What is the Philosophy of Healing? Thousands in the United States, and very many in Europe, have read this volume with delight. The author's description of "The Philosophy of Death" is alone worth more than the price of the book. No one can read and remain unmoved. The volume is especially useful to every family as a work on medicine and the science of disease and health. Price, $1.50; Postage, 20 cents.

Vol. II. THE TEACHER, Contents of Vol. II.—My Early Experience; My Preacher and his Church; The True Reformer; Philosophy of Charity; Individual and Social Culture; The Mission of Woman; The True Marriage; Moral Freedom; Philosophy of Immortality; The Spirit's Destiny; Concerning the Deity. In this volume is presented the new and wonderful principles of "Spirit, and its Culture;" also, a comprehensive and systematic argument on the "Existence of God." Price, $1.50; postage, 20 cents.

Vol. III. THE SEER. This volume is composed of twenty-seven Lectures on every phase of Magnetism and Clairvoyance in the past and present of human history. Swedenborg's condition is thoroughly examined. Among the subjects treated are, Philosophy of Clairvoyance and Inspiration; Man's Ordinary State, considered in Connection with the External World and to the Spiritual Universe; Dependencies existing between the Body and the Soul; Action of the Mind upon the Body in Disease; Manifestations of a Universal Sympathy; On the Historical Evidences of the Psycho-sympathetic State; Condition of Ancient Prophets, Seers, and Religious Chieftains; The Phenomena and History of Clairvoyance; The Spiritual State and its External Manifestations; Concerning the Principles and Causes of True Inspiration; The Philosophy of Ordinary and Extraordinary Dreaming; The Sources of Human Happiness and Misery Philosophically Considered; A Brief Exposition of the Satan which Tempted Jesus of Nazareth; The Authority of the Harmonial Philosophy; On the Uses and the Abuses of the Sabbath. Price, $1.50; postage, 20 cents.

Vol. IV. THE REFORMER. This volume contains truths eminently serviceable in the elevation of the race. It is devoted to the consideration of "Physiological Vices and Virtues, and the Seven Phases of Marriage." It covers ground never before occupied by any reformatory writer, and teaches the most important truths upon the most vital questions that can agitate any mind—those of *Marriage* and *Parentage*. It is a work that appeals first to man's consciousness, by a clear representation of existing evils; and next to the higher faculties, by pointing out the "highway of freedom" from all these evils. Satisfying as it does the understanding, it affords valuable aid to the individual in rooting out bad habits and reforming vicious tendencies. It is a safe book for youth, for it has not the least indelicacy of sentiment or expression; and it furnishes just such knowledge, and inculcates such principles, as are calculated to preserve the youthful mind from contamination, and insure the practice of virtue. It is an invaluable book for the newly-married, for it points out the danger and consequences of extremism and inversionism, and imparts that information concerning the reproductive functions necessary to avoid conjugal misdirections. Price, $1.50; postage, 20 cents.

Vol. V. THE THINKER. This volume is by numerous readers pronounced the most comprehensive and best sustained of the series. Read it, and you will become acquainted with all the great central "Ideas" which, aided by the minds by whom they were unfolded, have carried forward the mighty growth of humanity. Read it, and you will learn of the "Origin of Life, and the Law of Immortality." In this volume you will also find very many new and instructive diagrams. Price, $1.50; postage, 20 cents.

THE PRESENT AGE, AND INNER LIFE:

Ancient and Modern Mysteries Classified and Explained.

The best critics have pronounced this work one of the most classically pure of all the volumes of the author. It abounds with thrilling passages; and no one can fail to be instructed by the systematic "classification" of all the wonderful developments of modern days. The work is, in itself, almost a demonstration of the claims of Spiritualism. Price, $1.50; postage, 20 cents.

THE PENETRALIA.

This work, which at the time was styled by the author, "the wisest book" from his pen, deserves to be brought prominently before the American public. The importance of the subjects considered, and the peculiarly terse and original style in which they are handled, combine to give the book a most noticeable character. While the topics are mainly theological, many questions of practical interest and value are answered, thus rendering the volume an acquisition to the student and philosopher, as well as the theologian. Price, $1.75; postage, 24 cents.

THE HARBINGER OF HEALTH:

Containing Medical Prescriptions for the Human Body and Mind.

This new and rare volume contains more than three hundred prescriptions for the treatment and cure of over one hundred different diseases, and forms of disease, incident to mankind in all parts of the world. The author's prescriptions are given in the light of the "Superior Condition." The Harbinger of Health has never failed to awaken intense interest in the minds of the most intelligent of the Medical Profession, and it is invaluable to the general reader, containing as it does, information concerning methods of treatment hitherto unknown to the world, and imparting important suggestions respecting the Will Power and the Self-Healing Energies, which are better than medicine. It is a plain, simple guide to health, with no quackery, no humbug, no universal panacea. Price, $1.50; postage, 20 cents.

ANSWERS TO EVER-RECURRING QUESTIONS FROM THE PEOPLE.

During the period which has elapsed since the publication of the author's work entitled the "Penetralia," a multitude of questions have been propounded to him. From this list of several hundred interrogatories, those of the most permanent interest and highest value have been carefully selected, and the result is the present volume, comprising well-considered and intelligent replies to more than two hundred important questions. It is believed by hundreds that this work is one of the most interesting and useful volumes that has been issued. It invites the perusal not only of those vitally interested in the topics discussed, but of all persons capable of putting a question. It awakens inquiry and develops thought. The wide range of subjects embraced can be inferred from the table of contents. An examination of the book itself will reveal the clearness of style and vigor of method characterizing the replies. Price, $1.50; postage, 20 cents.

MORNING LECTURES:

Twenty Discourses, delivered in the City of New York, in the Winter and Spring of 1863.

This volume is overflowing with that peculiar inspiration which carries the reader into the region of new ideas. The discourses are clothed in language plain and forcible, and the arguments and illustrations convey conviction. Among the subjects treated are:—"The World's True Redeemer;" "The End of the World;" "The Reign of Anti-Christ;" "The Spirit, and its Circumstances;" "Eternal Value of Pure Purposes;" "Wars of Blood, Brain, and Spirit;" "False and True Education;" "Social Life in the Summer Land;" &c. This volume of plain lectures is just the book to put into the hands of skeptics and new beginners in Spiritualism. Price, $1.50; postage, 20 cents.

A STELLAR KEY TO THE SUMMER LAND.

Part I. Illustrated with Diagrams and Engravings of Celestial Scenery.

The author has heretofore explained the wonders of creation, the mysteries of science and philosophy, the order, progress, and harmony of Nature in thousands of pages of living inspiration. He has solved the mystery of death, and revealed the connection between the world of matter and the world of spirits. Mr. Davis opens wide the door of future human life, and shows us where we are to dwell when we put aside the garments of mortality for the vestments of angels. The account of the spiritual universe; the immortal mind looking into the heavens; the existence of a spiritual zone—its possibilities and probabilities—its formation and scientific certainty; the harmonies of the universe; the physical scenery and constitution of the Summer Land—its location, and domestic life in the spheres, are new and wonderfully interesting. Price, $1.00; postage, 16 cents.

ARABULA; OR, THE DIVINE GUEST.

This fresh and beautiful volume is selling rapidly, because it supplies a deep religious want in the hearts of the people. Best literary minds are gratified, while truly religious readers are spiritually fed with the contents of this volume. All who want to understand and enjoy the grand central truths of the Harmonial Philosophy, and all who would investigate the teachings and religion of Spiritualism, should read this inspired book. It contains a New Collection of Gospels by Saints not before canonized, and its chapters are teeming with truths for humanity, and with fresh tidings from the beloved beyond the tomb. The names of the new Saints are:—St. Rishis, St. Menu, St. Confucius, St. Siamer, St. Syrus, St. Gabriel, St. John, St. Pneuma, St. James, St. Gerrit, St. Theodore, St. Octavius, St. Samuel, St. Eliza, St. Emma, St. Ralph, St. Asaph, St. Mary, St. Selden, St. Lotta. **Price**, $1.50; postage, 20 cents.

THE MAGIC STAFF:

An Autobiography of Andrew Jackson Davis.

"This most singular biography of a most singular person," has been extensively read in this country, and is now translated and published in the German language. It is a complete personal history of the clairvoyant experiences of the author from his earliest childhood to 1856. All important details are carefully and conscientiously given. Every statement is authentic and beyond controversy. In this volume (including the autobiographical parts of "Arabula" and "Memoranda" which enter largely into the author's personal experiences), the public will find *a final answer to all slanders and misrepresentations.* Thousands of copies of the "Magic Staff" have been sold in the United States, and the demand, instead of being supplied, is increasing. Price, $1.75; postage, 24 cents.

MEMORANDA OF PERSONS, PLACES, AND EVENTS:

Embracing Authentic Facts, Visions, Impressions, Discoveries in Magnetism, Clairvoyance, and Spiritualism.

This volume of transcripts from the observation and experience of Mr. Davis will be welcomed with great pleasure by his tens of thousands of readers, in which they will find a great variety of those fresh and fleeting "impressions" of the inspired seer, carefully set down by his own hand for a period of over twenty-two years, that can not but let them further than ever into his own nature, and the mysterious realms which his vision is permitted to penetrate and search. There is a peculiar freshness about this latest book from Mr. Davis that makes it specially attractive to the general reader. His off-hand characterization of persons of note will strike all as peculiarly apt and effective. In fact, it is a sort of mirror for all to look into. This volume should be read by all who have perused the "Magic Staff." The Appendix, containing the fine translation of Zschokke's tale of the "Transfiguration," will attract all to its perusal, since it illustrates the curative powers of human magnetism, and the spiritual beauty and purity of the superior condition. This book is also particularly valuable to history, because it contains a chapter written by Mary F. Davis, concerning the "Introduction of the Harmonial Philosophy into Germany." Price, $1.50; Postage, 20 cents.

THE PHILOSOPHY OF SPECIAL PROVIDENCES.

This is a small pamphlet of fifty-five pages, but is living with thought. The author considers the question, "Are there Special Providences?" and no one can fail to be instructed and elevated by its perusal. The pamphlet contains Two Visions, and An Argument. Price, 20 cents.

THE PHILOSOPHY OF SPIRITUAL INTERCOURSE.

CONTENTS.—Truth and Mystery; God's Universal Providence; The Miracles of this Age; The Decay of Superstition; The Guardianship of Spirits; The Discernment of Spirits; The Stratford Mysteries; The Doctrine of Evil Spirits; The Origin of Spirit Sounds; Concerning Sympathetic Spirits; The Formation of Circles; The Resurrection of the Dead; A Voice from the Spirit Land; The True Religion. In this thrilling work the reader is presented with an account of the very wonderful Spiritual Developments at the house of the Rev. Dr. Phelphs, of Stratford, Connecticut; and besides these, the work is replete with similar cases in all parts of the country. This work is completed by its sequel, entitled "Present Age and Inner Life." Price, in paper, 60 cents; cloth, $1.00; postage, 16 cents.

FREE THOUGHTS CONCERNING RELIGION.

This pamphlet contains short arguments, fresh and vigorous, substantiated by plain historical and geological facts, against the popularly received idea that the "Bible is the word of God." Infallibility is demolished, and creeds finely pulverized in the mill of truth. As a little pamphlet, it is calculated to "stir up thought" in a bigoted neighborhood. We recommend "Free Thoughts Concerning Religion." Price, 20 cents.

THE HARMONIAL MAN.

CONTENTS.—How shall we Improve Society? The Influence of Churches; The Necessity of Organic Liberty; Mankind's Natural Needs; The Means by which to Secure Them; The Philosophy of Producing Rain; A Statement of Popular Theories; The Causes of Rain Explained; The Philosophy of Controlling Rain; Answer to Scientific Objections; Plagiarism; Clairvoyance Illustrated; What will People Say; The Pirate's Simple Narrative. The contents of this little work are designed to enlarge man's views concerning the political and ecclesiastical condition of our country, and to point out, or at least to suggest, the paths of reform which the true Harmonial Man shall tread. We might add many commendatory notices of the press, but it is deemed sufficient to give the reader an idea of the work, by

www.ingramcontent.com/pod-product-compliance
Lightning Source LLC
LaVergne TN
LVHW010211110826
845151LV00004B/1052

* 9 7 8 1 4 2 5 5 2 8 5 9 1 *

CATALOGUE

OF THE

PUBLICATIONS

OF

RUDD & CARLETON,

130 GRAND STREET,

(BROOKS BUILDING, COR. OF BROADWAY,)

NEW YORK.

VERNON GROVE;

By Mrs. Caroline H. Glover. "A Novel which will give its author high rank among the novelists of the day."—*Atlantic Monthly.* 12mo., Muslin, price $1 00

BALLAD OF BABIE BELL,

And other Poems. By Thomas Bailey Aldrich. The first selected collection of verses by this author. 12mo. Exquisitely printed, and bound in muslin, price 75 cents.

TRUE LOVE NEVER DID RUN SMOOTH.

An Eastern Tale, in Verse. By Thomas Bailey Aldrich, author of "Babie Bell, and other Poems." Printed on colored plate paper. Muslin, price 50 cents

BEATRICE CENCI.

A Historical Novel. By F. D. Guerrazzi. Translated from the original Italian by Luigi Monti. Muslin, two volumes in one, with steel portrait price $1 25.

ISABELLA ORSINI.

A new historical novel. By F. D. Guerrazzi, author of "Beatrice Cenci." Translated by Monti, of Harvard College. With steel portrait. Muslin, price $1 25.

DOCTOR ANTONIO.

A charming Love Tale of Italy. By G. Ruffini, author of "Lorenzo Benoni," "Dear Experience," &c From the last London edition. Muslin, price $1 00.

DEAR EXPERIENCE.

A Tale. By G. Ruffini, author of "Doctor Antonio," "Lorenzo Benoni," &c. With illustrations by Leech, *of the London Punch.* 12mo. Muslin, price $1 00

LECTURES OF LOLA MONTEZ.

Including her "Autobiography," "Wits and Women of Paris," "Comic Aspect of Love," "Gallantry," &c. A new edition, large 12mo. Muslin, price $1 25.

EDGAR POE AND HIS CRITICS.

By Mrs. SARAH HELEN WHITMAN. A volume possessing many attractions and which has created considerable interest among the *literati*. 12mo. Muslin, price 75 cts

THE GREAT TRIBULATION;

Or Things coming on the Earth. By Rev. JOHN CUMMING, D.D., author of "Apocalyptic Sketches," &c. From the English edition. FIRST SERIES. Muslin, price $1 00.

THE GREAT TRIBULATION.

SECOND SERIES of the new work by Rev. DR. CUMMING, which has awakened such an excitement throughout the religious community. 12mo. Muslin, price $1 00.

ADVENTURES OF VERDANT GREEN.

By CUTHBERT BEDE, B.A. The best humorous story of College Life ever published. 80*th edition*, from English plates. Nearly 200 original illustrations, price $1 00

CURIOSITIES OF NATURAL HISTORY.

By FRANCIS T. BUCKLAND, M.A. A sparkling collection of surprises in Natural History, and the charm of a lively narrative. From 4th London edition, price $1 25.

BROWN'S CARPENTER'S ASSISTANT.

The best practical work on Architecture; with Plans for every description of Building. Illustrated with over 200 Plates. Strongly bound in leather, price $5 00

THE VAGABOND.

A volume of Miscellaneous Papers, treating in colloquial sketches upon Literature, Society, and Art. By ADAM BADEAU. Bound in muslin, 12mo, price $1 00.

ALEXANDER VON HUMBOLDT.

A new and popular Biography of this celebrated *Savant*, including his travels and labors, with an introduction by BAYARD TAYLOR. One vol., steel portrait, price $1 25.

LOVE (L'AMOUR).

By M. JULES MICHELET. Author of "A History of France," &c. Translated from the French by J. W. Palmer, M.D. One vol., 12mo. Muslin, price $1 00.

WOMAN (LA FEMME).

A sequel and companion to "Love" (L'Amour) by the same author, MICHELET. Translated from the French by Dr. J. W. Palmer. 12mo. Muslin, price $1 00.

LIFE OF HUGH MILLER.

Author of "Schools and Schoolmasters," "Old Red Sandstone," &c. Reprinted from the English edition. One large 12mo. Muslin, new edition, price $1 25.

AFTERNOON OF UNMARRIED LIFE.

An interesting theme admirably treated. Companion to Miss Muloch's "Woman's Thoughts about Women." From London edition. 12mo. Muslin, price, $1 00.

SOUTHWOLD.

By MRS. LILLIE DEVEREUX UMSTED. "A spirited and well drawn Society novel—somewhat intensified but bold and clever." 12mo. Muslin, price $1 00.

DOESTICKS' LETTERS.

Being a compilation of the Original Letters of O K. P. DOESTICKS, P. B. With many comic tinted illustrations by John McLenan. 12mo. Muslin. price $1 00

PLU-RI-BUS-TAH.

A song that's by-no-author. *Not* a parody on "Hiawatha." By DOESTICKS. With 150 humorous illustrations by McLenan. 12mo. Muslin, price $1 00

THE ELEPHANT CLUB.

An irresistibly droll volume. By DOESTICKS, assisted by KNIGHT RUSS OCKSIDE, M.D. One of his best works Profusely illustrated by McLenan. Muslin, price $1 00.

THE WITCHES OF NEW YORK.

A new humorous work by DOESTICKS; being minute, particular, and faithful Revelations of Black Art Mysteries in Gotham. 12mo. Muslin, price $1 00

TWO WAYS TO WEDLOCK.

A Novellette. Reprinted from the columns of Morris & Willis' *New York Home Journal*. 12mo. Handsomely bound in muslin. Price $ 00,

HAMMOND'S POLITICAL HISTORY.

A History of Political Parties in the State of New York. By JABEZ B. HAMMOND, L.L.D. 3 vols., octavo, with steel portraits of all the Governors. Muslin. Price, $6 00.

ROMANCE OF A POOR YOUNG MAN.

From the French of OCTAVE FEUILLET. An admirable and striking work of fiction. Translated from the Seventh Paris edition. 12mo. Muslin, price $1 00

THE CULPRIT FAY.

By Joseph Rodman Drake. A charming edition of this world-celebrated Faery Poem. Printed on colored plate paper. Muslin, 12mo. Frontispiece. Price, 50 cts.

THE NEW AND THE OLD;

Or, California and India in Romantic Aspects. By J. W. Palmer, M.D., author of "Up and Down the Irrawaddi." Abundantly illustrated. Muslin, 12mo. $1,25.

UP AND DOWN THE IRRAWADDI;

Or, the Golden Dagon. Being passages of adventure in the Burman Empire. By J. W. Palmer, M.D., author of "The New and the Old." Illustrated. Price, $1,00.

THE HABITS OF GOOD SOCIETY.

An interesting handbook for Ladies and Gentlemen; with thoughts, hints, and anecdotes, concerning social observances, taste, and good manners. Muslin, price $1 25.

RECOLLECTIONS OF THE REVOLUTION.

A private manuscript journal of home events, kept during the American Revolution by the Daughter of a Clergyman. Printed in unique style. Muslin. Price, $1,00

HARTLEY NORMAN.

A New Novel. "Close and accurate observation, enables the author to present the scenes of everyday life with great spirit and originality." Muslin, 12mo. Price, $1,25.

MOTHER GOOSE FOR GROWN FOLKS.

An unique and attractive little Holiday volume. Printed on tinted paper, with frontispiece by Billings. 12mo. Elegantly bound in fancy colored muslin, price 75 cts.

www.ingramcontent.com/pod-product-compliance
Lightning Source LLC
LaVergne TN
LVHW010211110826
845151LV00004B/1055